Change Your Mind, Not Your Child

Loving Your Child by Raising Your Consciousness

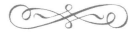

A new paradigm for parenting

Michael Cavallaro

For parents and anyone who has ever been parented!

Published By

Adele and Michael LLC
PO Box 374
Red Hill, PA 18076

Library of Congress Control Number

If you have any questions concerning the book contact us at:
Adele and Michael LLC
PO Box 374
Red Hill, PA 18076
admin@adeleandmichael.com

ADDITIONAL BOOKS AND EBOOKS
BY: MICHAEL CAVALLARO

The 55 Concepts

The 10 Commandments, A Modern Interpretation

Relationships – Making Them Work,
Making Them Last

Change Your Mind, Not Your Child

Ramblings

Seven Steps to Freedom

Thoughts, Beliefs, Knowings and More

Loving Yourself

Ego, Personality, Conscious and Unconscious

Overlays

TABLE OF CONTENTS

GRAMMER CHOICES

In this book the use of "they" and "them" instead of he or she and her or him when referring to the singular child, as well as plural children, has been done purposely.

Using he or she diverts your attention from the message for you and your child to the gender of you and your child. Throughout the ages, society has focused on the differences between the sexes, but every individual has both male and female traits to varying degrees. It is time to drop many of the stereotypes that keep us individually and collectively trapped in being less than a whole person.

Also, when this book refers to a child, it is referring to more than just the child in your home. It also often includes your inner child, the children you connect with, the children your child connects with and all children. As you change yourself and your relationship with your child, you change the world as well.

Though it may feel uncomfortable and strange to read the unfamiliar grammar in the beginning, realize that for a lifetime you have been programmed to see things through one lens. Reading this book with these grammar choices is an exercise in changing your perspective and opening to a new and unfamiliar way of doing things. This is not always easy or comfortable, but it can change and expand how you see yourself and your world.

Your reaction to these grammatical choices — whether it's curiosity, frustration, interest, or deciding it's wrong — is a metaphor for how you judge and open (or don't open) to what is unique and unfamiliar in your child and the way they perceive their life. Becoming aware of your reactions gives you the opportunity to change the ones that don't work. Parenting in a new way involves embracing change. It may not always be comfortable or easy, but it is well worth the effort.

This parenting book is for all gender, race and culture parents although in some examples we have used the traditional mother and father model.

THE HEART OF A CHILD

- The key to every human being is their heart.

- When you connect with the heart of your child, your child knows that you love them even without words.

- A child's heart is open and innocent when it comes into the world.

If you care for your child's heart and teach them to love themselves first, you open a world of unending joyful possibilities to them. Raised in this way, your child knows that they are loved, even if it is unspoken.

Loving your child does not mean allowing them to do whatever they want or not being firm when necessary. Loving your child means teaching them to be functional in life while loving themselves.

This applies to yourself and your own "inner child".

You are the guardian of your child's heart and their guide in life. Preparing them for life, loving them and loving yourself is the greatest gift you have to offer.

This is what this book is about.

CHAPTER ONE

CONSCIOUS PARENTING

(Please read 'Grammar Choices' on page three before continuing.)

You may have picked up this book and believed that you were reading it for your child's benefit. If so, you may be surprised by how much you learn about yourself and how much you, your child and your relationships grow.

When you use the ideas and tools in this book, you will have answers instead of going in endless circles. Instead of demanding that your child change and making them feel wrong, you will begin to see your part in creating problems. As you accept your part without judging yourself, you will continue to become more centered and calm, changing yourself and facilitating change in your child. Keep in mind while you read through the book that what you are learning is an experiential process of evolution and not a call to be a perfect parent.

The best way to grow as an individual and become a model of what you want for your child is to observe them. Watch how they interact or speak to others or to you. When you feel upset by something they are doing, notice how you may have taught them to do that through your own behavior. You will see that the difficulties they have are because you have some version of these problems and difficulties that you may not have been aware of up until this point.

When you truly understand that change for your child begins by committing to changing yourself first, you will have a much easier and more gratifying time parenting. Teach by example rather than bribes, threats and lectures. Children learn by example. They feel everything around them. Be the change for you, and your children will learn from watching and listening. They will experience the joy as well and you will all become closer as a family.

This book will bring about an awareness of what stands in the way of you having a joyful human experience. It will provide tools and techniques to teach your child in ways that allow them the possibility of having a full and happy human life, too. Parenting this way becomes more of an enjoyable adventure rather than an exhausting struggle. It allows you to raise cooperative, well-balanced, loving, independent, self-actualized human beings.

Learn what it takes to be a conscious parent. Learn about the issues you have that may get in the way of your child's growth and wellbeing. And learn how to resolve these issues, which will impact your child in more ways than you can imagine. You will discover new information about children's feelings and emotions, as well as why to remove words such as good and bad from your vocabulary. You'll gain a new perspective on words such as boundaries, discipline and rules. And you will come to a new understanding about things like touch, relationships, communication and talking to your child about sex. Most of all, parenting will become a process that makes sense and you will begin to feel new confidence and ease.

Parenting will also bring up a lot of issues and things that don't work that you didn't even notice before having children. The key is to deal with the parts of your life that aren't working and be open to seeing other options without judgment.

Everything a person experiences from infancy on affects their beliefs and patterns. As you become more aware of how these beliefs and patterns affect your parenting and how your parenting affects the child long term, you become a more conscious parent. Issues, detrimental beliefs and patterns are all unresolved conscious or unconscious problems or concerns that need to be addressed because they get in the way of having the experience you want.

As you recognize your patterns and beliefs, you can teach your child about those they have inherited rather than both of you allowing them to run your lives. You can keep the ones that work and consciously choose to change the ones that don't. Your self-awareness will enable you to teach your child to be aware of themselves, thereby making their journey through life easier.

WHAT'S FIRST

Many parents were raised to believe that their children should come first. In this book you'll learn to put yourself first. You won't do it in a selfish or egotistical way, but in a way that models for the child how to love themselves. In the end, this is what most of us want for our children.

When you have a partner, putting them next creates a deep connection for both of you and a strong, safe, consistent foundation for your child.

Understand that as a conscious parent, you are the child's guide, not their friend. Your job is to provide food, shelter, clothing and boundaries, and to give them the skills to prepare them for life. Your journey to becoming a conscious parent requires dedication, patience, kindness, awareness, inner reflection, courage, consistency and much more. While it is often challenging, you will find it rewarding beyond measure.

As the old saying goes, you must walk the walk in order to talk the talk. Be the living example and your child will follow your lead. This way, your child can grow and expand what they do know rather than compensating for what they don't know. They will become more responsible and independent, setting the stage for having better relationships later in life. This also enables you and your child to create a close and rewarding relationship with each other. Obviously, a child who grows up this way enriches their own world and the world around them as well.

As you grow through this process, remember to be kind and patient with yourself. Be aware that judging yourself keeps you from fully loving yourself. Loving yourself is the most important and beautiful example you can give to your child. Learn from your mistakes and keep going! You will not be perfect and there is no end goal. Yet when you step into the journey with love and without judgment, the possibilities are endless.

Everything you have known up to now is about to be questioned. So doubt nothing, question everything. Open your heart and mind to receive the information. Most of all, find the beauty and joy for yourself in this new life you are about to experience!

Change the way you parent
to the way you WANT to parent

A WARNING ABOUT POSITIVE PARENTING

Some tell you to be 'positive' as a parent. Yet to be positive often means you look for positive behaviors and reward the child for what they do right. Although positive parenting techniques are usually well-intended, some of these techniques are designed to manipulate the child. They could be labeled "bribery parenting," as rewards are simply a form of bribery. You reward the good behaviors of your child but don't reward their negative behaviors. This is manipulation that teaches the child that they should be rewarded for doing what others consider right and gives the child no skills to deal with the negative. It teaches your child how to manipulate, be manipulated and be well-trained, like a pet. This may take care of the situation in the moment but undermines the real growth of the child's abilities to cope in the world.

Conscious parenting instead assists the child in being a healthy, well-functioning, well-rounded, self-directed human being. It helps them learn from their own thought processes, feelings, experiences and results, rather than from rewards and punishments.

As a conscious parent, sit down and write
what you would like your family to look like ideally.

LOVE YOUR CHILD WITH ALL YOUR HEART

Love yourself with all your heart. By doing this, you set an example for your child so that they can love themselves. Loving yourself is about accepting all of yourself — even the parts you believe are unlovable. Unconditionally accept that your body looks the way it does, that you are the age or gender you are, that you have the talents you do. When you do this, you show your child that they have the right and the ability to love themselves unconditionally as well.

There is no greater act of love!

When your child sees you loving and caring for yourself, they will know that they can do this for themselves also. The child needs to see that to love one's self is possible. By giving them the space and a living example, they will know how much you really love them.

Children learn by example and use what has been modeled for them. If you show them that you do not love yourself with all your heart, they will come to believe that they do not deserve to be loved. How so?

A true loving heart is one that has loved itself first and shares/radiates that love with others. Sharing or radiating love is different than giving love. When you radiate love it is because you have become the love. When you are the love then you can be nothing but loving. In this model, love is effortless because you are the living expression of love.

When you show a child that you do not have love for yourself and that only others matter, they reflect and adopt this behavior and belief system. What you teach them by not loving yourself is that self doesn't matter — only loving others matters. Loving others is a nice idea, but being the love that others then feel is to love without effort or sacrifice. Real love is effortless.

Teaching a child to love themselves first is the sign of a truly loving heart. Loving themselves first means not putting other people's needs and wants before their own. This is a tricky one for most parents to teach, as parents themselves have had no role models. As you model this, the child learns that you love them so much that your personal needs are not part of the equation in them loving themselves. You give them the freedom to consider their needs over yours and let them know that your love is absolute and pure. The key to teaching this to your child is learning to love yourself without conditions. You'll learn more about what this looks like throughout the book.

Traditionally people have been taught that the expression and display of love is the most important way to communicate it. In truth, love is a feeling. Love is not a display or a communication. You can feel if someone loves you or not, no matter what their words are. This is especially true for children. They feel your love no matter what you do or say. As they become older, they begin to understand the concept of love as it is explained, but this does not change their experience of what love is.

How is this related to loving yourself first? Well, loving yourself first makes you a hub of love. The children will feel the love that is inside you and automatically feel and be loved because they feel the love in your heart. Love your child so much that you dare to love yourself first!

REMEMBER:

Love your child with all your heart!

CHAPTER TWO

LOOKING WITHIN

Parents and their issues
What parents need to look at and why

To really be an effective parent you must work on your own personal issues. If you don't you only pass your baggage on to your children like your parents passed theirs on to you. This isn't to say that your parents were evil, only that they had dysfunctional behaviors and beliefs that they passed on to you and now you can choose whether you want to pass these traits on to your children or not. You have the opportunity to break the cycle — you can end it now.

Please do not think you do not have any issues. We all have issues, whether we know it or not and whether we like it or not. By clearing your issues, your life gets easier and you and your children will be happier.

The healthiest parents in the world are parents who work on their own personal issues or inefficient and dysfunctional programs, behaviors or beliefs. Sometimes it is hard for people to do this simply because they are unconscious of these problems or because it hurts their pride. These people do not want to admit that they have difficulties, because admitting to them feels like admitting that they are flawed and that they are not good enough. This can then trigger beliefs about not being good enough or being unlovable.

This is not about you being flawed. It is about your behaviors and beliefs being flawed. By correcting your behaviors and addressing your beliefs, you will teach your children healthy behaviors and they will not have to believe that they are flawed.

To resolve issues, you need to look at:

1. Things that were done to you.

2. How you felt about your mother and father when you were growing up.

3. Things that you disliked.

4. How and where your child brings up your issues, sets you off or irritates you. (These are about you, not them!)

5. Where you are seeing your past as a child rather than your child's present.

You can begin looking at these through journaling. Writing things down makes them concrete and easier to consider than just ideas swirling in your head. By journaling, you can really see what you are thinking and doing. Some ideas for looking at these behaviors are at the end of the chapter.

You:

- Must love yourself, for you cannot give what you do not have.

- Must love your partner if you have one and be a living example (herein "love" is a verb).

- Must love your child in the way the child needs it — not the way you would want to be loved or believe it should be.

YOUR ISSUES

Feel a tightening in your gut at this one? Don't want to look? Relax. That's how most people feel. You may feel that way because you may have always believed there was something wrong with you, and that things you did were wrong. You'd rather not look at your issues because you either think there's no solution, it's impossible or that the solution is difficult. Let's address the "wrongness" first.

Nobody's bad. Things aren't necessarily wrong. Some things just don't work. When behaviors don't work, you typically want to change them. You're not bad and you're not wrong, but you certainly have habits, behaviors and belief patterns that aren't optimally functional, as we all do. Try to remember, people tend to feel wrong or not good enough because they accepted this belief when they were young. Sometimes because they were told this and sometimes they just felt they could never do enough to be loved the way they wanted or loved for who they were. Know that your parents could only love as much as they were capable — it wasn't your fault! You did nothing wrong! You were a beautiful innocent child; your parents lost touch with their inner beauty and parented you from their beliefs, patterns, judgments and wounds.

These dysfunctional habits or patterns aren't innately yours; in fact they are not yours at all. They come from your parents and your parent's parents and on down the line. You pick up traits and don't even realize it. What you also don't realize is that you have a choice as to whether or not to make these patterned behaviors yours and a choice of whether or not to pass them on to your children and continue these patterns.

Your parents have all the habits that they learned from their parents: how to survive in the world, how to maintain things, what hurts you, what doesn't hurt you, what is good for you, what is good for the children, how life should be, etc. They don't even know where all these beliefs came from. But they have them, so they believe they are real. In fact, they don't even see them as beliefs but think this is just how things are. Because of this, they can't even see how these beliefs and patterns are totally dysfunctional and don't work. Each belief may contain little bits of truth and because your parents got by using them, you say, "These must work! I'll pass these on to my children." These are the ones that are consciously passed on — this doesn't even include the ones unconsciously passed on.

As a child, you were a recorder. You sat there and recorded everything that happened. Everything they did — every feeling, every sensation, every motion, every gesture, every phrase, every intonation that they had — you recorded. Then you thought or decided (consciously or unconsciously), "This is how the world works. This is how I need to behave. This is how I manage these situations." And then you added your own little spin on it.

Around the start of puberty, somewhere between the ages of 10 and 12, you began practicing all the skills your parents gave you that they didn't even know they gave you. When they saw this, they said, "What happened to my child?" What happened to their child is that you took all their traits, patterned behaviors and belief systems and made them your own, with your own little twists, and started acting just like them.

Then you practiced these patterned behaviors until you were in your 20s. In your 20s you unconsciously thought, "Okay, I've kind of perfected these patterns and behaviors, and now I'm going to live by them." So you do. Then when you hit your 30s, or late 40s, or sometimes even your 50s, all of a sudden you wake up and say, "This stuff's not working! I don't even know what's going on. All I know is that I'm not happy and my life isn't the way I want it to be." This is what you might call a midlife crisis.

At that point you have to look inside and say, "Whoa, what's going on?" Most people don't. Most people blame everything else: "It's my partner, it's my job, it's my kids, it's everything else." Nobody ever teaches you that your beliefs and patterned behaviors are what are getting in the way. Of course you would think it can't be you! Denial is a common response. Justification is also a common response. Basically these are ego defense mechanisms to salvage your sense of worth and value and to avoid your own judgment of self.

Commonly people are taught to be responsible for their action but rarely for the way they believe. Their beliefs are usually associated with their identity and therefore rarely questioned. Now if their beliefs are questioned then their identity is in question, this then brings up all their beliefs about who they are and their sense of value and worth as a person. This is very scary for most people, so it is easier to blame circumstances, people, things and events than to approach these threatening feelings.

Let's look at it another way that is maybe less threatening. Imagine you are a computer. The patterns, behaviors and beliefs are the software. There is nothing wrong with the computer. The computer and its hardware are perfect, but the software is defective. Would you buy a new computer if you knew this? Probably not. So now you have to reprogram the computer or replace the software. There is no need to judge the computer or the software. This would be a waste of money and time. Simply changing the software would painlessly make everything different. It's the same with you, your beliefs are the faulty software and you are the perfect computer!

The first and most common thing most people do is believe that they are at fault, that they are to blame. Nobody is at fault and no one is to blame. These are passed-on traits/beliefs that run a muck. Nobody educated you about them and now you believe you are stuck with them. In fact, most people believe they are the problem and that they are their beliefs and their behaviors, since they are the problem, they are somehow broken, flawed or faulty. You must separate yourself from your beliefs and behaviors both for yourself and your child. Just as your parents passed these dysfunctional beliefs and behaviors on to you, you will pass them on to your child — unless you choose to change them and end it here. Become conscious. Consciousness cures everything!

This is important: *You are not your behaviors*. Your behaviors are choices you make based on your beliefs, whether consciously or unconsciously. It is those behaviors and patterns that get in your way. The computer needs to be reprogrammed and you have to take time to reprogram it. When you do that, your life begins to run the way you want it to run. It takes time, so be patient. It took you time to get here. You didn't develop this overnight, so it's going to take a little time to resolve it. With a lot of practice and application, it will start to move much faster. And don't worry; if you slip back into old habits sometimes, this is common and is just part of the process.

As you become aware of your own beliefs and patterning be kind to yourself; do not judge yourself. Awareness is the first step to changing these beliefs and patterns. The second step is stopping these behaviors in their tracks and choosing alternate behaviors. The third step is the discovery of where these patterns began. The fourth and final step is finding a technique or process that allows you to make these changes permanent. This can be as simple as self-forgiveness and conscious awareness of all that you do. Always remember that these beliefs and patterns were passed on to you and they are not who you are but merely things that you do while your unconscious of them.

GUILT AND WRONGNESS

It is important for you to know that even though you understand this mentally you may still feel guilty or wrong. Know that you don't need to keep your guilt or feeling of wrongness, but you do still have to feel them. Feeling, not wallowing in them is required for you to move beyond them. Don't deny the feelings. When you deny them, they are still there. Ignoring them doesn't make them go away, it only creates the illusion they are gone. Instead they keep coming up, and usually at the most inconvenient time, like when your child is acting up and you most need to be calm and consistent, or late at night when you could really use some sleep. The feelings cloud your decision-making process; interfere with your parenting and the rest of your life.

You have to feel these feelings. Own them. Say, "Yes, I feel guilt and wrongness. Yes, I believe I'm messing up my child and I feel like I am a failure as a parent." Don't judge it, just feel it. Though you may feel alone, you've just joined 99% of parents. You're just like everyone else, so this is common. Chill. It's okay. You don't have to judge yourself and judging yourself serves no purpose except to punish yourself which will support the guilt and wrongness.

While you are judging yourself for being wrong or not good enough, you can't fully own those feelings, clear them or get past them. They stay with you and come out in other ways. (I.e., you manipulate and justify things to your partner so you don't feel wrong; you do things that boost your ego to compensate for the wrongness etc.) As you suppress your feelings, you teach your child to do the same. Even if they look like they're doing well, they still inherit your pattern of feeling like they are wrong or not good enough. One indicator is if your child or you are a pleaser or identifies themselves by their grades, accomplishments or people's approval.

So own it. Just say, "Yes, these feelings are mine. I didn't consciously create this pattern, but I'm doing it. I'm not going to judge it. That's just the way it is." Saying, "That's just the way it is" isn't saying that's just the way you're going to let it remain. It's simply acknowledging that you accept that's the way it is, right now. Understand: it's just software. It's changeable. It's simply old, outmoded, outdated, improperly distorted programs that you can change if you want. By changing them, your child changes and so does the situation. However, if you are afraid to see how incorrect or distorted your ways are and you judge them as wrong, then you'll have great difficulties in making absolute change and life will turn out pretty much as it was headed or how it was for your parents.

You want to be able to see *everything* in a different light. Instead of being the judge of things, be the observer. All you really need to do is observe what isn't working. Watch what's going on. Ask yourself, "Is what I'm seeing logical, reasonable and rational? Is it working?" If not, change it. You don't have to judge it, get emotional or irrational. All those things will cause more difficulties. If it's working enjoy it; if it's not, change it. That's all you have to do. It's not about right or wrong. It's about is it working or not.

LIVING THROUGH THE CHILD

One of the things many parents do is live their life through their child. Unconsciously, many parents see their child as an opportunity to do the things they were not able to do as a child. For example, the parent may have wanted to do better in school and may have wished they had gone to college or taken a different career path. Now they take all their unhappiness and unfulfilled dreams and project them onto their own children. They consciously or unconsciously see the child as an avenue to live through and experience what they perceive they missed. Thereby often funneling their child in the direction they now wish they had gone. The child will at some point feel this unspoken or spoken pressure and feel a need to measure up. This is projected onto many areas of the child's life: academics, sports, social activities, friends, etc. all the while the parent thinks they are "helping" their child and can justify it by pointing out how it all makes sense.

For example: Growing up, Rachel's mother always dressed her in jeans and casual clothes so she could enjoy playing outside. Rachel loved frills and bangles and lace and longed for them. She promised herself that her daughter wouldn't miss those things. So when she had a daughter, she dressed her daughter in frills, bangles and lace and was thrilled to finally get what she wanted. She was so thrilled that she failed to notice her daughter's tears and frustration when dressed that way or when scolded for messing up her clothes while climbing a tree or playing outside. Can you guess how Rachel's daughter might dress her daughter?

Another way of living through the child is when a parent gets their sense of value or worth from what the child accomplishes. They see the child as a projection or identity of themselves. Many parents are hung up on the child's performance in school. They use the grades the child gets as a way to feel a certain way about themselves or their child. They think, "If my child is smart and successful then I have parented well. If my child does well academically I can be proud of my child." Don't be proud of your child, just love and accept them as they are. Pride can't exist without its opposite, shame. If you teach your child about pride, then you also indicate that there is shame. If taught this the child will struggle, consciously or unconsciously, to stay away from shame which in turn may create an unhealthy prideful person. If they become too focused on pride then needing to be right or perfect may be a side effect which usually creates anxiety. This anxiety will be covering the cause, which was the pride/shame, and you may have noticed there are many people being medicated for anxiety with no apparent cause.

Observe how you feel when your child succeeds. When they are on a sports team, for example, and they do something well, do you feel good about it? When they do not excel in something, do you have a feeling about that too? This is where you are identifying through your child the unresolved issues of your past. Working through this means you'll have to become conscious and aware of your own issues that are tied up in your child. It requires you to be honest with yourself and really look within at where your issues are and the patterns or beliefs you may have from your own birth family experiences and history.

Simply love your child with all your heart and say, "Good job", "I love that you are having fun". That's enough. When you are overly concerned about your child's performance, realize these beliefs run deep in almost every parent and that they are not wrong to have, but they create dysfunction and many unexpected beliefs to be created by your child. The beliefs and patterns are different for every individual but they do occur. Take a close hard look at this and feel deeply within yourself to see where these patterns are running in your life and where they were in your birth family.

It is your identification with and attachment to these patterns that needs to be considered. In the feelings of attachment are many of your own beliefs, needs and unresolved issues. An effective parent loves and guides their child to be able to function on their own, while allowing them to create their own individual identity rather than molding them into something that meets only the parent's needs.

When parents live through their children the children have no life of their own.

When a child is imposed upon this way their adult life will often feel inexplicably empty. This is because they have lived a life created and molded by someone else.

Love your child so much that you teach and allow your child to be self-directed, self-sustaining, self-maintaining and free-thinking!

Love yourself so much that you are the model of those qualities!

YOUR CHILDREN DO NOT BELONG TO YOU

Parenting is a relationship, not a dictatorship. Your children are unique human beings with their own agenda, rights, purpose and destiny. They are not indentured slaves or possessions. They do not need to be molded, only directed so they can consciously choose. You do not own your children, they don't belong to you, nor do you have the right to boss your children around. Your children are not things or objects. You do have the privilege of guiding, caring for, and teaching your children how to function in the world, while you love and enjoy them.

Before anyone gets too upset let's clarify this possession thing. To think or say "they are my child" is common. But if you see your child as part of you then it is ownership. Many parents unconsciously see their child as a part of them. Mainly because you created their bodies through an act of love through the donation of your egg and sperm or gave birth to them.

If you could truly see your child as a separate individual both in feeling and mental understanding then the attachment would begin to dissipate. All too often parents feel that if they separate from their child in this way it is being cold or not loving. Let's say that it actually is the most loving act you can do! Love your child with all your heart by setting them free from your own attachments. Love and attachment are two different things. Look them up in the dictionary if you are not sure.

Saying or thinking "You are *mine*" or "You are *my* child" implies possession. Remember you do not own your child. When you teach your child that they belong to you, the child starts to believe that they belong to others and not to themselves. This turns the child into a puppet who can be controlled or manipulated by other people. Usually these things are said with no ill intent but they eventually become habits, beliefs and assumptions that a child often takes literally.

The child may even reciprocate and say, you're my possession by saying "you're my mother, you're my father, and you own me. You should take care of me. You have to take care of me and I'm never leaving home." This is a result of a needy or unconscious parent who unwittingly taught the child to be needy and dependent, then can't figure out what went wrong.

Many parents use their children to have an experience which they themselves are not having. These experiences may include joy, pride, satisfaction, success, attention, acknowledgment and of course love. Parents love to love their children; they love to protect their children; they love to speak for, about, to or at their children; they love to think for their children. They love to make their children feel safe and to make them feel creative. They get their sense of meaning or satisfaction from their children's exploits because they are not living life and experiencing it themselves. Instead, they live off the feelings their children are having and experiencing. This way the parents don't have to do it themselves or maybe they never learned how to do it themselves. It often appears socially acceptable and others may even say, "Wow, you are a wonderful parent! You just so love your child."

Maybe so, but this can be really distorted at the same time. Everyone is like this, to some degree, until they get clearer or more mature. We'll label it as living your life by proxy through the child. You can live by proxy through someone else too, but it's very common for parents to do it through their children. Keep in mind this is not to say these parents are bad. It is however to say they may have dysfunctional beliefs and behaviors that are so socially or familiarly acceptable they appear healthy but in actuality are not.

If you have the attitude that your child belongs to you, then a) you are not paying attention to yourself, and b) you are turning your child into an emotional cripple who will look for someone to take care of them when they are older rather than be self-directed.

Grandparents are often just as responsible for this as parents. They can really get off on trying to experience life through the child if they are not matured grandparents. They may be mature in handling their own lives, but not yet internally mature. And since they passed the patterns to the parent then they may not be aware of this pattern therefore it will be assumed "normal".

If you've cleared your issues or whatever you want to call them, then you can love your children or grandchildren purely, just the way they are, without feeling pride or ownership of their accomplishments. But 95–99% of grandparents are doing exactly what their parents did and haven't cleared a lot of those processes or beliefs from their lives.

Learn to believe and accept that you and your child are equal human beings allowed to have your own likes and dislikes. You simply have two different positions at this time. They are to learn to be a functioning human being and you are their guide and nourish them until they are old enough to do that on their own. Other than this you are equals!

The following concept is often hard for most parents: *your child does not have to obey you.* What the child must learn is to make cooperative choices. If they just obey you, you have taught them to blindly obey authority and not think for themselves. Your job as a parent is to assist in connecting your children to their own answers and inner awareness so they can have their own experiences and gain wisdom from those experiences with your guidance.

While you teach your children human skills, they will teach you about your human issues. Your children will inevitably show you what your weaknesses and strengths are, and their behaviors and questions will often force you to grow. How your child irritates you or creates joy for you is a reflection of what you must change or feel within yourself. Raising your child is an adventure not a task!

PROGRAMMING THE CHILD

Imagine, your child is a blank canvas and everything that happens in their world, seen or unseen, becomes part of their canvas. Knowing this, you are responsible to be conscious as a parent. Your lack of awareness alters your child's life. Children do not have mature discernment skills and rely on you to model healthy human skills. Please, understand that the programmed behaviors and beliefs are 80% unconsciously taught and learned. Human behavioral and patterned learning is 20% mental and 80% feeling.

You must be as aware of your behaviors, words and feelings as possible, for you set the standard by which your child will view and respond to life!

A parent is a teacher, a mentor and a model, not the owner or boss of a child. Parents commonly go into the unconscious pattern of controlling children because that is often the way they were taught by their own parents. That way, however, is not very functional. It is not that your parents were bad parents — we are not going to blame them. Instead, we are going to look at the facts and the functionality of what is actually happening in order to understand yourself and, in turn, your children. Keep in mind everything you do, say, think and feel affects your child and becomes part of their programming. One of the biggest keys to being a healthy parent is understanding yourself.

A parent's self-discovery and self –awareness is critical to a well-adjusted child.

Do your own inner work: Understand why you act the way you do and why you say the things you say. Then interpret it and see if it makes sense. Let's go to the idea of analyzing something to see if it's logical, reasonable and rational. If it doesn't fit those criteria, it's just emotional. Realize that if it's emotional it makes no sense to the child. When you program the child with things that make no sense, they just become robots who respond rather than healthy human beings who figure things out for themselves.

We said earlier that children are individual human beings. You really have to grasp the concept that your child does not 'belong' to you — the child is not 'yours.' You have to see and *feel* the child as a separate individual and treat them that way. Begin to understand how the child thinks, behaves and most of all how they feel.

DO NOT assume, judge or disregard how they feel inside! This does not mean you must agree with them or feel the same way. It does mean that you respect them as a human being. By modeling this they will *feel* your love. It is up to you to assist them from a mature adult stand as to whether or not their opinion or perspective is functional. Notice we said 'functional' and not 'makes sense.'

Feelings will often not make sense but they are real and must be honored. Now notice we said honored NOT validated. This is important for you can never validate someone's feelings, this only they can do! If they look to you for validation then you have created a puppet and they will become dependent on others to validate them. This is called "giving yourself away." When a child gets the program of giving themselves away they are now subject to other peoples manipulations, whether well intended or ill intended. You now have created a victim child program. After their feelings are honored then they are observed to see if they are functional. Really get to know your child. All too often parents expect the child to understand the parent. Love your child enough to understand and honor them.

Children can learn choice and cooperation or they can learn fear. When you constantly tell your child that what they are doing is bad, you give the child the impression that if they do something bad, you do not approve of them. Then the fear comes in: "If I do this, I am not going to be loved, liked or accepted by my parents. So guess what? I am going to do what my parents say whether I agree with it or not. I will not risk not being loved."

In this model, your child has again learned that to be loved they must give themselves away to others. Your child is a drone for others to control and use because they haven't gained the ability to be free thinkers. They are simply obedient humans unable to have a will or choice of their own without some painful repercussions.

This type of programming is very common, subtle and often unintended. Because of a fast paced life, when parents focus on the physical needs or their own inner life under stress it is easy to have these subtle unconscious programs being taught. It is important for a child to be freethinking, to have thoughts of their own creation and the ability to discern if they are functional or not. Children should act not because they were told how to behave, but because they were able to sit down, explore, discern and choose what is functional or not, what they like, don't like, what they want to do and become.

For example: You see your child playing with a fire truck. You always thought you'd like to be a fireman and you think it's a good career. You ask them, "Do you want to be a fireman?" or tell them, "You want to be a fireman, don't you?" Maybe that idea never even crossed the child's mind, but because they like fire trucks, you program them for the next five years to believe they want to be a fireman. They will grow up to be a fireman and only then realize that it is not what they really loved to do or wanted to do all along. They will have chosen that job just because they were told as a child what to feel or do. So now they have a job that they really don't like and they don't know why they chose it. They didn't. It was due to a very subtle almost hypnotic suggestion that became the direction of their life; all this from your preference, personal needs and desires while you observed them playing with a fire truck.

Suggestion is very powerful for the parent and the child. You have to remember that as their parent, your child sees you as the god of their universe and this is no exaggeration. To your child, you are absolute power. The young child is completely dependent on you. There is nothing greater than you and your power for a long time. Anything you say to your child is taken as fact and becomes an internal belief for the child unless they become conscious enough to figure out that your beliefs are flawed. That usually doesn't take place until they are much older.

They may live 40 years or more before figuring out that they have been programmed with beliefs that aren't even helpful, and only then realize why their life was difficult or challenging.

When asking your child questions never ask them questions that imply what to do. Always ask them questions that allow for their choice. When asking choice questions try to give them at least three or more options to choose from as this creates an opportunity to develop critical thinking skills.

PARENTS' REACTIONS AND PERCEPTIONS

AND THEIR EFFECT ON THE CHILD

Parents must be aware of how their own reactions and perceptions interfere with their parenting skills. When a parent sees something in the child, they usually judge it through their own perceptions and then act or respond according to those judgments. This is not conscious parenting.

For example: Your child falls off a chair, bangs their head, gets hurt and cries. Next time the child gets on a chair and looks like they will fall, you yell at them and say, "Sit down, it's not safe!" or "Sit down!" without any explanation. The child just feels your hostility and wonders why you are being so mean. They may not listen because you make no sense to them; they do not feel as if they are in any danger. You yell again and get even more forceful. The child thinks they are being bad and now sits.

So what has actually happened? You just taught them that you are unreasonable, erratic, unstable and mean. You've also taught them that they are bad, must do as you say to be accepted and loved, and that you can get your way by bullying. Look at what you have created unintentionally. Look at the patterns that were created: bullying, control, bossiness, moody erratic behavior, unreasonable requests, emotional demanding to name a few.

Why did you do this? In a normal parent's mind, this is protecting the child. Why? Because you are afraid the child will get hurt.

What you did not do in this situation is explain to the child what happened before and express your concern about the situation happening again. What could you have done instead? You might have said, "Honey, the last time you did that in a chair you fell and got hurt. I am concerned it might happen again. Please sit down." If they don't, you might add, "I asked you already and now I am telling you — you must sit down now so I do not have to be concerned about another fall and you getting hurt. My job as your parent is to keep you safe from hurting yourself if possible." Explained to them in detail what you were feeling and why you are saying it.

Too often adults think that the children do not understand. However, children understand and feel more than you know or what is measurable. If you explain in detail early on in the child's life it will create a greater bond and connection between you and your child as they grow older which will make your relationship richer. This, of course, is just one example of how your fears or judgments interfere with your parenting skills.

An example of another type of perception that may influence the child is when a parent dislikes a task — say, making a meal for the family — and expresses how unpleasant it is for them to do. The children form a belief that doing things for each other is unpleasant. This will cause the children to not want to do things for anyone because it inconveniences them or is somehow otherwise unpleasant. On the flip side of this a child must understand that they are part of the family and as a part of the family there are tasks that are done because the family is a team and everyone must work together.

We are in no way suggesting that you become a passive parent. You must be the leader but not the dictator. A parent should know what logical reasonable and rational requests are and see to it that the child participates as best as they can. To allow the child to become the leader by being too passive with them creates a whole other type of programming that is unhealthy.

Commonly parents who have been in a dictatorship as a child will be the opposite as parents. There must be a balance. You must be kind, understanding and yet the maintainer of family rules and systems that make sense. These rules and systems should be equal and age relative for everyone including the parents and must be practical and logical. Rules that are based upon emotions are rules to be eliminated. Rules and systems that are in place just because that's the way you have always done them or your family did them when you grew up should be eliminated or modified to fit with current day needs and logic. Rest assured if they don't make sense your children will question them or oppose them.

THE ROLE OF THE ADULT

A child looks to you as the adult for your reaction and will copy your response to a situation. Young children will accept the adult's reaction without question.

For example, watch toddlers playing in a kiddie pool. Once in a while, a child falls and goes under the water for a second or two. For a split second after they get up, they will look for their parent and gauge their reaction. The child of parents who respond with fear and drama will cry. On the other hand, if the parent claps, smiles or responds calmly, the child will most likely smile as well or just get back to playing.

Young children are primarily sensorial, meaning that they experience their world through senses and feelings directly. If you are scared or shocked, the child will be scared and shocked, won't know why and will come to see these reactions as their own rather than something they have imitated. If you remain calm and centered, the child will remain calm or have the opportunity to calm down. What if you start to react and then remember to be calm? Explain to the child, "Oops. This isn't something to be afraid of and I shouldn't have responded that way I apologize if I frightened you." Remember the more you explain to a child the better and the richer your long-term relationship will be. When explaining to your child, please remember to speak to them in age-appropriate words.

Instead of thinking of how you feel and projecting your feelings and experiences onto the child, view this is an opportunity to instruct children on how to handle their own feelings. Put your personal feelings and issues aside and then teach your children that they have choices which give them tools for an easier life. Do not condone or allow children to deny their feelings. They should never feel bad, guilty, ashamed or wrong about what they feel. It is perfectly okay for children to have the emotion they choose. If they decide to experience a feeling, guide them to find an appropriate way and words in which to express it. Practice asking questions and actually listening and responding to the feeling the child is communicating to you.

CONSCIOUS PARENTING

Conscious parenting requires constant awareness. This doesn't mean paranoid, crazy attention, but vigilance so you're aware of whether your patterns are seeping through in a way that you don't realize. The key is to start to develop your feelings. Feelings aren't emotions. Feelings are a sense of what's going on, an intuition. They go beyond thinking and the mind.

Feelings are not emotions
Emotions are felt
Feelings are an unseen sensory experience
Emotions are based upon beliefs and perceptions

Mentally, it's challenging to be aware of your patterns. By the time you mentally recognize the signs and signals, your old pattern may be running and have affected your child as well. When you see your child in some sort of pattern you must recognize that it has already been years in the making. The majority of patterns and belief systems have been established in the child by the time they are six or eight years old.

When you start to become more feeling/intuitive/in tune with your environment, your child and raising your child, you will be more in tune with how they feel. With this new consciousness, you will start a pattern or be in the middle of one and feel that something is off. You will realize, "Something is going on here" and be able to change.

You have to be feeling, or as some people call it, intuitive. Intuition is just sensing/feeling, not emotional feeling. When you begin to develop your sensate abilities and integrate mental awareness with appropriate human skills, you will naturally be in tune with your child.

When your patterns run, your mind will justify them. When you are feeling without a balance of intellect and human skills, the patterns may just take over because there is a lack of discernment. As you develop your intuition you will feel and be aware of more than you ever thought possible. If you already have a good sense of intuition, learn to trust it. Intuition is one of the greatest and under estimated human skills available. Contrary to popular belief everyone is intuitive!

DIFFICULTIES IN CHANGING

Sometimes it is hard for people to change because they are unconscious of their patterns or they are too prideful and they do not want to admit that they have difficulties or are not perfect. Change also can be challenging to a person's identity. To change often means that what they have been doing is wrong or not good enough. However, change is simply the conscious awareness that something isn't working and you are choosing a fluid, flexible lifestyle rather than a rigid controlled lifestyle.

Behaviors are like clothes — you can put them on and take them off. When you believe you are the roles you play in life, i.e., parent, husband, wife, mother, father, employee, boss, etc., or that you are your behaviors they become identities and identities are much harder to change than behaviors.

Change your behaviors without judging them to be wrong. See them as functional or not functional and you will teach your children healthy behaviors — they will not grow up believing they are flawed. You will have shown them that self-reflection is a safe and positive thing.

Some challenges to effectively parent and change are parents who:

- have authority issues.
- have personal power issues.
- have power issues between themselves, their children or their partners.
- are too rigid and blame others.
- do not take responsibility for their own behaviors and the creation of their own world;
- who are victims or victimizers (mental, emotional or physical)
- are in denial of their own unresolved issues, whether they

are mental, emotional or health issues.

- are too wimpy or passive

- too aggressive, controlling, rigid or demanding

- smothering, fearful or protective

- non-communicative or communicate poorly

- are too needy, emotional or mental

- have worth and value issues

- feel empty, unloved or unlovable

Areas where issues arise in connection with your child

- Do you get upset or want to cry when your child wants to cry?

- Do you defend or blame your child without hearing the facts?

- Do you cushion your child or control their actions when you believe their actions may result in emotional pain, or lead them down a path that you think is wrong?

- Do you sometimes look at your partner and child and see a reenactment of your father or mother and yourself from a scene from your past?

- When telling your child a consequence, do you feel guilty or are you fearful that they are not getting what they want and will not be happy?

- Do you emotionally choose sides when mediating a confrontation between two or more of your children?

- When teaching or reprimanding your child, do you do it with emotion?

- Do you ever bring up the past when speaking to or confronting your child?

- Do you speak or treat your child differently when you are alone than when you are with your whole family?

- Do you ever feel or notice that you and your partner equally don't want to be the bad guy, and therefore no one parents?

- Do you allow your partner to be the primary disciplinarian?

- Do you preferred to be the "nice guy" parent?

- Do you repeat yourself over and over, saying the same things to your children?

- Do you try to control everything they do, believing you know what's best?

- Do you allow your child to be emotionally in between you and your partner?

- Do you manipulate your child in any way?

- Do you treat your child like your friend or as an adult in regards to your personal life?

- Do you yell at your child?

- Do you lose your temper?

- Do you focus on grades/performance in school or sports?

- Do you give your child personal space?

- Do you truly listen to your child's inner feelings and thoughts without imposing yours?

Remember that your child learns how to behave from you. They will use your own issues and manipulations to manipulate you. You show them by example how to react to situations. They then put this into practice and experiment with how the world works.

Children use the tools they have learned to find their way. If their tools are faulty, their journey will be difficult. Your child will be a reflection of your own inner or outer struggles. Your child will show you your own patterned behaviors by acting them out. Have compassion for yourself by having compassion for them.

Learn from them. Know that whatever they do that you don't like, somewhere you behave, have behaved, think the same way, or have done something similar. Otherwise they would not be doing it. That's a difficult concept for many parents to swallow but it's true. Also know that if you deny that this is true or even a possibility then it is definitely true. The upside is that as you change what you're doing, you model the change for your child. Ninety percent of a child's adult patterned behaviors are established by the time they are six years old. However, these behaviors are reversible with your guidance and modeling.

The way you relate to your child
becomes your child's way of the world.

A lot of parents don't want to do the hands-on work. They want someone else like a teacher, a therapist or some sort of professional to fix the child. You must know right now, no child is broken! Some children's emotions and psyche can be or have been wounded but this can be changed. Unfortunately no professional can fix a child. They can assist them in their own recovery but the parent is required to participate in order for the child to heal their wounds. All children deserve the unconditional love of their parents! All children should know that they are lovable! All parents theoretically should communicate to their child in multiple ways that they love them!

PARENTING, GROWTH, MATURITY AND FUN

Most people believe that the child within must go away in order to become an adult. As a child, you were often taught that playful wildness was a sign of immaturity or annoyance to the adults. In order to grow up, you assumed that it wasn't allowed or that it simply wasn't acceptable to have fun. As one grows into adulthood and prepares to become a parent, there is an unconscious assumption that all of your fun, joy and reverence for life must be subdued and held under wraps in order to be mature and become an adult.

You don't have to subdue the child within in order to be a functioning adult, but you may suppress this playfulness (both your own and that of your child's) if you are not a healthy functioning adult. Achieving functioning adulthood simply means that you understand how the world works and can make it work for you. But to become a mature man or woman, you must become a functioning human being and love yourself. Those are the only two qualities necessary everything else will come naturally if you have achieved these two things.

A mature adult is a functioning adult who knows how the world works and loves themselves. Mature healthy adults retain the joyful and wondrous feelings they had as children. They are still playful, they are still wild at times, but most of all they are loving and they are functioning in the world. This allows you to enjoy life on earth, which is exactly what you are here for.

A REFLECTION: WHY DID YOU BECOME A PARENT?

Ask yourself these questions:
- Why did I want to have a child?
- Did I want to have a child so I could be a parent?
- Did I have a child just to have a child?
- Did I have a child because I thought I was supposed to have a child?
- Did I have a child because that is what my parents wanted?
- Did I have a child because it's something most people do?
- Did I have a child because I was "born to be a mom or dad"?
- Was I prepared to be a parent?
- Did I have a child for another reason?

Whatever you decide was your reason, you now have to take this into account for some of the difficulties you may be having as a parent. The reason you had a child was your choice but that reason also affects those around you. If you made being a parent an identity — if being a parent is what you believe you are in life — then you have lost your inner self. Your partner and child have lost the real you. Your child has learned from you that it is okay to ignore their real self and become an identity: a mom, a doctor, a perfectionist, or any other label that a person may apply to themselves.

Parenting is something you do, not something you become. If you had a child because you were supposed to or because it was expected of you, you have given up your own free will to choose and become something for someone else instead. This is not to say that after having children, you don't really enjoy being a parent. It is to say that you're living your life based on someone else's ideas and not your own.

Most people cannot distinguish between being a parent and having a child. Most people have children without thought as to what it really means to be a parent. By choosing to be a parent you already know that parenting is a lot of work and not always fun. Although the joy of being a parent far exceeds the work, it's often forgotten in times of stress or change.

Often times, people approach having a child with "new puppy syndrome": once the puppy is in the house, it is not as much fun. The puppy becomes an obligation and can cause feelings of being overwhelmed. Many parents feel this way about their children. When you have children, the work and possible problems that may come along are usually not considered. There may be ADHD, autism, emotional or physical problems, to name a few. It is best if the parents don't think negatively and be totally accepting of whatever comes, whether it is perceived as positive or negative. If you love your child you accept them and their circumstances. You might even ask "How is this situation giving me the opportunity to grow as a human being?"

Children are the bearers of the information and a reflection of what you yourself need to understand, change or heal.

Be thankful for the gift of the reflection and do not judge the messenger or your perception of the message.

MAKING LASTING CHANGE

Be patient with yourself. It takes time to change — you can't instantly transform your life. Keep in mind that it's not possible to simply think yourself happy. If it were, we could erase a bad day just by thinking happy thoughts. Unfortunately, thinking happy thoughts is only a quick fix to an ongoing problem and never a permanent fix.

The key to making lasting change, to truly finding happiness and fulfillment, is actually quite simple, though not always easy. You have to fully commit to changing, taking responsibility, being truthful and honest with yourself and uncover the beliefs that are limiting you. Once you uncover your limiting beliefs, you can begin to change them so you can create the YOU that you want to experience.

Begin keeping a journal. This is beneficial for you as an individual, for it grounds your feelings and experiences, and often shows you issues that you may not have been fully aware of up until this point. When you write your experiences down on paper, they become more clear and concrete. These notes are a reference for you to really see where your difficulties are as a parent and as a person. Remember that everything and anything can be changed! The key to this exercise is to do it without judgment. Observe yourself and your experiences and change the behaviors and patterns that no longer serve you.

Journaling can provide new insights. Journal about what you liked and disliked growing up, what you promised to do differently than your parents and when, where, how and why your child irritates or frustrates you. Realize that all of these frustrations are about you and that recognizing them is the first step to changing them. Journal about why you wanted to be a parent. These too will give you new insights. The best gift you can give your children is a list of your beliefs so they can know what to look for in themselves. Of course we must give it to them when we feel they are ready for them, but this is the way patterns are broken.

Five things you can do:

1. Journal what you feel about your parenting, child and partner
2. Be aware of what emotions and emotional attachments you have with your child
3. Be aware of what thoughts you have
4. List the beliefs you have about parenting
5. List the beliefs you have about yourself as a parent

Use these exercises to become more conscious about you. Change what is not working and recognize how much you picked up from your childhood experience. This will create a much more fulfilling parenting experience. Most of all do not blame or judge yourself.

CHAPTER THREE

HABITS & SKILLS OF A CONSCIOUS PARENT

21 habits of conscious parenting

1. Be persistent and consistent. Be firm and do not give in under pressure. A child will continue to push for something as long as they feel you are not firm in the psychic boundaries you have set. Set boundaries mentally, emotionally, physically and verbally. Once boundaries are set, they do not change! You may set and reset boundaries with each topic but they should never change once they are set. They may however evolve as your child gets older to be more age appropriate. Be balanced, firm but not rigid, flexible yet not wishy washy.

2. Be patient, lovingly kind and firm without being emotional. You can be firm without being rigid. Kindness should always begin and remain in the home. Most people are more courteous to and treat strangers with more compassion than they show to their own family members.

Ask yourself these questions:

Am I nicer or more patient with people outside of my family?

If people in your family see you being nicer and more patient with outsiders, you are sending them the message that other people matter more than they do. Is this what you are doing?

***If so, can you see how your family members might learn
not to be nice to you or each other?***

3. Be aware of and understand your feelings. Also have the ability to verbalize your feelings. Teach your child to do the same with their feelings.

4. Speak in age-appropriate language. The way you speak to your 10-year-old is different than the way you speak to your three-year-old. Explain in language that is appropriate to their age and ask them if they understand and what you have said. Have them explain it back to you to be sure they understand. You may be surprised at how often they nod their head but really don't understand.

Remember to change your style and your techniques during each new stage the child goes through. Every time the child changes to a new stage or a new state of growth, your techniques, your style and the way you do things has to be repeated in a different way. You have to adjust. Your parenting style evolves with the child. This supports and reinforces the first habit.

The two things that are important are their age-appropriate maturity and their ability to comprehend at the time you are instructing them. These are key because they might be mature enough to handle it, but they can't comprehend what you are saying, and now you've made a mess. Vice versa, they may comprehend what you're saying but can't handle it maturely.

5. Be present. You may often be distracted with worries, plans or what's going on somewhere else. Many people spend more time in the past and future than in the present. The only place to truly be with your child, the only place where change can happen, is in the present.

6. Be the living example for your child of how to live as a functional human being who is balanced, logical, reasonable and rational. Realize you are a model your children learn from, whether you are a healthy one or not. Work on you and admit when you're wrong — let them know you're not perfect but are always learning and growing as they are.

7. Be a director, not an authority; be a guide and guardian, not a commander. Treat your child as an individual, not as someone you are controlling.

8. Treat everyone equally, not fairly. Everyone has a different definition of what is fair, but equal can usually be agreed upon by all. Equal balances the age and personality differences. Each age and personality has different needs and requirements for equality.

9. Be solution and result oriented. Always seek a solution. Be aware of the results and assist the child in being aware and understanding the solution and how it was attained.

10. Seek conscious cooperation, not conformity. Create an atmosphere of conscious cooperation and seek solutions that are mutually agreeable. Never attempt to get your child to conform. Allow them to make their own choices in their own style.

11. Allow the child to do for themselves rather than you doing things for them as much as possible. Don't mother your child. Doing for them because it is easier for you creates emotional cripples. Even if it takes a little longer allow your child to do the doing.

12. Help them find their own answers. Rather than tell them the answers lead them to discovery through the appropriate questions and logical deductions. If you give them the answers the experiences are never theirs and you create dependency. If you lead them to their own self-discovery of the answers it is theirs for a lifetime and you have empowered them.

13. Give them choices. Make almost everything a choice for them. This teaches decision-making, discernment and critical thinking skills. If there are no choices to be made and what must be done must be done, do not give them choices, be honest. It confuses them when you tell them they have a choice and then tell them they have to do it regardless of what they chose — then you have betrayed them and created patterns of mistrust. This also teaches them that you set them up for a fall, which looks like a power trip. When something must be done and there are no choices and they don't want to do it; give them the choice of the end result.

Example: if you don't mow the lawn then you won't have any privileges this weekend, if you do mow the lawn then you're free to go out this weekend. You choose what you would like to experience.

Always give options when you can and allow them to choose even if you do not agree with their choice. This enables them to see the results of their choices and choose hopefully more wisely in the future based on their own experience.

14. Promise nothing. Do not promise children anything. Tell them you will do the best you possibly can to meet the desired goal. If you cannot fulfill a promise, you are literally teaching your children to lie and not trust you. After many years of disappointment they will decide you are not to be trusted and are not honest, which then complicates the relationship and destroys any chance of real cooperation. Broken promises equal broken trust. What you can trust about this is that they will eventually do the same to you.

15. Make home a haven, a safe place where everyone wants to be. Make your home a place of cooperation, not conformity, a place of discussion not argument, a place of trust and honesty not manipulation and broken promises. In this case safety means a stable consistent environment and the feeling of knowing what is most likely to happen based on trust and consistency.

A common understanding of safety is to hold onto, protect or be familiar with, this is limiting. True safety is expansive. True safety is actually awareness — not protection. "Being aware" means being an explorer. You can train your child to be an explorer, or you can protect your child in a fortress. Explorers expand and fortresses imprison. What type of life do you wish for your child?

Home should be the place where everyone wants to be. (This may change a bit when your child becomes a teenager, but it should always remain the safe place they can come to in times of crisis.) It should be a safe place where there is no judgment (this does not mean total agreement), violence, rejection, screaming, invalidation, ignoring, denial, lying, etc. There should be kindness, acceptance, confirmation, compassion, love and understanding. Home is where one should not have to have one's guard up; on the contrary, it should be the place where you do not need to guard at all. You need to create this for yourself and for your children.

16. Do not argue. Arguing is a sign of weakness, power issues, lack of confidence, insecurity and instability. Instead, there should be discussions. Discussions can be amicable or in disagreement and can sometimes become a little heated, but never allow it to deteriorate into an argument. Approach all discussions with logical, reasonable and rational thinking as well as communication. Discussing things in this way opens a dialog and creates trust. Arguing creates animosity, power struggles and an adversarial relationship.

17. Never yell! There is never a good time or reason to yell. Yelling only separates and distances people from each other. Yelling is a sure way to make your child dislike, distrust or even worse case scenario, hate you. Yelling is an indicator that something is wrong. Use as calm a voice as you can and if necessary a firm or stern voice is absolutely acceptable.

18. Never bring up the past. When something is done, let it go. Do not bring it back up. Do not be vindictive or hold a grudge. This only teaches children to do the same. People only do this when they do not get what they want and are still feeling the hurt of an event, when they are attempting to degrade or hurt someone else or justify their behaviors. Be kind and understanding, even if you do not agree. You may disagree without holding a grudge. Express how you feel and never bring up old dirt. Old dirt equals all the pain. Old pain equals new pain.

19. Be aware of environmental influences. Your children are influenced not just by you, but by friends, peers, school, media and more. Educate and guide your child about outside influences: TV, peer pressure, electronic devices and cultural attitudes. Do not do this from a place of fear or for overprotection, but from a place of consciousness, love and understanding of the world around them.

20. Love your child unconditionally for who they are, not for the version you want them to be. Always conclude an encounter with a child with an explanation that what you have spoken about or done is your opinion about what you feel is best and you are sharing it with them because it is your job to prepare them for the world. Also let them know that those things may change in the future but for now, this is how it will be. Be open and let them know that if they can show you a logical, rational reason to consider a change, you will take it under consideration.

21. Love Yourself. The type of love we're referring to here is internal. It is not about the things you do for yourself or how you take care of yourself physically. Those are important, however how you feel inside about yourself as a human being and an individual is of equal or greater importance. How you feel about yourself internally is psychically reflected to your children even if it is never spoken about. If you take the time to love yourself, your love will radiate to your child. Loving yourself is the greatest act of love you can give to your child.

NEW PARADIGM PARENTING EXAMPLE

The following example — a parent bringing a child to an unfamiliar environment — shows how several of these habits can work together to guide a child to independence and self-reliance.

Background: Vanessa and her son, Jake who is 5, begin to gather their belongings for their weekly neighborhood play date experience. While packing his backpack, Vanessa anticipates Jake's anxiety about going to a home that is not his own. She feels Jake's anxiety escalate while walking towards her neighbor's house. Sometimes she can't discern whether they are his feelings or her own. Jake does the same thing every time. They walk in and Jake hides behind Vanessa. When she encourages him to play with the other children, he tightens his grip around her leg. She asks him several more times to go play with the children before giving up and allowing him to stay with her and the other parents. Vanessa does not enjoy this experience, but feels sorry for her son. She allows this behavior from Jake and he continues to repeat these patterned behaviors. Both believe that there seems to be no other option.

After attending a parent group, Vanessa decides that the next play date will be different for both of them. She prepares Jake ahead of time, using language he will understand. She is kind, but her tone is firm.

Their first discussion happens a few days before the next event. It goes something like this: "Jake every time we go to the play date you hold onto my leg and refused to be with the other children. Why do you do this?" Jake responds "I don't know". Vanessa says to Jake "well honey, feel it out and see what feelings were going on inside of you and your body when we have been over there". Jake says, "My body feels funny and I don't want to be without you". Vanessa says, "That sounds like something that adults call being afraid, your body sometimes feels funny and you really don't want to do something or feel something. Almost everybody feels that at some time in their life. You can learn how to make that change but you have to do something different. I am telling these things to you because I have to prepare you for when you're a grown up. So next time we are going to do something different and I know you will probably be a little bit afraid but were going to do it anyway."

The next discussion happens either the night before or the morning of. And it goes something like this: "Jake, I want to remind you that we are doing something different today and I want you to know that you will not be allowed to stay with me during the play date. It won't matter if you whine, argue; hold onto my leg, cry or scream. I will be placing you in the room with the other children and I am going into the other room with the grown-ups. To prepare yourself, you may want to tell yourself or imagine yourself playing with the other children now to get used to the idea. We will not leave because you are whining, arguing, crying or screaming and you will have to be with the other children. I will have fun with my friends and you will be with the children. Jake, you will choose whether you want to have fun or not. It is up to you. Do you understand? Whatever you choose is alright but remember I will be doing what I have just discussed with you."

Vanessa waits for Jake to respond. He looks at her for a few moments and then shakes his head "yes" acknowledging that he understands what is expected of him.

At the next play date, Jake moves behind Vanessa as soon as they walk in the front door of the neighbor's house. Before grabbing her leg, he hesitates and looks at her.

He wonders, "Did Mom really mean what she said? What will she do? Will she feel sorry for me? Will she do what she always does? She said these things before, but gave up and didn't follow through.

"I would rather play with the toys and games with the other kids. I don't want to be with Mom and those boring adults. I am just afraid that I won't know how to play with these new toys or children. I don't feel afraid when I am with Mom. So instead of trying something new that feels scary, I'll stay with Mom because I am safe with her. I will stick with what I know."

Jake grabs Mom's leg tightly. This is the moment for Vanessa to be consistent with the expectations she previously set with Jake. Kindly, patiently and without intensity, Vanessa repeats what she wants. "Jake, remember what I told you. You will go with the other kids." Jake says, "No" and tightens his grip. He feels Mom, but wonders, "Will she insist in front of other people? Does she really mean it this time?" Mom looks Jake in the eye, and firmly and calmly says in front of her friends, "Jake, remove your hands from my leg." She continues to look at him, but does not say anything else. It seems like a long time for both Vanessa and Jake. Firmly and kindly she repeats "Jake, your hands, remove them, dear." She finally pries his hands off of her leg. Jake starts to cry. Vanessa takes him into the room with the other children. He returns to her twice but both times Vanessa persists. She gently takes him back to the children and then sits with the parents. Although this is hard for both of them, Vanessa realizes that there is a bigger picture that outweighs their current discomfort.

The following week, Vanessa and Jake prepare to go to the next neighbor's home. Part of consistent parenting is repeating the exact same guidance with Jake every time until he gets it. This is important because he is not used to Mom being consistent. Mom reminds Jake, in age-appropriate language, what will occur for the two of them at their next visit.

"Jake, I just want to remind you that you will not stay with me today during the play date. It won't matter if you whine, argue, cry or scream. I will be placing you in the room with the other children. So prepare yourself. It may help to imagine yourself playing with the other children ahead of time. Just so we are clear, we will not leave because you are whining, arguing, crying or screaming. I will have fun with my friends and you will be with the other children. You will choose whether you want to have fun or not. It is up to you. Do you understand?"

Vanessa waits for Jake to respond that he understands. He makes a face and shakes his head "yes." This happens several times; sometimes with improvement, sometimes with no change and sometimes it feels like he regresses. But Vanessa stays consistent.

Eventually, when Vanessa and Jake enter their neighbor's home, Jake hides behind Mom but he hesitates. He looks at and feels Mom. Vanessa looks Jake in the eye and connects with him. Kindly and firmly she says, "Remember what we said. Remember what will happen. I will have fun with my friends and you will be with the children. You can choose to have fun with the other children or not." She notices that Jake didn't grab her leg so she says less than what she said the previous time. She guides him over to the children. He stays with the children, but keeps staring at Mom. Mom talks with her friends and does not make eye contact.

As Vanessa remains consistent and persistent, Jake's hiding and leg grabbing decrease with each play date until eventually he goes to play with the children on his own.

A typical problem with parents and consistency is that parents often see this consistent behavior as too much work and find it is easier just to give in or command the child. If you do this you are missing the point. The point is; you are teaching your child skills and preparing them for life. This means that until the day they move out you are an instructor on duty in every interaction. However as they get older the teaching is less and you become more of a guide; making sure they use the skills you taught them appropriately.

PARENTING SKILLS

Parenting using these skills will be much easier. If you parent a child this way from birth, you will raise a very healthy child with well-developed human skills. This in turn will make for a very smooth and happy life for both you and your child.

Use common sense — good judgment founded on sound, practical experience rather than on opinion, theory or study.

Be logical — understand and communicate the relationship between specific events, objects or situations and the definite consequences or results of their interaction.

Use reason — the ability to think and communicate clearly and coherently or in a logical way.

Be aware — gain knowledge of something by observing it. Awareness is the state of being fully conscious of what's going on around you.

Communicate clearly — Use the other skills to communicate with your child in a way that is true, kind and clear, and in language they can grasp.

In communication, it's important to listen, listen and listen. Listen single-focused to what is being said. Do not form questions or rebuttals while the other person is speaking. You want to verbally acknowledge what is said or done to indicate that you heard and to ensure that you understand.

Be neutral — don't judge or take sides. This includes neutral communication. Make neutral statements rather than be authoritative or act wishy-washy. Basically be lovingly matter of fact and not emotional.

Love unconditionally – love and accept your child no matter what they do, say or become. Never withhold love or require anything to love them. But you may put conditions on behaviors.

TELLING CHILDREN WHY YOU ARE INSTRUCTING THEM

When doing things with children, such as teaching them, instructing them, telling them what to do and why things are done, explain to them why you are doing what you are doing.

Always provide a child with a reasonable, rational and logical reason why they must do or learn something. Do this even when you do not think the child will understand. A child is never too young to hear the words. Although they may not cognitively understand what you are saying at the moment, they will associate the action with those words. Later, when they understand the words, the associated actions and the words will come together as a complete understanding. You should never tell a child to do something or that they must learn something just because you said so or that they have to.

Some simple examples are:

- "I'm asking you to do these things because it is going to make your life easier when you grow up."
- "You have to do this because then you will understand how it works."
- "You have to learn to do this because when no one is here to help you, you will be able to do it all by yourself."
- "Everything I teach you or ask you to do is so that you can do things on your own."
- "I am teaching you and asking you to do these things because I care about you and want you to be able to help yourself."

Chapter Four

Family Patterns

Family patterns are ways of thinking and behaving based upon belief systems that are passed from generation to generation. These belief systems can be either conscious or unconscious. A belief is defined as an assumed truth. Knowing this, just take a moment and think about all of the assumed truths you have in your life.

- What do you believe just because you believe it to be true?
- What do you think is true just because you've seen it before?
- What have you seen your whole life and have never thought could be different?
- What do you do that you do not really know why you do it?
- What factual evidence do you have for everything you believe?

Once you start to look at these assumed truths you can see how limiting these can be to your life. But many families think the same from generation to generation. They take the things that are working for them and carry them on to the next generation and pass it on as wisdom. The things that they did not like they attempt to stop. What if everything your family taught you was slightly inaccurate? That inaccuracy could change everything.

Children are the most perfect reflection of your own patterns and belief systems. Notice we use the word reflection. Early on they do not yet have the same beliefs or patterned behaviors as you do; until about the age of six they are still practicing and discovering how to behave or think about their world. You must realize this about your child. You may see your child as your greatest teacher or your biggest problem, it's all perspective.

Reflect for a moment about the things you dislike or like about your child and their behaviors. First you must know that your child is not their behaviors. Their behaviors are simply responses to their environment based upon the patterning and beliefs they have been taught. When you see something you like or dislike about your child you must recognize that you are seeing yourself, your own patterned behaviors and beliefs systems at work. They may be different and not quite look like yours but the foundation that creates them comes from the same belief system.

Unfortunately, parents don't recognize that the child is their mirror. Most people haven't been taught any of this information so this may seem a bit far fetched. We would like for you to just be open to the possibility that what we are sharing is true. What we are sharing here is the energy or quantum physics of behavior. What is commonly held in society is to deal with ways of thinking, behaviors and emotions. What is typically used is a punishment and/or reward system in an attempt to change the behaviors. This is high maintenance and never a complete solution. If you understand the quantum physics of behavior and the human being you will be able to make permanent generational change.

Imagine that the young child has no brain or mind capabilities and all they have is a video recorder inside of their head. Until about the age of five they are simply videotaping their entire experience. Then at this age they begin to mimic that which is on the videotape in their head. The child simply sees an event and goes through the videotapes they have recorded to find a response appropriate to that event. Then the child acts out based upon the scene they have just replayed. This is the child experimenting to see what works and what does not work in their world. They are basically testing the responses they have recorded. Once they have decided if the responses work or not they will repeat them or modify them. The main way they decide if they work or not is does it feel good or is there a negative response to their choice of action. Based upon this methodology you must understand that the child has a very limited option of responses and has no idea that there are other possibilities. In this way maybe you can understand that the child is simply subject to the patterned behaviors or emotions that they have witnessed.

What we were trying to give you is an example of is how family belief systems and patterned behaviors are simply passed on and repeated unconsciously until there is conscious choice to modify or change them. If you understand this as a parent you will be able to model and teach them different options. The key here is that you must model the changes. That means you must change your behaviors and patterns so that the child can witness that it can be done and feel the new options.

The bottom line is that the parent has to be responsible. If the parent is not responsible enough to make these changes, then you have a bunch of children running the house in adult bodies and child bodies. If the parent doesn't become the model then misinterpretations, misunderstandings and inappropriate behaviors or inappropriate parenting abound.

Patterned behaviors and beliefs systems are just the symptoms of the quantum energetic patterning that is going on underneath. As not to over complicate this quantum energetic patterning let's simplify; the energy or feeling behind behaviors and beliefs is the real source of all human behavior. The behavior patterns and belief systems are just a way to see this in everyday life. It is a way for you to understand and discover your conscious or unconscious family patterns without having to have a degree in quantum physics. This is all very practical logical and simple if you allow it to be. We understand that an introduction of something new like this might take a little bit to wrap your head around, so be patient and open.

Energetic patterning is the key. If you get that, you can stop the energetic patterning at its source without having to go through all the beliefs, behaviors and tracking everything. But until people begin to understand energetics and energetic patterning, they are not going to be able to do this. For now, looking at patterned behaviors and beliefs is the simplest way to achieve the desired result.

Children going through stages and phases energetically can completely irritate the parents. They can stimulate everything adults don't want to know about themselves: everything they don't like about themselves, everything they've been hiding. Now the child will mirror and spin all that energy back to them.

If you can look at your child as a teacher, you will both be able to learn from one another. Your child will teach you a lot about yourself. If you can eliminate the judgment and control factors (the should and the should not) and guide your child, they will teach you many things about yourself.

PATTERNED BEHAVIORS WITHIN THE FAMILY

In this section we will deal with patterned behaviors it a little more detail.

Within each family, there is a set of patterned behaviors, beliefs, thoughts and attitudes that influence the development of the child and the family dynamic. Remember, when we talk about patterned behaviors, beliefs, thoughts and attitudes, we mean the energetic dynamics of these things not just the display or psychological factors.

Each parent brings to the family a set of their own patterned behaviors and beliefs. When two people join together, there are now two sets of patterned behaviors and beliefs systems that must integrate. Patterned behaviors and beliefs systems of both parents can spawn multiple new and unique behaviors on top of the ones that each brought into the relationship thereby creating their own unique system. The system is similar to both parents' family systems but is unique unto itself.

In the case of single parents, your individual set of patterned behaviors interacts with those of anyone you bring into your household, including family, partners and friends. Anyone who spends a reasonable amount of time within the household adds to the patterned behavioral dynamics and influences the system.

- *Patterned behaviors are unconscious and conscious responses to external stimuli.*
- *Patterned behaviors are learned and assimilated from examples or modeling.*
- *Patterned behaviors do not have to be seen in order to be*

assimilated.

- *Patterned behaviors at some point are always believed to belong to you.*

- *Patterned behaviors can be felt intuitively and thereby unknowingly made into an aspect of a person's personality.*

- *Patterned behaviors are usually predictable and seen as the individual's personality.*

- *Patterned behaviors can always be changed.*

From conception, the child begins to experience and develop the patterned behaviors that are within the family. This may seem a bit far-fetched, but if you've ever talked to a child in the womb, you notice that they move when you speak to them. They may even feel you touch them through the mother's belly. Children are sensitive to the environment from the moment life begins, but especially seem to develop this awareness after the third month. This is not to say that there is any cognitive thought, but there is a sensory awareness that the fetus experiences even though their minds are not yet functioning in the way they will once the child is born. Once born the child's mind does not truly begin to function in a cognitive sense for the first few years. Up until then the child is mainly sensate and intuitive.

Unborn children feel the patterned behaviors of their mothers directly through the chemistry of the body and through the mother's mental and emotional experiences. An unborn child also feels the interaction between the mother and father or the mother and the environment in which she is living. Everything that the mother feels while carrying the child the child also feels. Once the child is born, they are directly affected by all of the patterned behaviors that go on within the household and environment. The interactions between the mother and father, how they treat each other, the way they feel toward each other and the way in which they speak to each other are all assimilated by the child. This all becomes part of the child's patterned behavior. Patterned behaviors are not acquired solely from seen behaviors. At least 50% of the child's patterned behaviors are acquired from the unseen intuitive experience.

PATTERNING FROM OLD FAMILY PATTERNS

RATHER THAN FROM CONSCIOUSNESS

As a parent, it's important to understand that you parent through your issues. In the way that if you wore glasses with colored lenses it would color your vision. In the same way your patterned behaviors and beliefs systems color your vision of the world you experience. In order for change to happen, you need to learn new behaviors and skills to deal with your issues and to eventually identify and get rid of them.

Be conscious of what you are passing on to your children in the form of patterned behaviors and beliefs systems. Most of your patterned behaviors and beliefs systems lie in the unconscious so don't be fooled into thinking that you are aware of what your patterns and beliefs are. We would estimate you are only conscious of 20% of your belief systems. Whatever you are not or have not been happy about with your life know that you must change first in order to be able to be the model for your child. You have to become a conscious parent in order to raise responsible conscious human beings.

Unconscious parents raise unconscious children. You have to be aware of what your patterns and beliefs are in order to become conscious. Family patterns and habits passed on unconsciously are simply programs. Think of it like a software program — you install it on to one computer after another and there may be a few variations based on the culture of the machine, but ultimately it is the same software. Once you become conscious you are actually rewriting the software or deleting the outmoded and installing the new.

Rewriting your patterns will change your life and that of future generations. They may not use the new patterns immediately or the way you want them to, but they will eventually be used and become the new system.

During this process you will be changing problems that stem from the past. Do not feel guilty or wrong about the past or what you have done. You did all you could do then, and now you're learning how to do differently. Part of changing is understanding and accepting the past.

Let's address the guilty parent syndrome. What a waste of time and energy! No one benefits from a parent feeling guilty. What's done is done, and if you don't like it, change it. You passed on what you were given without conscious thought. Now that you are becoming conscious, anything is possible. Guilt changes nothing, but it does keep you busy so you do not change, which in turn causes more guilt. See the cycle? To some, change is a four-letter word to be feared and avoided. The conscious parent welcomes change with all of its adjustments and challenges.

Guilt's cousins, blame and shame, often rear their ugly heads as a way to avoid changing and so pass the burden on. Many blame their parents to lessen the load. Some blame themselves as a way to pay for their guilt. Both of these strategies keep you trapped in the cycle of guilt and victim-hood, rather than facing perceived frightening changes.

Be aware of the child who wants to blame, as they are avoiding the responsibility for their choices and avoiding the admission of their lack of skills. Remember that their poor reasoning and problem-solving skills are the problem, not you. This is another ploy to get you to do something for them. Your job as a guardian is to allow them to figure it out themselves through trial and error with clues, not answers. Trial and error are the only real teachers. Through trial and error the learning becomes the individual's not something an authority gave to them. It is then something that they can own and carry for the rest of their life.

Did your school teachers give you answers or questions? If they gave you the answers, did you really learn anything or become a mimic of some authority figure. Allowing others to govern your life is a victim mentality. Do you want your child to be a victim or the creator of their life?

Rewrite your patterns and change your child's life.

As you rewrite your patterns which will change your parenting style, you may believe you seem hard or mean. You may not like saying no, but you have to. Children have to have these boundaries and guidelines in order to be functional human beings. If you don't provide boundaries for them as children, they will become dysfunctional adults.

At some point you have to accept the position of guardian and guide. You are the guardian of their heart until they are old enough to do it for themselves. You are the guide that helps them become functional adults. They are not your friends. Although you can be friend like. Do not confuse the two if you do you will lose their respect and lose yourself in your own issues. Being the guide means saying no. But that means saying no with a logical reasonable and rational reason that you can explain to them. Explanation is critical to your success as a parent and theirs in becoming a functional adult.

If you have a hard time saying 'no' you need to know that is a patterned behavior and a belief that you must change in order to be the best parent you can be. There will be times when you must say, "No, you can't do that, you may choose to cry if you would like, you can accept this decision or not etc." When you say these things always follow with an explanation. Once you have explained it and they can repeat the explanation to you than there is no longer any need to explain because they have comprehended and understood.

Now if it is a new topic then an explanation or the additional reasons must be explained. However, don't expect them to like or accept your explanation. You are simply looking for them to understand it and be able to repeat it with understanding. Keep in mind you are the parents/ guide and remember to tell them, "It is my job to prepare you for life and to live independently as an adult."

Too often, children are worked by the system rather than being the creators of their own systems. They are told at a very young age, "If you do what we tell you to do in the way in which we tell you to do it, you will be rewarded at whatever level we feel is necessary."

This is not freedom!   This is slavery!
Freedom is the ability to create and change or
work within the system in order to create
what you want to experience.

The biggest problem for parents is that they can't discern the difference between childhood experiences and adult experiences. There is often conflict within the parents: "It doesn't make sense, but I feel this way." Do you ever experience that? This is often because you are running your life based on preprogrammed behaviors or responses that you picked up as a very young child and now they conflict with your adult mind. This is where the conscious mind and the unconscious mind come into conflict and it's hard to discern which is which. The conditioning of your childhood and your other life experiences impact how you react and respond to life and the life of your child.

You learned patterns from your parents and your children learn them from you. The best thing any parent can do for their child is to recognize their own behavioral patterns and beliefs. This way, you can teach your child to recognize negative patterns and make conscious choices to change them or use the ones that actually work in present day.

Your feelings are not about your parenting, they are about
how you perceived being parented and the judgments
you have of your experiences.

When you use your behavior patterns and beliefs unconsciously, you are not in control of your destiny or your life. You are subject to the outcomes thrust upon you by the behaviors and beliefs you are not aware of that are often repeating outcomes of the past. Choosing to be aware of yourself will enable you to teach your children to be aware of themselves and make their journey in life easier.

PARENTING AND DISCORDANT

ENERGETIC BEHAVIOR PATTERNS

There is an old phrase; "The sins of the father are carried on for seven generations" this simply means that the energetic patterning of parents is carried by each set of children in the next generation until someone breaks that pattern. In a healthy system by the seventh generation someone breaks the patterns.

If the parents break the pattern, the children no longer will have to carry those patterns. They will feel relief and will be able to become who they really are. Otherwise, they will be living out the patterns of all those previous generations and will not live their own life until they become conscious enough to break the cycle.

If the parent breaks the patterns, the child will intuitively feel that release. If the child is older and the patterns have already been established in their life and then the parent breaks them, the child is shown that that possibility exists. This enables the child to pursue the further breaking of them and actually be free of them in this lifetime.

When you break your patterned behaviors, you release your children — no matter what age they are — from those patterns by providing them with the experience of seeing you do it. They'll know that they can change those patterns because you have changed. You've created the potential and opportunity for them to be free. It is now up to them to change or perpetuate the cycle.

The younger your children are when you break your patterns, the greater opportunity for long-term freedom you create for your child. As you break a pattern, you should teach your child how to break their own patterns by consciously and verbally communicating what the pattern was, why it was there, how you got it, how you misperceived it, how you passed it to them, how they got it, how they misperceive it and how they integrated it into their life. Then explain to them how you changed it and how they can too, step by step. This will expedite their freedom because you have not only broken the pattern, you have given them the keys to open any door they want and fulfill their life's potential.

One of the greatest acts of love is freeing yourself and your child from limited familial patterns.

The act of breaking the pattern is a magnificent gift to your child and to yourself. By teaching your child how to do it, you have given them a gift beyond their understanding. That is how a parent bequeaths to their children an inheritance more valuable than gold. You've passed on the gift of consciousness and freedom. That's how the cycle ends.

Chapter Five

Independence, Chores and Family Participation

Skills not answers

Your job as a parent is to teach your child skills they need for life. It's not about giving your child your direction; it's about allowing them to find their own. It's not telling them how to make your choices; it's about allowing them to make their own choices. It's not teaching them the right way, your way to do something or the way you learned to do it. It's not about teaching them any agendas or giving them answers to life.

Your job as a parent is to teach them skills and allow their own discovery by making choices. Of course you may offer them options from which to choose thereby allowing them to make their own choices. When you attempt to influence your child, you teach them to follow others and that their choices are not their own. In a very subtle way this creates a rebellious attitude internally.

When you teach them the skills provide them with options and allow them to choose on their own they develop very important life skills. Some of these skills are: critical thinking, self-direction, self-discovery, independence, reasoning skills and more. Many parents find it very difficult to sit back and allow their children to choose especially when they think they are going to get hurt or do something wrong. The only time you really need to step in is if there is any physical or traumatic emotional danger. Otherwise disappointments, failures or challenges should be allowed. This creates a strong and integrit personality.

Keep your agendas out of everything that you share with your child. This is not to say that you may not give opinions, but it is to say do not have ulterior motives behind your opinions. Children are far more sensitive than you realize and commonly absorb your agendas without you even having to speak them. Be transparent, open and integrit in your motives with your child.

If you are manipulative or have hidden agendas your child will intuitively sense this and eventually figure it out. Honesty and transparency is the best policy for a long-term open, loving and healthy relationship.

FAMILY PARTICIPATION AND WHY IT'S IMPORTANT

Many families today do not require their children to participate in household duties. We suggest that if you are not having your child participate in household duties that you begin immediately. We also suggest that it is time to change the concept of chores or duties to family participation. It's important to sit down and explain to your child that since they are part of the family, they participate in the things that the family needs or that are required to have the household function fluidly. This includes, but is not limited to, cleaning up after themselves, assisting in making dinner, grocery shopping, laundry, taking out the trash, cleaning up the yard and any requests that you may make that will assist in allowing the family to function smoothly.

Allowances are not necessary and create a program and belief system about money that will haunt them for the rest of their life. Money is never a good motivator. Teaching them about the desire to acquire something while knowing that money is only a means to an end takes the focus off of money. This then allows for them to focus on to their own desire and ability to create. Teaching them that there are other ways to create and not be solely dependent on money will free your child from the shackled mentality of money. In case you happen to have these issues do your research on what money really is and reflect on your own beliefs about money. Where did they come from? How accurate are they versus how real they are to you and many other people?

All too often, parents take on everything as their job and believe the children are just children and should not be required to do things around the house. Sometimes parents do not even imagine that their children should be participating in family cooperative duties. Conversely, some parents believe the child should work around the house because working is good for their soul. Let us address all three of these positions. When reading the following please try to suspend judgment of what we are suggesting and be open to the possibility of hidden family patterning.

The child should/can do nothing because they are a child mentality.

This type of parent typically has assumed the identity of caretaker. Once having assumed the identity of caretaker; they cannot even begin to understand or consider that the child must be taught to be their own caretaker. Sometimes, this type of parent uses the act of caring for their child as a self-esteem booster for themselves and a false sense of loving that loses sight of the child's need for independence and self-direction. Sometimes caretaking makes the parent feel good about themselves. There is a difference between a loving act and feeling good about yourself. Oftentimes this type of parent was raised in a household where dependency was common and even instilled under the guise of love.

This is not to say that your parents didn't love you; it is just to say that this style of parenting is dysfunctional.

There is also the mentality that the child is a child and therefore must be taken care of. Along with that comes the mentality that says the child is not capable, they are not old enough or are too young to do what needs to be done. This limits the child and creates what some call low self-esteem.

If you are this type of parent, you must understand that loving your child is teaching your child and preparing them for a life on their own. This includes teaching them how to discern, understand and make decisions from their own perspective and, most of all, from their heart. To expect nothing from your child and to do everything for your child, in the long term, creates an emotionally crippled adult with long-term damaging effects.

Love your child. Require your child to do things for themselves age appropriately. Never underestimate a child's capabilities. Age has nothing to do with capability!

Empower your child by teaching them that they are individuals with choices first and that they are part of a family. Individuals within a family work together cooperatively and do their share in order to create a joyful family experience. You must make all tasks age appropriately equal among members of the family. Otherwise dissension will always occur. Love is equal not fair.

It's the parent's job mentality.

While the child is very young and too small to do jobs or assist in cooperative family tasks, it is understandable that the parents do everything. As early as the age of one or two, you may begin asking your child to participate in doing things around the house. This is as simple as, "Johnny, will you take this napkin and give it to Daddy?" This begins the understanding that the child is part of the family and they participate because they are a family member not because it's their job or their duty and not because they have to. At such an early age you will find that most children love being part of the family or helping. They participate simply because they live in a house where everyone is part of the family and assists each other out of love and courtesy. This is called teamwork. When you create a mentality of teamwork then no one is overburdened.

You must remember that it is not your job to do everything for your children. It is only a task that you perform while they are too young to do some things. As they get older parents often find it quite burdensome to do everything for your child and you will long to have your own life. This will, in the long run, affect your ability to patiently and lovingly interact with your children. If this burdensome caretaking is taken beyond an early age it will create stress and conscious or unconscious resentment toward your child or towards doing any tasks whatsoever. Often times this frustration is turned on the partner in the relationship or other children.

Everyone shares in the family. They share the benefits and they share the cooperative tasks that enable the family and household to operate as a unit. This sharing must be explained in detail and reinforced throughout the child's life. The mentality of "it's the parent's job" often comes from the parent's childhood whether they believe mom and dad should do everything for them or when mom and dad did not do enough for them and they felt slighted. It is not your job to do everything! It is your job to teach your child to do everything for themselves, age appropriately.

Hard work is good for you mentality.

This type of parenting leads to authority issues and power struggles. It takes the fun out of life. This type of parenting sets the child up for a future of a lot of work and very little play or joy. This mentality says a child must work hard because it prepares them for a hard life or because somehow working hard is good for them.

From this perspective, you create the belief system that home is not a fun-loving, safe place. It is a place of strife, difficulty and power struggles. This mentality teaches the child that they are under someone else's control or they must learn to control others. This also teaches them that life and the world are hard and painful. In the end, this type of parenting creates bitterness, resentment, struggle and control issues. Commonly the child sees the family as restrictive, controlling and not nurturing, so they fight against it or give up. It is common for a child raised under these conditions to act out or want to leave home as soon as possible.

There must be some type of balance between these three types of parenting.

Balanced parenting

Balanced parenting in the area of family cooperative participation is a combination of having expectations of your child's participation, being a guide and doing things to assist them in becoming self-directed, freethinking individuals by assigning them age-appropriate cooperative tasks. It is suggested that you begin at a very early age.

Beginning as early as the age of two, teach your child to pick up after themselves and assist in doing things that benefit the family as a whole. Do not expect the child to do it perfectly or accurately, as this is an ongoing practice that eventually will build lifelong skills. You're teaching the child the value of these skills for later in life. Whether the child likes the task, dislikes it or voluntarily wants to do it, you must help your child understand the concept and participate. If this is done at such an early age tasks and self-care will become a normal part of life and will lessen the likelihood of conflict.

Participation will vary based upon age and the cooperative duties assigned. These duties should be alternated and changed on a frequent basis in order to avoid boredom and resentment toward what they are doing. Alternating the duties allows for a variation that will keep them at least temporarily stimulated and teaches them a variety of skills. If you can teach them in an age-appropriate, fun and interesting way that the things they are doing are skills for the human experience, you will find that your children still may not enjoy doing them but have a greater feel and appreciation for what they are doing.

A balanced parent is emotionally stable, physically dependable and consistent in their parenting style. Becoming a balanced parent takes time. You are not given these skills as a child. In fact most people do not have balanced parents as models. Be patient with yourself you will learn on the fly. Balance parenting occurs only through experience. In order to become a balanced parent you must be able to look at your own beliefs, patterns and emotions in order to change that which is dysfunctional. Some people are afraid to look at their dysfunctions. It is suggested that looking at your dysfunctions is the best thing you can do for yourself and your child.

Now you can't just look at them. You must do something about them. If you do not know how to do it yourself than set off on a task of self-discovery and solution finding. There is plenty of information and ideas in today's modern world that will assist you. Changing your dysfunctional patterns, beliefs and behaviors is a magnificent loving gift that you give to your child and yourself. Always keep in mind; anything that bothers you is your issue. You have the power and ability to change anything you so choose to change. Change yourself and you change the way you experience the world. Change yourself not your child!

DOING FOR YOUR CHILD

Many parents do things for the child that the child can do for themselves, like getting them a drink. You can start to lessen this behavior early, because it's fun for them to have increased responsibility and it teaches them to do for themselves. Also understand that responsibility equals freedom for your child. Responsibility in society is often a negative word in the sense that it is related to an authority position. By teaching your child to do things for themselves you free them from dependency and limitation.

Beginning at the age of two, teach your child age-appropriate, do-it-yourself tasks.

- When your child asks for or motions for their bottle or food, tell them to go ahead and get it or at least force them to verbally express it as best as they can. Doing this allows for the healthy development of communication skills.

- When your child whines or cries to get your attention, teach them to say "excuse me" instead. This forces your child to develop communication and discernment skills.

- When your child wants to watch a TV show, give them the remote and show them which button to push. Then begin to ask them to change the channels for you. This develops hand -eye coordination.

- When you child is mad and sulks, teach them how to say they are unhappy. This develops the ability to express emotions clearly and safely.

- When your child wants you to do anything for them, teach them and then have them do it themselves. This creates self-reliance and independence.

From the time they are old enough to walk, begin to teach your children to dress themselves, pick up after themselves and get their own snack. As they get older, teach them to get themselves up for school, do their laundry and manage their allowance. Give them the skills and then let them experiment and learn. You want to always be alert for areas where your child can take over something you've done for them. If you wait too long to teach these basic skills you will most likely have conflict with your child. This is because they have formed a belief systems and habit patterns based upon dependence and you as their caretaker and now change is difficult because you must break habits, change beliefs and establish new ones.

You must find the fine line between doing things for them because you're just being kind and helpful versus doing things for them because you're the servant or controlling parent. Parents who wait on their child's every whim usually have children who grow up feeling entitled and ungrateful. Why should they be grateful? ... You've made them dependent on others and unable to take care of themselves; at this point they may even be demanding. Confident children are self-sufficient. Self-sufficient children are low maintenance.

The opposite is also true. The child is not your servant. Home should be a place where everyone can take care of themselves and yet be willing to share or do a favor or kindness for each other.

When you baby your child, you create dependencies both physical and psychological. Know the difference between facilitating self-advocacy and caretaking. Don't take care of your child — teach your child to care for themselves by facilitating their independence. This empowers them and stimulates curiosity, adventure, accomplishment, creativity, self-direction and self-reliance.

Children train you, the way you have trained them. They will use the behaviors and patterns you have taught them on you, unconsciously or consciously, testing these patterns and behaviors to see how and where they work. Every parent should know that loving your child is not the same thing as letting them do whatever they want, giving them everything or being their best friend. Many parents mistake or blend being a child's friend and being their parent and guide.

Remember, doing things for your child rather than teaching them to do for themselves creates an emotional cripple. It teaches them that they don't have to do things they don't want to do, things they don't like to do or things that are challenging. It also discourages them from stretching and doing new things. If you do too much for your child it also inhibits neural development/brain development from occurring due to the lack of use in certain sectors of the brain.

Integrity, functionality, social skills and their own personal spirituality are the greatest lessons you can teach your child. Create situations where your child must ask for what they need or want as this will develop critical thinking, communication and self-confidence.

Too many parents just do for their child early on, forming a habit where the child does not communicate but simply demands and expects things to be done by the parents or others. Create as many situations for them to think and discern on their own. When they are in a situation where they don't know what to do ask them; what do you think you should do now? How would you do that? Why would you do that? Allow them to explain to you the answers and require them to be clear and concise in their communication.

Do not give them the answers or accept vague answers and then fill in the blanks for them. Too many parents give in to this because they wanted answers when they were a child or because they remember how hard it was for them as a child and the worst reason of all is because it's easier than taking the time to work through the situation.

By taking your time and working through as many of these situations as you can your child will notice the love and care given to them during this process even if they don't recognize it until later. Never tell your children what you yourself do not believe or things that are not factual — tell your children only facts and then give them your opinion. But clearly communicate the difference between the facts and your opinions or beliefs. This is a sign of integrity and builds trust.

If you have done things for your child without making them think you will find that when they get older and you want them to do things for themselves, they will use phrases like, "This isn't fair." "Why can't you just tell me?" and "It's not my fault." When you hear these phrases, you should know that somewhere along the line you have allowed them to avoid responsibility for their actions and choices. They are dependent on other people to do for or take care of them; they lack personal responsibility and self-direction.

Remember whatever you have allowed them to do you were the model for. Keep in mind that you have passed on some form of family patterning that has allowed this behavior and belief system to take place. We cannot emphasize enough your own personal responsibility as to changing your dysfunctional patterned behaviors and beliefs systems. Yes, sometimes this is not easy. Sometimes it is very challenging to face your own fears, anxiety, regrets and feelings of shame. Do not let this deter you. Everyone is capable to make these changes. The only question is; are you willing? Have confidence in yourself which then translates into confidence for your child about themselves.

Sometimes the best thing to do for a child in this situation is allow them to fail. This quite often is too difficult for the parents to bear, so they cover for the child and think they are helping them. They push them and coach them, forcing them to succeed. In actuality they are supporting their dependency and creating emotional cripples.

No one likes to see their child fail but sometimes it's what the child needs. What a child learns from this is that they can manipulate the system if they exhibit the correct emotions. Parents sometimes feel that their child's failure is a reflection on them. Never confuse your worth and value with your child's. Again this is up to the role model and the child intuitively will know what is going on even if you hide what you are feeling. Keep in mind that failure is a value judgment. It has no bearing on the child's actual quality, beauty of their spirit or essence.

No human being is a failure. The only thing you can ever fail at is some standard that some other human being made up. Yes, many people may agree to the standard and buy into it as a belief system but it still doesn't make it real. It's only real to people who believe in it. And if you teach your child to believe in it too they will have to measure up to some false standard in order to find their own worth and value. By doing this you ultimately set your child up for failure.

Note: All of the information provided in this book is to be discerned and used in a way that is helpful to your own life. This information should be appropriately used based upon the age and emotional maturity of your child. You should also understand that at whatever age your child is when you begin to use these concepts there will be different results and will take different amounts of time for the results to be seen or used by the child.

THE CHILD THAT WON'T LEAVE HOME

Quite often there is the child that does not leave the house. This child has graduated high school and may be into their 20s or 30s still living at home. If you happen to have one of these children here are a few reasons why they are still at home and what you can do about it. There are so many complications to the causes of the situation we could fill an entire book on examples, so here we will just lightly cover this topic.

These children are typically one of two things:

1. They are afraid of the real world and having to be on their own.
2. They are so comfortable at home that they have no reason to leave.

Those who are afraid to leave and go out into the world and actually be self-sufficient often disguise themselves through intellectual bantering and justifications. They will tell you that they know what they're doing or they just haven't found their niche yet. They may tell you there are no jobs or apartments are too expensive and anything else to give you a logical explanation so that you will allow them to remain at home. Some will downright refuse to leave home.

Those who are so comfortable will appear almost lazy. They may have no interests or love to play video games all day and visit their friends at leisure. These children often have no real logical excuse and they tend to give you answers to appease you so that you will leave them alone and then they will proceed to do nothing.

Both types of these children may seem like they need to be taken care of and they may play on your weakness of caretaking or fear that they may not make it in the world. Do not be deceived by their acting. Unless the child is severely mentally, emotionally or physically handicapped your child knows better and will be able to figure out how to make it in the world if they are pushed to do so. Many parents are too afraid to push their child out of the nest and force them to fly, especially when the child feigns weakness, vulnerability or logical understanding.

In most cases the children are in this position because of the lack of appropriate parenting. The parent either is not emotionally prepared to be a little "hard" on their child or the parent has the need to take care of their child because they did not receive the emotional nurturing they desired as children themselves. And of course, there are several other possibilities for these situations; these are but two. If you were one of these parents do not be hard on yourself because you were not yet skilled enough to parent your child as they needed earlier on. You must now see yourself in a position to learn and teach or force your child to become independent and self-sustaining. If you do not have the courage to do this now then your child is destined to a life of dependency, manipulation and misery.

If you are beginning now then things will be quite difficult as you begin to make the appropriate changes. Be patient with yourself and the situation. Realize that both you and your child created this circumstance. Blame no one and focus on taking action to rectify this situation. Be prepared to be "hard-nosed" with your child. This may go against everything inside of you but it is required for you to make change in this situation.

1. Make a decision and commitment to change this situation.
2. Be in alignment with your partner in this decision and how you will proceed.
3. Lay out a plan with your child to leave the house.

4. Give them a deadline to get a job or move out of the house.

5. Make the child uncomfortable by not taking care of them or paying for anything other than the roof over their head.

6. Once they have gotten the job tell the child that they have a certain amount of time or due date in which they must move from the house.

7. Do not argue with the child and stay consistent in moving forward no matter what they say or how they behave.

8. Do not be afraid to be "mean." Often times parents feel that giving deadlines and being firm is being mean. It is actually more cruel to allow them to remain at home without these pressures.

9. Follow these steps with your own style and modifications as are necessary to communicate your seriousness to the child.

10. Never change the plan. Often times the child will begin the proces and once they have movement the parent is so pleased that they allow for negotiating the plan and the child then stays.

Understand that the child is a lot smarter than you give them credit for. They know all of your patterns, buttons and triggers. They will manipulate you and their circumstances in any way possible to prevent themselves from having to go out into the world or do the things that they fear. It is actually more loving of you to push them to face their fears than it is to coddle them and allow them to hide in your household. Allowing your child to stay in your household without them participating in life is to create an emotional cripple and lifelong dependent.

It is your responsibility as a parent no matter what stage you are at to prepare your child to leave home and start their own life. If you are a parent with a child out of high school that is still at home you need to do something to force them into an uncomfortable experience so that they will desire to leave and if they do not you must demand and require that they leave. You do them no service by allowing them to hide from their fears. As a parent you must consider, 'What will happen to my child when I am gone?'

If you are in the early years of child raising then you must prepare them from approximately the age of 12 to know that they will be moving out of the house either at 18 or when they have graduated college, whatever you collectively decide. By preparing them early when the time comes it is much easier for you to let them go and for them to venture out into the world.

No matter what stage you are at as the parent you must make sure that your child has all of the basic skills such as understanding bills, expenses, food and shelter costs, using a checkbook, banking and the required necessities to live on their own.

Do not let your fear of what will happen to your child stop you from taking the steps necessary for your child to become a self-sustaining adult.

LOVING FREEDOM

True freedom for a child comes when the parent allows or requires them to do things on their own out of love, not duty. Because in their early years they were dependent and catered to, they sometimes tend to argue and fight when they're first given a job to do on their own. Often, however, they are delighted and — if not criticized for their first, sometimes bumbling efforts— they feel quite good about themselves even if they don't admit it. Always provide your child with the opportunity to experience emotional, physical and mental tasks on their own at age-appropriate times. They are often ready and able to do things long before most parents believe that it's possible. Doing these things for your child is an act of love, even when your child doesn't see it that way.

If you do not encourage children to do things on their own early enough and you wait until they're older, even teenagers, then this whole process becomes more difficult for them. They will struggle and flounder. Then what do they do? Typically they look to the outside world to feed, nourish and care for them. They find unscrupulous people who take advantage of them and use them for their own benefit. Even though sometimes this process may sound harsh, the harsh reality is that if you don't do this process or something similar your child's life will be difficult at best.

Too many times parents have childhood issues that they project onto their child when they are parenting. These could be positive or negative issues. Attempt to remain neutral, logical, reasonable and rational in your parenting at all times. This will allow you to do things that are practical and have foresight about the probable outcomes of your parenting. All of this hard work that you do as a parent by remaining conscious sets the stage for healthy generations to come in your family lineage. Love yourself and your child enough to envision the future and plant the seeds for a beautifully experienced life.

CHILDREN AND INDEPENDENCE

Give your child choices which will result in an outcome, not commands that may result in punishments if disobeyed. Teach your children to govern themselves. Remind them that they are in charge of their own life and their own decisions. This being said, the child must also understand that the parent has the final say until the child is of legal age.

There are only three times when you take full control as a parent:

1. If children are in real danger of physical harm
2. If they endanger someone else
3. To prevent damage to someone else's property.

When you give children choices, you empower them

Start early. As early as age one, a child can make choices: "Would you like a cracker or a cookie? The big one or the little one?" As the child gets older, look for opportunities to give them choices and learn to make decisions. You will not only strengthen your child's ability to make decisions, you will strengthen your skill in giving them choices and your confidence in their ability to make decisions.

Be sure your children know that they and only they control their behaviors, feelings and responses. They must know that they are responsible for whatever choices they make in regards to their behaviors and responses in life, even if they did not know better at the time. Allow them to choose their own direction, not yours, even if it takes longer or is not the direction you think they should take.

How to give children options:

• When you find yourself elevating your voice, say, "This is the third time I've told you to do this. I can either talk to you this way (calmly), or I can raise my voice. Which do you prefer?"

• When children are behaving wildly and they get hurt, say something like, "This is what can happen if you are so wild. If you choose to be wild, I'm not going to referee because I warned you what could happen. You need to decide whether you want to continue to be wild or not. If you don't want to be wild, separate. If you don't separate and you choose to be wild, whatever happens… happens."

It is important that you take yourself out of the position as referee. If you remain as the referee you become the authority that they will rebel against or blame for telling them what to do. Give them the choice to decide for themselves and you do not have to get involved in any unnecessary drama. At this point there is no one to blame except themselves.

Making decisions is empowering, builds confidence and character. Let them become who they will and use their own voice. If you stifle their voice you shut down their heart. If you shut down their heart you stop their creativity. Allow them to be creative under your loving guidance. Then they will find their own way in life. They will become the magnificent being they were born to be. By making decisions, they can forge their own path. That is the beauty of letting this take place, even though at times it's hard for parents to watch.

You have to adjust. You have to break free from the old beliefs that you hold about what a parent is supposed to do or be. By remaining neutral without getting emotional you can be centered in your love not your mind.

> *Independence for your child is scary,*
> *challenging and exciting*
> *Independence for the parent is scary,*
> *challenging and exciting*

Never become attached to or dependent on your child's choices. Doing so leads to disappointment and judgment on your part, which then affects your relationship with your child, your child's concept of themselves and your ability to love them purely. Independence equals freedom. Freedom equals self-discovery. Self-discovery creates self-direction.

PARENTING IS A FULL-TIME JOB

Sometimes parenting seems like a lot of work, and that's because it is a lot of work. It is a lot of psychic work, physical work and emotional work because your primary focus is on your child and you are always on duty. Once you become a parent, you stay a parent until your children are 18 and released from your charge. Being a parent is your role not your identity so it is wise for you to know what it entails.

Try to view parenting as an act of love not work. Remember that being a parent is something you chose. Saying parenting is too much work is like saying, "Life is too hard." Life/parenting is as hard as you perceive it. That's not to say it's not tiring, maybe even exhausting while trying to manage a career or a relationship. When things get tough try to see the humor in things; don't be so serious and learn to laugh.

It takes effort and commitment to be a conscious parent, but conscious parenting is required to have conscious self-directed children. They only know what they see and what you are teaching them. If you are unconscious in your behaviors and actions, they will be unconscious, too. You must teach them to be conscious by being conscious yourself, aware of what you're feeling aware of the purpose in what you are doing at all times.

When you ask them something, say, "I'm purposely asking you this." Always remind your children that you're making conscious purposeful choices to teach them. Tell them, "It is my job to teach you and prepare you for life. That is my number-one objective. I love you unconditionally no matter what you do." This way they know love is not even a question.

If your children *feel* that you love them, you don't have to tell them you love them. Saying it is not enough, it's the feeling that is conveyed that really counts. Please continue to say it but really begin to feel it in your own heart. They will always know they are loved if they *feel* loved, no matter what your behaviors are. They may still dislike your behaviors, but they will always feel loved and that sets the foundation for your communication and your relationship.

Real love is felt not spoken!

If they *feel* the love they will be open to you no matter what you say, whether they like it or not. You can't measure the effectiveness of what you're telling them by whether they like it or not, if you do you may feel like a failure, judge them or judge your parenting abilities.

Your only measurable success is did you love them unconditionally. That's it. There is no other success in parenting. Love them with all your heart, teach them self-direction and discernment, do the things you need to do as a conscious parent, teach them how to function in the world; now that's perfect parenting.

Expect disagreements, differing opinions, temper tantrums, sulking and being disliked at times. They all are normal experiences of a parent. Funny thing is, the more they dislike you the more you know they feel safe and loved. If your ego gets bruised, don't sweat it... it happens to the best of parents. The bruising however gives you the opportunity to resolve your own childhood issues to become a healthier adult and better parent.

Consistency is the key to parenting — if you change the rules, they'll know you are full of hot air and they will manipulate you until they leave the home, if they ever leave. Being consistent is imperative. Consistency models stability and builds trust. They may not always like what you are consistent about, but they will intuitively appreciate it. Your consistency allows them to become consistent themselves and develop self-confidence.

Three Fundamental Parenting Tools:

1. Love
2. Human Skills
3. Consistency

These are your fundamental parenting tools. Apply these three things and you will create a beautiful foundation for your child to experience a wonderful adulthood. Remember that they have to make their own choices and that you may not like a lot of choices they make.

Honesty is another important parenting tool. You need to be as honest with them as possible based on their level of maturity and their ability to comprehend. For example, you cannot be honest with a six-year-old about sexual topics. There are some things that must wait until they are at the right maturity to be totally honest about. What you teach them has to be age and/or maturity appropriate. You may have a six-year-old who is more mature than a ten-year-old. You also need to be aware of their ability to comprehend and understand information accurately.

Sometimes it will feel like you just need time for yourself. Take it! You deserve it. Make time for you and your partner, if you have one. These things are necessary for you. Your relationship will hopefully last long after the kids leave home. Do not let your relationship drift apart for the sake of the child! Even though parenting is a full time role you should never neglect your personal life or needs!

CHAPTER SIX

ASSITING YOUR CHILD'S GROWTH

Children, feeing and their environment

Children act and react according to their environment. You may have heard the expression that children are sponges — this is true. Children are energetically sensitive. They are open and feel everything that they experience in their environment. Then they attempt to interpret it and apply it to their own human experience by using the beliefs and patterns they have learned. This means that everything that goes on in the family, in the household, school and anywhere else affects them.

Energy is invisible
Energy is the feeling and physics of the physical world
Physics is the science of matter and energy and their interactions

There is an old adage that says, "Be careful of the company you keep." For our purposes this means; the energy of the people and places you choose affect you and reflect the level of consciousness you experience.

Energy is felt by the human sensate system

Because of a child's energetic, sensate and emotional sensitivity they will unconsciously make attempts to transmute and balance the energy in their environment. This may appear in the way that they behave, respond or feel at any given moment. Parents must determine whether it is the environment or their own behavior patterns that the child is struggling with, then act accordingly to assist the child in understanding their behavior or directing it in an appropriate fashion.

Children's behavior is the reflection of their environment. This includes but is not limited to their physical, mental and emotional environment, familial behaviors, beliefs, attitudes and thoughts. The environment that affects them is both the physical and nonphysical. The average person believes that if the child doesn't see it, hear it or understand it, they are unaffected. This is false! Your child is affected by everything.

Energy is interpreted by the human using their beliefs
Energy is responded to using patterned behaviors

Children reflect, imitate, channel and respond to the energy, behaviors and belief patterning they experience in their immediate surroundings. Which they then use and experiment with their learned human skills to understand and master their world. This then allows them to become functional as adults. This does not necessarily mean the behavior skills they develop are optimal, healthy or functional. Children develop with whatever the level of consciousness in the household or their environment is. When your child is born, they are not familiar with this world. They simply integrate and interpret their experiences and environment the best they can. Remember that your child is a stranger to this world, experimenting and doing their best to understand, imitate and function with a limited concept of what life on Earth is really like.

Physics states that everything in the
physical world is energy
Energy is light, sound and frequency
made up of quantum particles

Adults have developed skills to cope with what they feel. Children are in the process of learning how to deal with this invisible experience while often adults tell them it does not exist. When adults do this the child is invalidated and learns to disregard themselves and their feelings. It is often proven to them that they are wrong or are not feeling what they are feeling by reinforcing that it can't be seen and if it can't be seen then it can't be real. If these adults were physicists then this would never happen.

Human beings feel energy consciously and unconsciously. Children are hypersensitive to energy. Since energy is invisible it is often discounted from having any effect in a person's life. Please know that energy is real, it is a science and you and your child feel it. It is an everyday experience. Please do not discount what your child feels. Do not "baby" your child either. Consider what they feel and deal with it logically, reasonably, rationally and functionally.

There is much more to life than meets the eye!

SPINNING OFF ENERGY

Your child will intuitively attempt to work out your problems for you if you do not work them out yourself. The child will pick up on your unconscious patterns, inabilities, downfalls and flaws in an attempt to balance them out.

If Mommy is the caretaker and Mommy is sick, the child may take up being the caretaker. Which child of yours does this? Maybe the oldest child, maybe the middle child — it depends on what each child formed as their identity. One child will realize that something must be done and this will activate the patterned behavior that they have consciously or unconsciously learned, "When someone is sick, I have to take care of the family in order for it to remain functional."

Children also pick up on what is invisible to the eye. In the same way that you can walk into a room and know if there's just been an argument, children pick up on these invisible energies in the home as well.

Children who are very sensitive cannot experience this energy without doing something about it. They intuitively need to act on it and often are not able to discern which feelings/energies are theirs or someone else's. A child intuitively knows that when there is an inharmonious energy in their environment it must be balanced. They will then kick into whatever patterned behavior allows them to defuse that energy in their environment.

As an example, a child may unconsciously feel that Daddy is angry; the child then will act out. This acting out could be as simple as caretaking or as drastic as becoming hostile and rageful. In another scenario the child feels the energy of their father and will spin off that energy and act out, run around the house, throw things and get in fights with their siblings. If the parent isn't showing their anger, they may not understand why the child is doing what they are doing. People who have suppressed their anger often don't understand they have it.

The child begins spinning because of that energy and out of nowhere may go up and pull their sister's hair, or punch their brother. When you ask the child why they did that, they say, "I don't know." At some level, the child really doesn't know why they did it. The parent may need to check the energy they've brought into the situation to see if that was a cause.

Often times the child is punished or rewarded for "spinning off" energy. Then typically the parents focus on the child and the child is commended or punished for their behavior. All this diffuses the inharmonious energy in the room. The worst part is the child almost always gets the brunt because parents typically only focus on behaviors and rarely on the awareness of the energy in the room. Be patient with yourself because this takes practice and awareness. This is something that is never taught to parents.

Children feel the energy in the house or the flow of energy in the house. They will act out on the flow. If there is something that needs to be released, the children will release it. If there is tension in the house, for instance, children will release that tension through some behavior, verbalization or act. As you learn to be aware of your own inner feelings and the energy in your household, start to correlate your child's behavior with your feelings or the feeling in the household or environment.

SENSITIVE CHILDREN

We do not mean emotional children. Emotional is often confused with sensitive. Being emotionally sensitive means: to respond to sensate feelings or experiences that are not pleasing using emotions. Sensitive children in the way it is used here are children who feel the invisible energy we described in the last section.

Sensitivity is the feeling of energy in a person's environment

There is energy in a person's intent, voice, actions, gestures, looks and physical presence

Children feel everything. Sensitive children are susceptible to acting out the repressed feelings of others and their imbalanced feeling in their environment. They often act out the repressed feelings or emotions of their parents or siblings. This begins at birth. If you have a child that is school age you may have noticed that when they first start school they often come home with behaviors that 'do not belong to them.' Many people disregard this as copying behaviors. This is only part of the reason. Here it's suggested that they are acting out the energy that they have encountered and are testing the associated behaviors that they witnessed went along with what they felt.

As they become teenagers, these sensitive children are exposed to other people who either are intense in their energy or have very suppressed energy. The sensitive teen starts to tune into or act out the energy of their friends. If they hang with them long enough they establish habit patterns that are similar. This is what is happening when a child seems to have been negatively influenced by their friends. Parents typically blame the other children, but the fact is that a child who has never acted out and begins to do so after hanging out with 'bad influences' is energetically sensitive. They spin off and act out the energies of the environment and the other kids they are surrounded by.

This is a normal part of the developing child, so don't worry, just monitor and guide them. This is how a child discovers their options in life and develops human skills. Experience is the best teacher, even if it is difficult for you to watch. Love them, guide them and advise them but never judge them. If you have planted the healthy skills discussed here they will turn out fine even if they take a slight detour once in a while.

Children act out for two subtle reasons. The first is the developmental stage of a child and the experiences that they are curious about. The second is their sensitivity to energy.

The energetic stimulation, combined with their developmental immaturity, lack of self-centeredness and curiosity often causes them to act out. Not to mention their own inner stress about what they feel and interpret.

If a sensitive child stays with negative influences long enough, they will eventually become labeled bad and incorporate this label into the identity they create for themselves. They will believe they are this identity or eventually change when they are finished with that part of their human experimentation. Remember that your child is always in the process of creating their identity. Having learned the skill of choice and discernment they will usually choose wisely in their identity traits. Your modeling will ensure a more likely wise choice.

What you say to your child on a regular basis or in times of intensity and high emotion becomes part of their identity, so be conscious of what you say and most importantly how you feel when you say it.

How you see your children

We mentioned in the beginning of the book that your reaction to our grammatical choices shows how you react to change. We have also introduced some new concepts and ideas for many of you, how are you doing?

Your reactions, if any, may also be a metaphor for how you see your child's behavior. If the grammar or these new concepts have distracted you from the message, what's to stop your child's behavior from distracting you from what's really going on inside them? If you were not distracted from the message, congratulations! Either way simply by reading this material you are on your way to becoming a more conscious parent.

What every child should know

The energy and influence of others

This might be a far stretch for many of you: The thoughts and feelings of others can influence everyone (especially sensitive people) and children must be taught to understand this.

All children must be taught to discern between their thoughts and feelings and the thoughts and feelings of others. They must learn how to check on their own thoughts and feelings. Then discern the difference between what they are thinking and feeling versus what seems to just pop into their head. Give your child exercises to train them to discern these differences. Otherwise the child will grow up to believe and respond to impulses that are not actually theirs thereby creating situations that may not be necessary.

Sensitive children and adults intuit the thoughts and feelings of others and often assume those thoughts and feelings are theirs. They then respond to those thoughts and feelings, which can unnecessarily complicate their own lives. This is the invisible world most people avoid or invalidate because there is no 'proof.' Everyone knows deep down that this invisible unexplainable world exists. Everyone has at some time had an intuitive or unexplained feeling that turned out to be valid. Intuition is an acceptable word used to describe the invisible unexplained experience you can't prove but know is real.

The sensitivity and the lack of consciousness of what is theirs or someone else's creates a dependency on the outside world for their own identity and validation. They must develop the skill of discernment between what is theirs and what is not. Because most children never learn to differentiate their own thoughts or experiences from the outside, they tend to assume they are their environment. It becomes an unconsciously assumed identity. Children commonly assume they are their family or their parents. This assumption creates a false dependent identity.

With this assumed identity they will never know who they really are inside and will always depend on other people or external circumstances for validation and identification. When they have an urge of wanting to be themselves there will be conflict within them and/or with others, their environment or circumstances. Because they had never learned discernment skills and do not know who they are, they will typically fight or withdraw from the outside world in an attempt to find their own identity.

This battle is an attempt to gain their own emotional and mental freedom so that they can establish and understand their own identity. From their perspective, conflict and resistance is the only way to do it; there seems to be only this one option. They must be taught that their own identity comes from within, not by resisting others or the world. They must know and understand that to have their own identity it is not necessary to be at war with the world. All this is not necessary and will take place minimally if they are educated about their inner life and given skills to handle these transitional times.

Children must be given exercises and taught skills to identify their thoughts and feelings from those of others or their environment in order for them to establish their real sense of identity. Otherwise they will just become subject to the pressures of others and their environment as a valid source of their identity.

This type of identification leaves the child feeling powerless, useless, not good enough, etc. because they can never meet the expectations of other people's thoughts or feelings no matter how hard they try. Without these skills of discernment, they will be constantly trying to meet the spoken and unspoken expectations of others or society.

If and when they give up seeking their own identity, at best they will be able to mimic the behaviors that society expects them to display. In the meantime they must surrender their own inner self to the outside world and its expectations. This will always leave them feeling empty and unsatisfied.

Please be clear here; this emptiness will never be satisfied because they have lost touch with their inner self and become dependent on an ever changing world that they cannot control. This many times leaves the sensitive child seeing the world and life as hopeless and that their happiness is subject to others. Teach your child early that they are the source of their own happiness and that when they feel complete within themselves then the world becomes a richer experience.

Children should be taught to focus on who they are and what they feel inside of themselves. You must take the time to allow them to experience and discern what they are feeling and what they desire. Teach them not to focus on everything they have heard, been told or thought they were supposed to be. Teach them to focus on what they feel and then integrate that feeling into appropriate social skills so that they may accomplish what they want through socially acceptable means as often as possible. Never tell them how they are feeling but instead teach them the current socially appropriate language to describe their feelings.

Sometimes their inability to discern the difference between themselves and the outside world comes from their unconscious remembrance of being in the one. When they come into the separateness or duality of this world, they often do not recognize where they are or what to do because they are so used to blending/being in the one. Therefore it is important that they learn discernment skills as well as appropriate human skills combined with the awakening of their inner knowing.

They should know that they are loved and have the divine right to make choices and enjoy their stay on earth. They should be able to identify their own feelings versus other people's feelings or what they have been told. They should know that at their core they are beautiful, loving and magnificent. They should know the difference between their ego and their divine loving heart. They should know and understand that human beings have multitudes of issues and belief systems that are often incorrect. They should know that they have the same challenges as other human beings. They should know that with your assistance and dedication to their own understanding they can see the world clearly and enjoy their life on earth.

EDUCATING YOUR CHILD

Parents must know how a child actually works versus the way they believe they work. With this understanding they must know methods and techniques on how to educate the child so the child absorbs and assimilates as much as possible. For our reference here educate is not a scholastic reference it is a reference to being educated in the ways of life.

Too many parents want the school system or some other authority to do the dirty work. As a parent you must know that this is a "hands on" project. You actually have to get completely involved. This means you will get mentally, emotionally, spiritually and physically involved. There is no shortcut!

Too many parents say, "I don't know what to do." Many parents who are not self-directed choose the medical route or go to the professionals for answers. They take their child who has challenges to the doctor and allow the doctor to medicate their child in order to modify their behavior rather than discover who the child is and assist the child in changing for themselves. A pill will not fix your child. It will however make them stoned enough to display the behavior that the system says is appropriate. Let's face it, you should be and are the expert when it comes to your child. And if you don't know, find out.

By educating your child about life you prepare them for living on their own. This education needs to include but are not limited to:

- What feelings are
- What emotions are
- Problem solving
- Making wise choices
- Listening to their heart/inner voice
- Intuition
- Understanding energy and its effects
- Communicating clearly
- Listening accurately
- Negotiation

We understand that many parents work and this makes the time available to educate your child more precious and shorter in duration. So all the more reason that you take advantage of the time you do have to continually educate your child and assist them in developing the skills we have mentioned thus far.

BE THE MODEL

The best thing you can do is to be the model for your children to follow. They will follow your example anyway, whether it is one that works or not, so be a healthy living example of what they can be. Work on your own issues, perceptions, judgments, patterns, behaviors and beliefs. There is always room for improvement. Teach them that you are not perfect and that you too are always learning.

The following are some of the most important phrases you can say to a child:

"I love you."

"I made a mistake."

"I apologize."

"Mistakes are how you discover what works."

"You don't have to please me."

"I love you no matter what."

"I don't know but I will find out."

"You don't have to like me but you do have to follow my guidance."

"You have a right to your feelings and choices."

If the parent is always right then there is no room for the child to grow. They will be forced to become a follower because they assume that everybody knows more than them or they will become your opponent because they just can't take being wrong all the time. Teach them to be explorers. Encourage them to explore their environment, their mental, emotional and physical capabilities. You help them learn to explore by teaching them that mistakes are actually discoveries. Be the example of this. Letting children know that you made a mistake and that by admitting it, you can now seek a better solution is among the greatest gifts you can give them.

Many parents get tired of hearing their children ask, "Why?" Exploration is about discovery and to discover, one must ask, "Why?" Welcome the question and be patient when they ask why and then direct them to find the answer or if it requires an explanation from you then give them a detailed explanation. Make the details pertinent to the conversation and topic, do not go off into some long-winded explanation and lose their attention.

When you have answered the whys enough times, make them think about it and re-explain it back to you. This way you can be assured that they did at least mentally or cognitively understand what you said. Once they have explained it sufficiently to you then when they ask you the question why, ask them to tell you why. This creates the need for them to self-reflect and it reinforces to them what they know and removes you from the authority position.

When they ask you why and you have already discovered that they know asked them questions like: "Why do you think?" "Remember what you told me last time?" "I don't know, you tell me." They may avoid answering you but don't let them off the hook by giving them the answer when you know that they know. If they refuse to give you the answer and you are positive they know because they have re-explained it to you previously, you may say something like "Well I guess you will just have to figure it out."

Do not give them the answers; at least not too easily. Make them think and feel for it. You need to teach them to be conscious decision-makers, not little puppets or responders. This does not help them — it only causes them to be emotionally dependent on other people to give them their worth and value. No parent wants to teach their child to be subject to others, wouldn't you agree? What you want to do is direct them, point them in the direction and allow them to figure it out. Anything less than that is not helping, it is enabling them.

Be consistent. Stick with what you say when you know it is the best and change when you find out there is something better. Do not be wishy-washy but be willing and capable of change. Do not give in to their pressure to get what they want when you have said no unless you made an error in judgment. Be able to say no even when you have said yes if you discover it was a mistake to say yes.

Tell your children, "If anything I do or say that you perceive as hurtful, please tell me. It is never my intent to hurt you and I want to correct any misstatements or misinterpretations."

And sometimes you may want to add: "However I will only change my mind if I find what I have said or done to be in error."

TEACHING A CHILD THEIR VALUE

Some see the academic grades the child receives as the child's identity and value or even that the child's grades reflect on the parent's identity or quality of parenting. If the child gets good grades, they perceive the child as intelligent, having value or even that the parent has done a good job. This then is accepted by the child as an identity of their own. If the child does not do so well academically in school, the parent may perceive them as unintelligent or not having value. The grades become the measuring stick for the child's identity, worth and value. At this point, learning has ceased and competing or pleasing others becomes the focus. The child intuitively begins to resent school, learning, the parent or, worst of all, themselves. And usually will resort to manipulating the system and the parents to compensate for their grades or neglect or refusal to participate in academic activities.

Egos are best left out of parenting

For example, when a child hears all the time how smart they are, it is often interpreted as an identity they must maintain. With this they will have their own assumptions of what smart really is and why they must maintain that. Sometimes the child feels that they must remain smart and produce results in order to be loved.

If the grades or their accomplishments do not match what standards the parents and they themselves hold, the child will often feel bad, wrong or like a failure. This is because successes and failures are tied up in the child's self-identity. This creates a great amount of unseen internal stress that may result in inappropriate behaviors and attitudes as well as physical illnesses. At this point the facts are that the child learning for their own benefit has been lost. Teach your child that learning is for them. It is for them to enjoy; and allow them to create the life they would like to experience when they are an adult.

In this example, if you saw your child begin to respond or become stressed because of not measuring up to some standards, this is where you will also see a reflection of your own identity or belief system. Always look to your child to teach you about your own belief systems and patterned behaviors. They are quite excellent educators themselves.

It is not necessarily the intent of any parent to actually mold their child, but it is often unconsciously done. If you remain conscious, the likelihood of molding is diminished. This creates an incredible bond in your relationship to your child and allows them to feel free to be themselves, whoever that may be and it creates a deep lifelong trust in your relationship.

A CHILD'S REALITY

When children unconsciously in their mind record an event, it becomes a reality instantly. This is because they have no idea how to question it or even if they should question it. They believe that the adults in their environment have the truth — truths that they acquire, assimilate and assume to be true for themselves.

Every child lives in their own reality. You must understand that every human being also lives in their own reality even though their reality overlaps with the reality of other people. This means that whatever one person perceives is never exactly the same as what another person perceives.

The challenge with this is that your child will have perceived their own experience of what you do or say and determine it to be their own truth. From this perspective they repeat what they perceive is the truth which may in fact have not been accurate or might conflict with other people's perceived realities. The inability to understand that what they thought they perceived as truth may in fact not have been accurate will cause many challenges later in life.

Do your best to require your child to repeat things and explain to you the reasoning behind their choices so that you may understand them and the reality in which they live. Quite often you will be surprised that your child sees things quite differently than you, especially when you have assumed they see everything the way that you have instructed or told them it is.

Typically in the child's reality there are what we call auto-responses. These auto-responses are the nodding of your head yes or the shaking of your head no. What a child learns early on is that when a parent wants you to understand or do something they nod their head and when they don't want you to do something they shake their head back and forth. Having learned this at the age of two the average child repeats this unconsciously throughout the rest of their life unless you have made a conscious effort to test whether there nodding or shaking of the head is accurate.

One way to test this is to do the opposite gesture when asking them yes or no. For example: when you say "Do you understand?" shake your head back and forth as if you are saying no when you would typically nod your head up and down for yes. Or when you say "No Suzy you can't do that." nod your head up and down as if you were saying yes. This will be confusing to the child at first. The purpose of this is to break the autopilot patterned behavior and force the child to be consciously aware of the question rather than follow the nodding or shaking of your head and responding.

This actually forces a reality check for the child and teaches them that they must be in the present moment paying attention. Anything that you do regularly that has become an automatic response for you and your child, change to something out of the usual. This begins to teach the child to be more conscious of the reality in which they live and assist in developing listening and discernment skills.

NEW BEHAVIORS

The first step is to teach them to be aware of their senses, of what they are doing and how they are behaving. This creates inner awareness and personal awareness skills. Secondly teach them about how those things affect their environment and how that environment responds to them. This teaches social and human skills

For example, if your child is barging into rooms and you want to change the behavior, you may have to model for them how to do it differently. Do it over and over again: "Okay, we're going in the room now and I want you to try to do it like I am doing it." Always have them explain to you that they have just been taught.

Never assume your child understands
Always require an explanation of what they do understand

You walk in very gently; you center yourself and walk in like that so they can get an idea of what that feels and looks like. Without this, you're asking them to model something that they can't understand or feel. You tell them the words and you expect them to know because when you ask them, they say, "Uh-huh" but they don't have a clue.

Never assume they understand, always require an explanation. With the explanation they must form the thought and verbally communicate what they understand. By doing this it anchors this information into their reality. Once they have explained it clearly then there is no need to have them explain the same understanding again. However some children need to explain it several times before it actually seats into their awareness and is available for their use.

You would be stunned how children often do not understand words, including the word "understand." All they know is that if you say, "Do you understand?" when you ask that question, they will nod and say yes. You really have to be conscious of what they really understand and ask them, "Do you know what understand means? Do you know what walk into the room gently means?"

Always assume your child doesn't understand anything until they explain it to you

Another example is when your child is too physically rough. Say to them, "Touch me gently please." "Do you know what touching gently means?" Then you model that. You hold them gently. You hug them and say, "Do you want to jump on me? There's a time when we're playing and there's a time where we're just being with each other so it's different." You'll have to physically show them what that was. Say something like, "This is what we do when we're wrestling or goofing around." and you grab them and you wrap around them tight, wrestle them around a little bit, then you put them down.

"Here's what it's like when you just want to be with me and hug. "Then you gently hold them in your arms so they can feel what that is. With this can they put together the feeling, the experience and your words. It will help them more and that will really assist you.

When your child is barging in the room, show them what it's like. Act it out and actually have them sit in the room and watch while you barge in like they do, or have your partner do it while you come in gently. You can even build up from coming in gently to being wild and do that deliberately. Now you start to show them exactly how it looks and feels. They feel and absorb everything and if you're just telling them things, they're not going to get it, it will only be a mental understanding not a felt experience. You have to model it so they can feel it. Seeing and feeling makes it real to them.

When you tell children not to do something, they have no other frame of reference and have to guess at what it means. When you tell them "Don't do it." and they think, "Well, what do I do now? Sit in the corner? Do I stand still? If I'm not doing that, am I bad?" Without an explanation this compounds their fears and then they often act the opposite of the way you wanted them to. You have to give them options and explanations when you want them to do something.

Don't just give them one option, because one will turn into an order. If you only give them one option, you're telling them what to do. If you give them three options, they have to make a choice. "You make a choice. Here are the three I suggest. Pick one of those three or try all three of them to see which one works for you." as they get older have them give you the three choices.

This allows them to be their own person and this is the key. Most parents parent from the authority position and don't give children many options or explanations. If you give them options, instead of having a dependent child you have a child who can think for themselves, make decisions for themselves. It will make your life easier. Otherwise before you know it they're fourteen and saying, "Dad, what do I do? Where should I go?" If they're not asking you because they can't trust you or are mad at you, guess who they're asking? Their friends and what do their friends know? They're asking people with little or no experience for advice. Guess what the likely results will be?

If your real intent is to teach them to be themselves, giving them different options and allowing choices is a great start. You must be aware of yourself and how you parent. Are you too talkative or not talkative enough? Do you really listen to your child or expect them to listen to you? You need to be balanced. If you're silent, you need to talk more because they are watching your silence and/or withdrawal. If you talk too much or do not listen to them, then they will most likely not listen to you. They will eventually do some version of everything you modeled for them. Keep in mind they are watching, listening and feeling everything you do!

If you have a partner then they're going to pick from both of your behaviors and decide which one works for them. They're going to watch the two of you and say, "Hmm, let me see. Dad gets his way most of the time. I think I'm going to use Dad's techniques over here. Mom gets her way with this. I'm going to use her techniques over here."

Be conscious of how you're interacting with your child and how you interact with other people. Do you shy away from people or are you a people pleaser? Find the balance. It's not that either is bad or wrong. It's just that you want to be aware that you are modeling.

When you want your child to have new behaviors you must model them, explain them and require the child to explain them to you. They need to have the visual, mental, auditory and felt experience. You must be patient and consistent in your efforts.

BEING PRESENT

Being present means being emotionally and consciously in the here and now. It's an important skill for both you and your child to practice. Being present is vital to an individual's ability to overcome difficulties. If one is not present then there is no past to remember and no future to come. The past is recorded in the subconscious and can be accessed, but it is not remembered by the conscious mind. This is a contributing factor as to why people with ADHD forget. Being present gives one a past they remember and something to build a future on.

Many people live in the past or think of the future to avoid the present. Many people detach emotionally to avoid the present. They then have difficulty remembering what has just been said, because they are not present. One reason for not being present is that there is a conscious or unconscious fear. It may be fear of a particular situation, of being in this world, their perceived faults or limitations, fear of being hurt, etc. This characteristic is unique to each individual.

Be aware of when you are not present. When do you check out, what triggers you? For example, maybe you are worrying, thinking of everything you have to do, your job, etc. Being present requires that you be in the moment and not in your head thinking about other things. Children are sensitive to this and feel when you are not there with them in the moment. Remember you are the model which they follow.

Know how to get back to being present. Be aware when you are lost in your thoughts and not fully in the moment, and then bring yourself back to the here and now.

"BE PRESENT"

"You must be present in the moment to be fully in the body and experience life to its fullest – to experience the moment.
You must also be mentally, emotionally, physically and spiritually in the now to be fully alive."

~ Excerpt from "the 55 Concepts, A Guide to Conscious Living" by Michael Cavallaro

GROUNDING YOUR CHILD

When you are not present in the moment, you are ungrounded. You need to be present to assist your child in being present. Be aware of your child's state of being. Be aware if you are present. The ultimate goal is for you and your child to admit and share with each other if you are present and if not, why not.

Have you ever driven somewhere and when you arrive, realize you do not remember how you got there? Most people have experienced something like this and it is a good example of not being present. Recognizing the feeling of being present or not is key to changing this in yourself and in your child. Observe your child. Many children will have a vacant look in their eyes or not be very responsive when they are not present. They may even be staring off into space. Use the observations to reflect on yourself or your partner.

When you have an understanding of what this looks like, you can start to feel when you or your child is not present. This is a sensory experience and may require some practice or assistance in order for you to discern the difference.

When you observe that your child is not present, you can easily bring them back. When you are talking with them and they are not 'there,' ask them to look at you in the eyes. You may have to do this a number of times during the conversation. Be kind yet firm with them if they repeatedly space out. This is about undoing patterns, not disciplining or controlling them. Breaking patterns or creating new ones takes time and effort.

When you are engaging with them in an activity and you sense they are somewhere else, direct them back to the present moment in what you are doing. Explain to them what you are doing and why. For example say, "Johnny, I am reminding you that we are playing cards right now. I felt that you were not here with me. When you are somewhere else you may miss what's happening in the card game."

Invite your child to let you know when they feel you are not present as well. It can become a fun game between the two of you as you both develop the skill.

Every child is unique so you really have to know your child. Some children may need a gentle tap or placement of a hand on the shoulder to feel the touch in order to bring them back to their body. For some the voice alone works. You may need to seek some third party assistance if you are not sure how to discern present and not present. We assure you that when you really get this and feel this for yourself, you'll be able to feel when your child is not present.

AGES AND STAGES

We are not going to cover physical, social or psychological development here. What we are going to briefly cover is the stages of belief, energetic and patterned behavioral development and their applications.

The following are the approximate ages and stages of inner development. Each child and parent will develop slightly differently.

Birth to five

During this stage a child is a sponge. They intuitively assimilate and experience every feeling in their environment. This includes but is not limited to: light, sound, vibrations, thoughts of others, feelings of others, voices, eye contact, touch, emotional and energetic tension or pleasure, the psychic interaction of others ,etc. Some children are more responsive or conscious of these experiences than others. During this phase they are not yet cognitively developed. Therefore almost all of their experience is recorded in the unconscious and rarely retrieved at an older age.

This is the stage where the child establishes 80 to 90% of their beliefs systems. The majority of these beliefs systems are unconscious. That is why when a child is often asked why they did something they will respond "I don't know." During the stages the child will sense and feel the energy of those around them and learn to respond by imitating the modeled behaviors and language.

During this stage the child is extremely psychically sensitive. This simply means; they are extremely sensitive to the energy and the invisible world in their environment. They at times will see 'invisible' friends or look around as if they are looking at something and yet there is nothing there. Many times the child is seeing things that adults no longer see.

This stage is mostly about feeling. (Keep in mind when we use the word feeling we are talking about the sensate experience not emotions. When we are referring to emotions we will use the word emotions.) This stage is where the child learns about themselves, using their body, being in touch with their inner-self and learning/intuiting the basics of the outside world. The child associates the energy of what they feel to their responses and patterns while creating lifelong habits. They then make meaning of what they feel and experience, consciously and unconsciously.

Children are psychically sensitive, intuitive beings

At this stage the child will decide semiconsciously whether the world is a safe or dangerous place. They will then begin to develop a personality that reflects their interpretation of their environment. This does not necessarily mean that their interpretation is accurate but it is real to them. At each stage the child will make a similar choice and a modified response based upon how they interpret their environment.

Six to eleven

This stage is spent learning about the outside, worldly skills/human skills while practicing the belief systems and patterns they learned in the previous stage. During this stage, many children lose sight of their inner knowing or connectedness and give themselves up to the outside world. Because they are so hyper-focused on the outside world and there is such a demand for them to act and behave a certain way, they tend to lose touch with their intuitive nature.

The high demand for attention on socialization, school, physical activity and becoming a participating member of the family consumes most of their focus. At this stage they still have intuitive insights but their interpretive and human skills are still in major development. This creates a challenge for them to completely understand what is actually happening to them.

At this stage they may run into conflicts with their siblings, parents and/or teachers. These conflicts stimulate and trigger beliefs systems and patterned behaviors. This is then often followed by emotional challenges or outbursts. Little does the child know that these emotions have nothing to do with them and that they are simply part of the early childhood programming and response mechanisms that they've witnessed or experienced.

As the parent you should know that most of your child's reactive behaviors come from belief systems and patterns formed prior to the age of six. This will assist you in understanding and being able to guide your child to a healthier interpretation in response to their world.

Along with this disconnect from their intuitive nature is the development of their physical body and pre-puberty hormonal changes. For boys this is often seen as a little bit more aggression and physical activity. For girls it can look like moodiness beginning somewhere around the age of 10. This moodiness is an energetic cycling in preparation for their menstrual cycle. Often times the menstrual cycle will start approximately two years after the moodiness cycle begins. These prepubescent hormonal changes sometimes trigger unexplained emotional or argumentative behaviors. This is because the chemical changes in the child's body is affecting their thought processes and triggering unconscious belief systems and patterning's that the child cannot control. It is as if that stare you just gave them push the button inside their psyche and they then uncontrollably act out or argue with you.

Please have patience with them and educate them on what is actually occurring in their body, emotions and belief systems. Of course to be able to do this you must know your child. If you have prepared your child about these topics at an early age communication and cooperation during puberty will be much easier. If you have not, begin immediately and it will at the least make it less challenging during this time.

Twelve to eighteen

At this point your child has so much going on within them and outside of them that life at times can be extremely challenging which often makes them miserable or have seeming personality changes.

At this stage the child begins to have the urge to become their own person. Couple this with more interactive social experiences, expectations that they take care of themselves more, academic pressures, body changes, disconnection from their intuitiveness, rules and regulations and finding their identity it's not surprising that they are often confused or moody. Do you remember when you were at this age? Sometimes it wasn't a whole lot of fun was it?

They are in between worlds and often feel alone and isolated even if there are people in their physical surroundings. Internally they feel like a foreigner in a foreign land. At this stage there is a lot of confusion, self-doubt and a sense of not having an identity. This is partially because they have lost their connection to their intuitive nature and inner guidance. The demands that require them to be certain ways that don't feel natural to them contribute to this confusion and self-doubt. The big question at this stage is "Who am I?"

This is also the stage when the hormones kick in and the "mating ritual" begins. If you have not educated your child on healthy sex, love and relationships they will be subject to experimentation based upon what they learn from friends and the internet. This additional pressure may cause a child to shut this aspect of their life down or delve deeply into it.

If you have established the trust and understanding with your child prior to this stage your love, reassurance and stories of when you were their age can at times be comforting for them.

Keep in mind that even though your child may intellectually be able to repeat the information that they have learned or think they know what they're doing, the truth is they still have underdeveloped discernment and interpretive skills. What skills they do have are based upon their interpretation of the belief systems and patterned behaviors that they have unconsciously learned. This typically makes the child highly inaccurate in their interpretations of what is going on within them and around them.

What compounds these stages for you as a parent is that the average parent is going through their own relationship issues, personal inner awakenings, financial issues and facing their own belief systems from their childhood. If you find it challenging just know that you're on the right track. The more you focus on your own personal growth and consciousness the easier parenting will be for you. If you happen to be in a relationship, never lose sight of your partner.

CRYSTAL, INDIGO AND STAR CHILDREN

All these labels merely identify certain qualities of children that are being born today. These labels are really not necessary. They are used to identify and bring to the awareness of humanity the changing consciousness and the souls that are arriving on planet earth. Whether you believe in this type of thing or not is irrelevant. The fact is that the children of today are quite different than they were in the 20th century.

These labels are not necessary and actually become a hindrance to some people as they make these labels their new "gods" to believe in.

It is not that we are not acknowledging the qualities that children with these labels have; it is that we are saying that the labels are not necessary and people too often identify with labels that in the end cause more problems than solutions. See the children as children and honor them for who they are and the gifts they bring to this life.

All you really need to do as a parent of today is parent your child with the concepts and the energy behind the information here. This will prepare your children to live in the world and the culture as it is today. These same human parenting principles will exist throughout time. These are permanent long-lasting principles that only change in the way they appear to acclimate to the current culture of the time.

SUGGESTIONS

Be conscious that you do not suggest to your child what their feelings and needs are. The first thing you have to remember is that children are responders. They will basically do what you tell them to do and feel what you tell them to feel, especially early on when they just want to please you or avoid experiences that make them uncomfortable. It is best if you do not say to your child these common phrases: "Are you cold?" "Are you hot?" "Are you hungry?" "You need to put a coat on because you will get sick." "Don't get wet because you'll catch cold."

All those common phrases tell a child what is going to happen before they even do something. It is best for you to say to the child, "Okay, do what you want to do." If the child goes outside and it's that cold they are not going to stay out there and die. They are just not that illogical. They will stay out there until they are really cold and then they will come in.

Remember cold does not make people sick. It is a false belief. There is no physical evidence that cold and wet creates illness. (We are not talking extreme, zero-degree weather.) All these things are untrue. Stop suggesting how the child will feel based upon a condition in their environment because you will create a responder and maybe even problems that would never exist. After you say it enough times, the child will respond by getting sick and you will say, "See, it's true. I told you." You programmed them to do that. This is not a physical truth. It is an old story, a fallacy.

YOUR UNCONSCIOUS INFLUENCE

Parents often unconsciously influence their children to respond a certain way, so that the child responds to what or the way the parent desires. Of course there is always the justification for doing this such as, "I want what is best for my child." Or "it makes perfect sense for me to want that for my child."

This is often done rather than allowing the child to give you an honest opinion. All too often unconsciously the child knows that if they don't give you the right answer there will be some sort of undesirable repercussion or they fear that one will occur.

Don't ask your child, "Did it feel good?" "Were you happy?" "Were you sad?" "Did you want to do it again?" Always give them multiple options, both positive and negative, so it's a choice.

If you say, "Did it feel good?" they will just say, "No." If you say, "Did you hate being there?" they will say, "Yes." You don't want to give them the answer that you are expecting them to give you in the form of a question — you want them to give them the opportunity to give you the answer they want about how they felt.

For example: "How was your trip to the museum?" or if you get no response try "Was your trip to the museum fun, not fun or just okay?"

There is a possibility they may not know how to say what they are feeling, so give them multiple choice questions and make sure they are balanced with positive and negative possibilities. Mix them up, because otherwise they'll figure out that every time Mommy asks something, she gives positive options the first three times and a negative option last. So they will eventually know or intuitively know that the answer you want them to pick is within the first three questions. They are often not conscious of trying to figure this out; they intuitively pick up on the pattern. They will hear you say it, they will respond, you will make a face and they will see, "Okay, this one! Mom is happy, good." After this has happened 50 times, they know the order, can feel you respond and know the answer you want.

Another thing to do is shake your head no when you are asking them a yes question. Shake your head when you say something like, "I would really like you to do this. Don't you want to?" It baffles them because they are so used to simply being responders.

Their attitude will be, "Nod the head 'yes,' I then say 'yes.' That way I don't have to think or be present. At this point they aren't making any real choices they are simply well-trained responders. They know that if mommy nods her head and they say yes and then mommy will smile and be happy. Daddy will give me a pat on the head. Everything is really good. Do you want a well-trained dog or do you want a freethinking child?

Keep in mind that your unconscious intent and agendas influence your child. Not necessarily because they're making real choices and following your direction, but mostly because they have figured out how to stay out of trouble or in your good graces. Intuitively your child knows the game and eventually will play your game on you. This is often where the parent says: "I don't know where Johnny got that behavior." or something similar.

SOCIAL APPROPRIATENESS

Do not ignore inappropriate behaviors or laugh at them as if they were cute or funny. If you do this you condone the behavior and eventually have to deal with that repercussion in the teenage years as well is creating social difficulties for your child. Parents who do this quite often end up punishing their children later for the types of behaviors they laughed at when they were little.

Point out socially unacceptable behaviors when they are occurring. Preface your conversation with, "This is not a criticism, this is to help you so people will not make fun of you." Have a discussion about it and ask the child what alternate behaviors are possible and maybe suggest a few they haven't thought of. Observe other people with your child and discuss their interactions and behaviors. See if your child can identify in others what is socially appropriate or not.

Differentiate between socially appropriate behaviors and required behaviors. Your child should never be required to have any particular behavior. Your child should always be required to exhibit socially appropriate behaviors that honor their own heart and not the feelings of others!

RESPECT OR AUTHORITY

A child must be taught the difference between blindly accepting authority and respectful behaviors. For these instructional purposes an authority is someone who controls, tells you what to do or bosses you around without your say. They must also know the difference between bossing as a verb and your boss as the employer or manager.

Respect is to know and recognize that someone knows what they are doing and knows how to do it. Respecting an authority figure means abiding by that person's limits and following their directions. It does not mean being controlled, manipulated or used.

Authority means that a person is in a position or job that gives them the right to direct people in order to get something done but never the right to make you do something.

They must know that they are respecting the person's skills and knowledge, but the person is not someone who has control over you — you don't have to do everything they say. The child must be taught that no one has more control over them than they do, but that sometimes people are in a position to be directing them and these people are to be treated with respect if they show respect to the child. The child must know that they do not need to respect people who do not respect them as human beings. This is especially true in regards to adults!

Adults who show no respect should not be respected.

BELIEVING AUTHORITY

You want to give your child a clear understanding of authority. The common belief for a child about authority is: "If I hear it or I am told it by somebody who is an adult or someone in charge/authority, I am supposed to and must believe them or do what they say." This comes from the child still feeling smaller than the adult and that the adults are supposed to know more than they do and because they have been told from early on that adults are supposed to be listened to. As a small child they also make assumptions that adults know everything because they don't really understand their world yet. This then sets in as a belief in authority as something to be followed or obeyed. Sometimes adults are just children in large bodies who have learned how to operate in society and sometimes adults actually know what they're talking about. The child must learn to question everything and then discern what is true, accurate or not.

Most adults don't get it either, mostly because they were taught this as a child and still assume it to be true. People in general seem to think that if an authority says it then it must be true. If they hear something from an "authority", it's assumed true, in many cases without question. They assume they are supposed to believe it if it comes from an authority they like, respect or is famous, a professional or a politician. Keep in mind people are just people. They don't necessarily know anything more than you just because they hold a title, hold a position or have an education. Many educated people or people in positions of power are extremely ignorant and know less about life than the indigenous peoples.

Children need to be taught that what is spoken by another person is simply something spoken by another person. It may or may not be true. It may or may not be factual. They should not believe what anyone says without their own investigation. So actually tell your child, "Always question what anyone says. Investigate for yourself whether what they say is true or not. Never believe something just because someone says it's true." When they question what is said tell them they may only be doing it in their mind and to not necessarily verbalize it or make it confrontational. Then teach them to do what is socially appropriate. Sometimes questioning the person immediately is appropriate and sometimes questioning it in your mind and then doing the investigation is appropriate. But they should question everything.

If it's true in the sense that it's a fact, they should understand that it is a fact but they do not have to believe it as your way of life — just know that it's a fact. There is a great difference and many people have this all mixed up. When something is a fact the only thing you must believe is that it's a fact. You don't have to believe that that fact is now your way of believing or your way of life. It is simply a fact. People don't usually do that. Typically if it is a fact or assumed to be a fact people make this a truth and a way of life. In a way, people are brainwashed as children and all the way through life to believe the things authority figures tell them. Some children resist but many just go along and others don't even question.

Freethinking self-directed individuals question everything and then choose what they want as their way of life. They never do something because an authority or authority figure has told him it must be done or it's true.

Teach your children to:

1. Know that no one has authority over you
2. Question everything
3. Find out the facts
4. Discern for yourself
5. Believe what you consciously choose to believe

MIRRORING TECHNIQUE FOR CHILDREN

Here are some exercises to do with children to help them become more aware of their behaviors, possible reactions, results and consequences. These will also teach your child to be more accurate and aware of their perceptions and themselves.

The mirror technique — Have the child stand in front of the mirror and look directly into their eyes and tell you what they see within themselves. Have the child look at their face, skin, hair and body and describe what they see.

Mirror the child's behavior — Imitate or reflect the child's behavior to them. Then ask them what they see or how they feel about the behaviors you have just imitated. This is so that they can see and feel why others might judge, react or have opinions of them.

Observation and solutions for behaviors — Next discuss the imitated behaviors. Talk about how they looked and how they felt from the outside as well is how one might feel inside themselves when acting that way. Then talk about the possibilities of how others might see them. Discuss solutions as to how the behaviors can be altered so that there are fewer repercussions that they have to deal with.

All this is done not to criticize but to create an awareness of self for your child. Make sure your child is told of this so that they don't assume this is a critical process.

PRACTICAL TOOLS AND TECHNIQUES FOR PARENTS

— Be consistent. It's been said before but can't be emphasized enough: Children need to know that you are there and that they can count on you, you are their guiding light. Guide them steadily. If you are inconsistent they will know that they cannot depend on you. Sometimes you are one way, and sometimes you are another way, so how can they trust you? This usually happens on an unconscious level. Being consistent is the foundation of trust.

— Remove yourself from the situation when you are feeling emotional or charged. Speaking to your child emotionally or charged breaks down trust and usually compounds the situation.

— Teach by example; make logical, rational, reasonable decisions. Teach your child decision making skills.

— Explain that feelings are a choice. Keep in mind however that feelings are based in beliefs and patterned behaviors. So the beliefs and patterned behaviors must also be addressed.

— Explain to your child the meaning of fairness, hurt, etc. Example: "For most people, fairness means getting what you want and hurt is not getting what you want."

— Clearly define privileges and what they are. Having a friend over, watching TV, etc. — these are all privileges. Basically, anything other than food, clothing and shelter is a privilege, not a right. Explain that privileges being taken away are a result of their behavior and choices not a punishment.

— Be aware of your responses: your voice, your tone, your gestures, your look, your words, and your attitude. They take it all in and make up their own stories about what they all mean.

— You want to explain the difference between what is factual and what is perceptual. "Someone attacked the child." and "Someone grabbed the child." are two different views. Grabbing may look like an attack, but to be labeled as an attack without more facts leads to a very different outcome and perception. The child may have been grabbed because they were stepping out into traffic, or about to fall. Be clear about what a fact is and what a perception is and thoroughly explain the difference to your child. A fact is what is, "I am human." A perception is how we interpret an event through our senses, judgments and beliefs, "Chocolate tastes good."

— Explain in the child's language but explain. Some people and professionals say that explaining is too complicated for children to understand. This is false. Don't underestimate their abilities. Begin explaining around the age of two. They may not cognitively understand your words but they will feel intuitively your explanation. Then when they are more cognitively developed and you explain the same thing the words will match the feelings that they received when they were younger. Remember children are intuitive beings.

— Assume nothing. Ask if the child understands and have them repeat back to you what it is they understand. Use the dictionary definition of words to be absolutely clear.

— Look into their eyes and be present when speaking to them, rather than whining or nagging. When you look into their eyes they feel you there with them. However if you are emotionally charged please do not look them in the eyes as you will convey those feelings to your child and this will create long-term difficulties. If you need to look at them while you are emotionally charged look at the bridge of their nose or on their forehead. This may sound ridiculous to you but we can assure you the intuitive nature of a child will be greatly affected by your emotional charges and the energy that your eyes convey. When you are loving your child look at them directly into their eyes and allow them to feel your essence speaking to theirs.

— When dealing with your child, you must take into consideration two things:

1. Their physical age – Treat them with the proper attitude and respect deserving of a person their age. Know the limit of their experience on this planet and teach them accordingly.

2. The age of their soul or spirit/their internal age – Did you ever now a child who was wise beyond their years? This is important. The wisdom of the soul has nothing to do with the age of the body. A wise old soul can assimilate and understand more information than a young one. But even with a wise old soul there are limits to what the human child mind can understand and interpret. So don't speak over their head.

— Misunderstandings – For example, a situation is sometimes taken too far. Everyone is joking, then all of a sudden they take it personally and get angry. Evaluate why. Let the child do the talking. Commonly this is a result of some belief system or patterned behavior being triggered.

— Love your child unconditionally do not judge them. Provide them with the opportunity to learn, grow and accept whatever their choices are. This empowers your child to become a creator of their own life.

Parenting is a long-term process and not about immediate results. Too many parents are looking for immediate results from their instruction of the child for their own satisfaction or relief. Most do not get them. Sometimes you are lucky, but for the most part it's planting the seeds for your child's own understanding, experimentation and later decisions. If you push for the immediate results, you will be sorely disappointed.

Forcing results will simply be a manipulation and will not empower the child. It will end up backfiring if you have an agenda. Your only agenda is to plant the seeds to allow the child to make a choice to become the creator of their own life.

POTENTIAL AND PURPOSE

Help your children find their path in life, not what you want them to be or think they should/could be. Support them in their interests and don't force them to do things for their own good. Teach your child the specialness of their differences. You need to identify the uniqueness of your children and help them develop it, not to conform and lose it. Teach and direct them to use it functionally in the current society.

Teach your child to feel: to balance their male and female aspects or qualities and to connect their head with their heart. Oftentimes you accidentally or purposefully step on your child's heart by not listening and then telling them what to do. You are usually well intended, but it is nonetheless hurtful and creates perceived realities and beliefs about the incidents. Trying to teach them by intellect alone and forgetting about their heart teaches the child to ignore their inner knowing and divine essence. You don't want them to be emotional cripples, but balanced, compassionate, self-aware individuals.

Teach them how to use their intellect to understand their emotions and be aware of the feelings underneath and in their heart. Teach them about their beliefs and patterned behaviors as well as where they come from. Present them with options and allow them to make choices and incur the results of their choices. Afterward, review their choices and point out other options.

Allow and guide your child to be who they are, not who you want or think they should be. Allow and guide them to discover what they love. Allow and guide them to discover and awaken their soul's purpose.

Encourage your child to discover who they are. Try to understand who your children are and let your children experiment with different things. Develop their sense of wonder and exploration. Don't expect them to stay with anything they try right away. Never say, "If you're going to start this project/sport/etc., then you have to stick with it." Let them try things. There are so many things that this stick to it mentality creates such as; disappointment, depression, sadness, setting themselves up to be victims or aggressors, lack of worth and value, being a people pleaser, feeling like they have no choice etc.

The pressure of too many expectations has many negative effects. However sometimes it is necessary to push your child to try or complete new things in order to develop human skills that will serve them later in life. The easiest way to discern the difference is: are you teaching them for the purpose of lifelong lessons or are you repeating what was done to you as a child. Be aware of what your true intent is, are you teaching or are you repeating patterns? Sometimes it's difficult to tell the difference between what you believe you are teaching and why you are actually teaching. When you do your own personal growth and become aware of your belief systems and patterned behaviors it is easier for you to discern the difference

Things to remember

- Let children know they are loved no matter what.

- Individual 1-on-1 quality time is essential.

- Fear and power have no place in parenting

- Family teamwork wins! Explain to them how the family works and how you all are part of the team.

- Stability creates trust. If you yell, are moody, wishy washy, or are inconsistent, you are unpredictable to your child and they will learn that they cannot trust you.

- Be very conscious of your attitude, because children live by example. You cannot be aware of everything. You can do the best you can. Think of it logically: if someone were using a power tool, would you be afraid of it and protect yourself from it, or would you be aware of how it works and use it properly?

- Never regret what has been done, simply change it in the present and move on.

Understand that life has tools and requires skills. Know that it is your job to give your child human skills, which are tools, and teach the child to be aware of these tools — not to protect themselves with them or from them.

Fear and awareness are not the same. Fearful people do not enjoy life. They are always worried that something is going to happen. They are always protecting, always making sure the back door is closed, making sure the front door is locked. Whatever it is, they are always on guard, always on duty. You want to create aware children, not fearful children.

Your child can and should experience joy in life. Awareness is the ultimate safety!

HOME AS A HAVEN

The total environment of the home creates the foundation of a child's behaviors and personality. It is not simply witnessing behaviors, instruction or being told what to do that creates a child's personality and future. Again the key factor here is the feeling of the environment. The feeling of the environment combined with the appropriate direction and instruction creates an emotionally and functionally healthy child.

A child raised in a neutral or non-loving home with proper instruction and direction will be a dysfunctional child. A child raised in a loving home without proper direction and instruction still becomes a dysfunctional child.

For a child to be emotionally and functionally healthy, they must be raised in a patient, tolerant and loving environment then given the proper direction and instructions on how to be a healthy and functional human being.

It is important as parents to remember and be aware of everything you experience and what everyone in the household is experiencing. If you do not pay attention to that, you are a) not a conscious parent and b) doing a disservice to everyone else in your household because psychically and energetically every experience and feeling gets transmitted to and through everyone in the household. At some level, everyone picks up all of the information and feeling in the household.

Everything you do, think and feel is energetically/psychically infused into your family unit and partnership. To be a conscious parent you must be open to both your children and whoever else lives in the household saying, "Hey, you know you just put that charge through the household with that comment. Could you tone that down or lighten up? Could you at least own that as your own by verbally admitting it to the other members of the family?"

You must be open to receive that information and feedback from your family members or child, or again, you are not a conscious parent. It is absolutely required. To do anything less is to continue the old way. Keep in mind that you are being a conscious parent for you, so that your life is more enjoyable. By being a conscious parent and imbuing those qualities you are creating a home that is a haven.

CHANGING PATTERNS

Your child witnesses you responding to things. The child sees what everybody gets away with and what everybody is allowed to do. The child sees the lack of boundaries (although they do not interpret it as lack of boundaries) and who is conscious of it or not. What the child has witnessed is exactly what the child's operating system includes now and with this experience a pattern and a belief is born.

If you don't catch these things in the child by the time he or she is six, you will have your hands full. If you catch them by 10 or 12, you can at least manage and educate them and their behaviors until they are out of the house. At this point you can at least give your child the skills they need.

> *All hope is not lost if you get this information a little later in your child's life. As long as they are in your household you can plant the seeds of understanding and wisdom for them to harvest if and when they are ready.*

So when your child is working the system with the patterns you taught them and acting in an inappropriate way, you wait until they are calm and talk to them in a casual, educational conversation. Part of that conversation is telling them why they are like that by admitting your part in the creation of these patterns. "Hey, I realize what I did… I realize how I let you, your brother, your sister, everybody get away with things. I realize that it's now a habit pattern. But I also want to tell you that these habit patterns are now your choice. So yes, you have the habit pattern, but now I am going to teach you new things. It's your choice whether you continue with these or change."

The next step is asking them if they really want to change. Tell them that you understand that it isn't going to be easy because they are going to have to learn a whole new set of skills. It is may be very challenging at times, but it can be done. The most important thing is to say, "I am going to have to learn, too. And know I may fall into my habit patterns and make some mistakes, but I'll be open to you making me aware so that I can make shifts too. This way we can both make these changes together."

The problem in a lot of situations is that the parents want the child to change so their life can be smoother and yet not look at their own issues, patterned behaviors or beliefs. It doesn't work that way. Children have learned to behave the way they do from you, whether you like it or not. And they have taken that basic foundation you have given them and modified it to create their own version. It may look completely different, but they learned the basics from you. They have to know that you're in it with them and that you own your dysfunctional patterns. Your honest and candid admission will create a new level of trust with your child whether they acknowledge it or not.

You also have to understand that every time you fall back, it's going to justify them behaving the old way also. You are the model! The do as I say not as I do attitude never works. You also have to understand that they will test you. Are you committed really? That's where the breakdown usually occurs, because they test you. A lot of parents get upset because the child is testing them and pulling the old stuff and then resort to their old behaviors.

This then proves to the child that you are not trustworthy and you don't really mean what you say. In spite of their testing you must remain consistent in your new way of being, at all costs. This is not to say you won't be frustrated or get angry, but you must not exhibit this to them in a hostile way. You may say something like "dealing with these old behaviors is quite frustrating to me and I am tempted to behave in my old ways as well. But I am choosing not to." This acknowledges the situation and your ownership of your feelings as well as acknowledgment of what is happening. This also creates trust. If they realize at a conscious and unconscious level that they can trust you their willingness to change is greater.

You are typically looking at two full years of consistent behavior on your part to even possibly notice a major shift in the child. Some changes may occur earlier, but the average major change seems to be in about two full years. Some parents say, "Wow, this is a long time I don't know if I can do this." Whatever you choose as the parent will be the model for the child and confirms your level of commitment to real change. As the saying goes "Rome wasn't built in a day." You must choose what you want, long-term; real change or temporary fixes. Although long-term change takes a lot of work, we can assure you that temporary fixes will be exhausting and never ending.

If you are inconsistent and you start over every day no real change will ever happen. That is the problem: A lot of parents don't stay committed to it. They lose their tempers, they have a bad day at work, and they go into their old patterns. The child sees this and behaves the same old way and it goes round and round. After watching this at some point the child thinks to themselves, "This is a sham." or even worse there is the subconscious message interpreted as, "My parents are liars and it is okay for me to lie to get what I want." So do not be disappointed if it takes two years for you to see a major change. Until then, little wins are your big victories.

It can't be expressed enough: consistency, consistency, consistency. If you are going to change and make up new rules of behavior, you have to stay with them no matter how bad it gets or how good it gets. You don't get lenient because it's good, and you don't get harder because it's bad. You stay with the program. It's really tough for parents but it truly does take that long. If you get lucky, you'll see changes sooner. The earlier you begin this style of parenting the faster you will see the changes. The two-year change is based upon a 12-year-old and older child beginning to experience this style of parenting.

Parents don't want to wait two full years. Realize it's not a quick fix because you are working with patterns they have had for 10 or 13 years and trying to change them in a couple of months. It just doesn't work. Don't expect the impossible. You will be disappointed. Don't set yourself up for failure and take every day, one day at a time. Stay present and be focused on the present moment. This makes it easier for you to do what you must do to be consistent.

Depending on the child's personality these changes work in different ways. Some children will succumb to the pressure but look for loopholes. Others will go straight at it. These are traits they learned from you. Your child will use all of the problem-solving skills that you have given them consciously or unconsciously. Your conversation with them needs to be neutral; not charged. Say, "I am going to be making a change too." Say to the child, "I am in it with you. I will remind you and you remind me." This type of conversation reinforces the teamwork concept of a family.

There is a possibility that they'll rage or rebel while you're reminding them. Then you say, "I see you are doing what we talked about. I am not going to get into it with you right now, but I'm reminding you, just like I would expect you to remind me."

At this point, you have to put your personal issues aside and be neutral, present and honest. "I am getting upset right now. I don't want to feel this way but this is what I feel. You have every right to feel the way that you are feeling. I understand that you are mad at me or hate me right now, and you're allowed to feel that way. I get it, but this is the situation." Then explain the situation. Don't explain yourself, explain the situation.

Let them know it's not okay to attack you with their anger but it is okay for them to express how they feel. Differentiate between expression and verbally or emotionally attacking someone. You must also discuss the energy of their expression and how it conveys what is really being said as well is how people might respond to energy of that expression. This is exposing the invisible world and is probably the most important part of understanding communication.

Lay the foundation, even if you don't think they are listening. That is your consistency. No matter what hold your consistency, stand in what you've told them you would be in and let them know you are there. That is the solidity it is integrity in action. If you have taught them up to now that they can wear you down, they are going to continue to do it. Stay strong and be conscious

You will have to modify your conversations for your child and each situation. It is impossible for us to put down in writing how many different scenarios are possible. Take the basic concepts from this information and use it wisely in your own situations in a way that works for you and your child.

THE FALLACY OF SELF-ESTEEM

Self-esteem is the level of self-confidence or value a person has about themselves. It has no basis in reality about a person's essence. Self-esteem is overrated and beaten to death, with no real resolution except continuous coping. All this focus on self-esteem is as effective as focusing on a flat tire and not changing it.

Fact: *Self-esteem comes from a belief system.*

Self-esteem is the belief you hold about yourself. The self-esteem a person holds is directly related and governed by their belief system. Changing the belief system changes the perception a person holds about them self. Changing behaviors to encourage a positive self-esteem is to create a false image to believe in, which is ultimately self-deception and never permanent. It is like putting on expensive clothes and then believing you are wealthy. It is an illusion.

Self-esteem comes from a judgment based on a perception that was made as a child that you accepted as the truth. You may have determined that something or someone outside of you determines your value. You may have decided that if you behaved a certain way you got attention or love. This all supported the belief that your behaviors determine your value and as such other people dictate the behaviors that make you loveable.

Behaviors do not determine worth or value
You are not your behaviors

You may be afraid to disagree or behave the way you really feel, so as not to be rejected, not accepted or even unloved. What you never really understood as a child was that you can never satisfy anyone else because their desires change based upon their own needs or issues of the moment and have nothing to do with you. You may have experienced the frustration of never being good enough for someone, and this is why.

No one or no thing determines your worth and value
You are divine in your nature and therefore innately
valuable

Don't create this same mess for your children. Don't teach them that their behaviors determine whether they are loved, liked or accepted. Teach them that their behaviors are socially acceptable or not and love the essence of your child. Do not judge them because they do not fit a mold you or someone else determined they should fit into. Let them create their own mold.

Again this does not mean you should let them get away with socially unacceptable or inappropriate behaviors. What it means is that you teach them social skills appropriate to their environment. Then allow them to choose to use those skills or not and experience the results of their choice. You are not fulfilling your parental duties if you are rescuing or saving them. Protect them physically, teach them emotional and social skills, and then allow them to experience their own life process. This is the greatest gift you can give them.

Always use common sense when parenting! Be logical, reasonable and rational and they will learn to do the same even if they choose not to use these qualities. Keep in mind that life is about choice and your child may make choices you do not agree with or like. Remember they make choices based on what they watch and feel you do, not just what you say.

Thoughts and beliefs are complicated
They distract you from living from your heart

Fact: If you get to the root when problem solving (the belief system), there is no need for the complications and life is simple.

Fact: The world and the mind loves complications. Complications make money, allow powerless people to feel powerful, keep you busy and allow the powers that be to control the show.

Fact: Connecting to your divinity and living through your heart simplifies life.

Life is simple
Live it that way

While you are getting to the root, managing skills are important. But do not make managing the focus or the endgame — make eliminating the root the focus. In management, most of the popular self-esteem skills written about are helpful, but using self-esteem as the driving force is like controlling a car with the tire: it can't be done. You need to get a hold of the steering wheel, which in this case is the belief about self and your value. Once you have done this, you can teach your child, too. Do not try to teach your child this if you are not in the process of mastering it yourself, otherwise it is the 'do as I say not as I do game again.'

CREATIVE POWER

Some adults have grown up and either don't like those in power or see those in power as needing to be suppressed, so they tend to give more leeway to those who seem to be being victimized or support those exerting power over another. Your child needs to be able to finds a proper or appropriate way to express their personal creative power. This power is not the power over others or the ability to influence others. This power is the power to create a world for themselves!

Expressing power is creating not controlling

Sometimes, a younger sibling will get out into another environment and try to exert their power and control in situations. This isn't because they're bad and abusing their power. They are simply trying to express their own creative power that's been suppressed or they have given away to older siblings or the parents. They need to be taught about their own creative power and their ability to direct and share.

Never allow anyone to control or exert power over your child including siblings or yourself. This teaches them that they are creatively powerless. Be as age appropriately fair and equal in all situations as much as possible.

A child should never be forced to share. Sharing that is forced upon them will teach them to shut down their creative power and become either passive or aggressive. They will fight you and not really understand how to use their own personal creative power or express themselves or they will give in and subject themselves to other people's wishes and whims. They should however be given choices to share or not and experience the results of sharing or not sharing.

It should also be understood that personal strength is also required. Maintaining that inner strength helps them develop a healthy personality and express their creative power. A child who knows they have creative power and that it can never be taken away becomes a confident and self-sustaining adult.

Your Journal

Remember journaling? It's time to start another chapter. This journaling is for you to write your experiences and questions about your children or the children you work with. Key things to write about:

- Your perceptions of them and their behaviors
- Your judgments about them and their behaviors
- Your feelings about them and their behaviors
- Your hopes, dreams and fears for or about them
- Areas in which you see they or you could use improvement
- What you have learned from them
- Your beliefs about what a parent's role is
- Beliefs and feelings about yourself as a parent

Read over your journal and what you have written about your child. Look inside yourself to see where, how and in what form you, too, may be experiencing these things. Feel the essence of the things you write about because the experience may appear different on the outside.

For example, you may see how your child whines outwardly about not wanting to do something. You may not outwardly whine, yet inside you may whine or complain to yourself about your job or parental responsibilities.

Do not make this exercise hard. This is a reference for you and a few words or sentences jotted down will assist you in uncovering the things you may want to change.

CHAPTER SEVEN
LEARNING, SCHOOL AND HOMEWORK
How children learn

Realize that learning is not about school and homework. While children can learn at school, they are learning every moment of every day. They learn from watching you, from watching others, their environment, their experiences, what they feel and more.

The first thing that you should understand about how a child learns is that they learn sensately. This means they learned through their sensory system which is more than the five commonly accepted senses. Often adults teaching children are attempting to stimulate or motivate children through the mind or a mental process. A child is optimally reached through their sensate system. This is a system that is all about feeling. This feeling we are referring to has nothing to do with emotions!

To understand what we are speaking about here, imagine some time when you were alone in a room, the lights were out and your eyes were closed. Could you feel or sense that something was in the room? Have you ever had a feeling that was not an emotion that you couldn't explain? Have you ever had an intuitive sense or feeling about a room or a building? You knew it felt creepy, dark, weird or strange but you couldn't put your finger on it. Have you ever had a feeling about someone without knowing anything about them but yet somehow you knew something was up, you didn't trust them, you really liked them etc.? Will this is the type of sensate feeling we are talking about.

These feelings are a major part of a child's learning and actually adults too. If something doesn't feel good to a child they will typically not be interested in learning. Now you must determine whether this is simply a resistance to something new or if it's some sort of inner feeling the child has about the subject matter. Once you have understood how a child feels it is much easier to teach them and for them to learn.

Unfortunately our school systems and society have little or no understanding of this part of the child. So you as the parent must learn about it in order to assist your child in his educational endeavors. The skill and understanding will help your child in all types of learning not just academic. The depths of this sensate system will not be explained in this book; it is far too comprehensive. But this should give you an idea and something new to expand your awareness in raising your child.

Keep in mind you are learning to teach your child *how* to be, not *who* to be.

If you are attempting to mold your child's personality, stop now. Nothing positive can come out of that except that you have created a little robot. Nor can you teach your child to make the choices you want them to make. You must truly get this. The best parent teaches their child how to be and then allows the child to experiment with that information.

A major part of the resistance children have in learning is when they feel you are trying to change them, when they feel they have no choice or they intuitively feel you are manipulating them. Once they feel any of these things they typically make one of three choices; first they resist they take an oppositional stance against you and it becomes a battle, second they surrender themselves emotionally and become easily manipulated, third they emotionally detach from themselves and their environment. If your child is aggressive or uncooperative they have taken choice one, if your child is a "yes" child they have made choice two and if they are spacey, unengaged, silent or unresponsive they have made choice three.

Now of course there are certain rules and things that they must learn that they will not like or even find interesting. These topics need to be explained to them logically reasonably and rationally so that you plant the seed of understanding that these things will assist them later in life.

Some children only like particular subjects because those subjects are fun for them. The other subjects are things that are not fun or easy for them, so they are not interested. They often then feel as if they are being forced to do something they don't want to do. At this point they begin to behave like exactly what they are, children.

This is the point when you have to explain to them about future use and how it will serve them. They probably won't understand or care because emotionally they have shut down either because it's too hard, they're not interested or they just don't care. Try to remember when you were a child. What did you do when you felt like you are being forced to do something, resist? At this point they will probably blame anyone or anything as well as have many excuses as to why. The major problem that exists here is that they are children. They have a child's mentality and perspective so they do not see the larger picture of life and what is needed or how if they don't learn these things how difficult their life will be. One of your jobs as a parent is to constantly educate and remind them of the larger picture. However don't be redundantly boring or nagging about the subject. We all know what most people do when they are confronted with a boring or nagging situation, don't we? Whatever you do as a parent, don't be boring or aggressive nags.

If you can give them logical explanations and examples than they will eventually understand. Even though they understand they still may not do what you want them to do. You as a parent must accept this as a possibility. All you can do is provide them with the information and opportunity and hope for the best. You cannot control what your child chooses to learn.

Because a child sees himself as a child and adults as authority they often cannot comprehend that learning or education is for them. You must constantly reiterate that everything that they learn and do is for them. It makes their life better or easier. What you want to tell them about learning is: "It is for you and about you. It is not for us or anyone else."

When children finally get that they are doing it for their own benefit — for themselves and not for somebody else — it's like they just woke up. They've realized the work is for and about them which now motivates them. Motivation is not done through manipulation, bribery or punishment.

You cannot motivate someone else. You can only teach them to motivate themselves. Reward parenting is a common method used by many parents. Keep in mind if you use rewards to motivate or manipulate your child that you are teaching them that bribery is an effective method to get what you want in life. This teaches them that the lack of integrity is acceptable. This also sets them up to be manipulated or used by others.

Money in particular should never be a motivator. However the knowledge that if they have money it will allow them to create or acquire something that they desire is acceptable. If they are taught in this way the motivation is to create or acquire something and money is just the resource.

Real learning comes when the child's heart is open. Any attempt to force something into their heart causes them to shut down. If you have built and maintained a heart connected relationship with your child the ability for them to receive information, even information they don't like, becomes easier for both you and your child. Do your best not to fall into your old programs or ideas about what learning should be. Allow your child to show you how they learned best and support them.

Should your child resist learning know that every child will have particular situations and reasons for resisting learning. Sometimes it is the way you deliver it, the way they receive it or have misinterpreted it, their fear, social pressures or any perceived traumatic experience associated with learning. We cannot emphasize enough; explain everything to your children no matter how young or how many times you have say it. This will have long-term rewards for both you and your child.

ALLOWING CHILDREN TO LEARN

Give the child permission to be themselves, whoever that it is, without judgment. That is what a real teacher does. A real teacher enables children to be and discover. After that a real teacher facilitates an understanding of the options and assists in awakening an awareness of the child.

Give your child the opportunity to be independent by allowing them to do things even when you are afraid, of course as long as the child's physical safety is not in jeopardy. It is optimal to let them do things a little at a time, yet not too slowly. Let the child learn to do things on their own while also letting the child know that you are still there as a safety backup. Knowing when to help and when to step back is a skill that takes time to develop. This way, when the child is old enough, you can give them their freedom and they will know and be confident that they can do things on their own. Once you know and witness that they have the tools you will be more comfortable when it is time to emotionally detach and allow them to live their own life.

If the child does not develop the skills of being self-directed, self-maintaining and self-sustaining they will constantly look for someone to take care of them in some way, shape or form. The caretaker may be someone they work with, an employer, a girlfriend, a wife/husband or even their child. If you happen to be emotionally or mentally dependent on your own child now is the best time to break this habit.

A child learns best through their own experience.

Giving your child freedom is letting them know that they can always come back to you for advice while making decisions, or even just to brainstorm with you when they are older. Some parents hold on to children when they want to break away. This creates tension and ruptures trust in the relationship.

A situation of an emotionally attached or controlling parent refusing to let go when the child wants their freedom can escalate to banishment ("And don't come back!"). At this point the child may feel abandoned, rejected, betrayed and alone. These children go on to build relationships with other people in order to compensate for the void left in the relationship with their parent. Often times the relationship that is built for compensation is created from a childhood belief and need system that usually results in an unhealthy adult relationship. Rebuilding the relationship with the parent is the best thing a child can do. But if the parent is still too attached or holds a grudge this may never happen. When the child at this point, even being an adult, rebuilds the relationship it resolves childhood issues which allows them to move on toward a healthy adult relationship with their partner or friends.

That is the parent's side of learning. A child, on the other hand, has the responsibility of trying to understand when and how to break away smoothly. A healthy parent knows, understands this and allows the child to do whatever they are going to do. Healthy parents do not attempt to get their child to do what they parent would like the child to do.

The child's responsibility is to be as cooperative as possible absorb and experiment with the information that the parent has been teaching. The absorption of information is best assimilated by the child during a calm, logical and rational conversation. When you or your child are upset know that it is not the time to have a clear responsible communication. The child is responsible to wait until the emotions have passed and then agree to a reasonable conversation. Sometimes their emotions will get the best of them. This is common. Remember they are learning to be human beings and are in the developmental stage of practicing and honing the skills that they have learned. Be patient!

When a child is upset or non-communicative it is usually because they are struggling with their own human skills. Typically they find their abilities very frustrating and less than adequate. Your patience allows them to learn the skill of patience and give them time to gather themselves together in order to communicate what they want in a more effective manner. Don't ever assume that their hostility or silence is about you. Most often there silence or hostility is their frustration with the world that they are learning about. Encouraging your child to talk about how they feel inside will eventually change this. However many children do not know the appropriate language to describe the sensate feelings that are going on inside of them. So you must educate them on the appropriate words to use when they describe their feelings to you.

After having been educated the child has the responsibility of communicating appropriately and as effectively as possible. It is also necessary for them to listen. Now let's clarify what we mean by listen. Most people think that when you say a child should listen that it means they should do what they are told. That is not an accurate definition of listening.

Listen: *to hear what someone has said in an attempt to understand, to give attention with the ear; attend closely for the purpose of hearing*

Children should know that the purpose of listening is for them to learn, understand and be able to use the information they have gained for their own personal satisfaction. They should also understand that they are not learning in order to please others, whether it be a parent, a teacher or someone else.

Keep in mind the children learn sensately and emotionally. If there sensory system or their emotions are compromised or out of whack then learning will be difficult. Many times if they are in a compromise position emotionally or sensately they will shut down and not be able to learn/absorb the information that is being shared with them. Also know that the information that you are teaching them needs to be rephrased: you share information with your child so that your child may learn skills and information useful to them. All too often teaching or teacher is viewed as an authority position. When you are the sharer of information you are not an authority you are simply the sharer of information.

To fulfill their need of sensate and emotional learning it is wise for you to understand that authority type teaching will it be intuitively felt by the child and usually reject it. Thereby they only can learn a limited amount of the information because they have emotionally or sensately shut themselves down to the authority type feeling/energy. You are the adult and they are the child there is more for you to know in order to patiently allow your child to learn in a way that suits their needs and style of learning.

The optimal mentality for learning is that the child receives the information. Imagine that the information that is being shared with them is a beam of light. They do not need to reach out be intensely focused and grab the information as is typically assumed in traditional teaching styles. What they do need to do is sit back relax and receive the beam of light and absorb the particles of information that bathe there sensate system. If you teach your child to learn in this way you will find that they will absorb things much more quickly and efficiently than trying to use the mental, controlled, intensely focused method. Children with ADHD intuitively know and understand this. Children with Asperger's mentally understand this and will often refuse information that is shoved down their throat. The patient and kind share your beam of light (knowledge and wisdom) with your child and allow them to bathe in the light that you share.

LEARNING IS FOR ME

Many children don't like school because they were never taught that learning for is for them. With the emphasis on testing and grades the real learning of the child is forgotten. The focus tends to be on standards and funding which means that the child must prove they have accomplished what the system says is learning. At some point in today's school system many children simply give up and have learned how to manipulate the system by giving them the answers that they want rather than learning for themselves.

How do I change this for my child?

First, do not make grades and testing a marker of their success or failure. Teach your child that whatever they do as far as grades and testing is simply a marker for how much they have learned for themselves. You may also explain to them, "Everything you learn is preparing you for when you become an adult so you will know how the world works. You are gaining basic skills you need for life. You might look at all the things done in school and ask yourself, 'What is the use? Why should I bother? Why should I write the paper? Why should I go to school? Why should I have a job?' If you resist this education then you will have limited choices and life will be quite a bit more difficult when you are an adult. While the topic of the paper may not be important later, knowing how to learn, express yourself and communicate through writing will be important.'

"You were born in order to experience being on earth. You won't enjoy the experience if you are struggling with things you didn't learn when you had a chance. When you don't see the value in what you are learning, it becomes drudgery. It's difficult and challenging. If you could see that everything that you are doing will teach you something to use in the next part of your life then the journey and life than will be easier.'

"So let's say you're writing a paper on Shakespeare, and you wonder, 'How is this going to help me? What use is it in my everyday life?' The important part may not be the story of Shakespeare. It may be the exercise of simply getting things done that you don't necessarily find interesting but which need to be done. Or there may be some hidden understandings within Shakespeare's work that you are not paying attention to that will teach you about life. Part of the thing that you are struggling with is seeing the value in what you are doing when you don't find it particularly interesting."

Admit to them that many of the topics in school were not interesting to you or you found that you do not use now that you are an adult. However there were many things that you did learn that you use every day. A few of the things you learned piqued your interest and gave you direction in your life. Tell them that all learning is for them even if they don't understand how that is true right now.

The next challenging thing for children in learning, especially in the school systems, is their interaction with teachers. Typically most children have a personality conflict with the teacher at some time. You must educate your children on how to handle these difficult situations. This includes what to say, how to act and who to take their problems to if they can't work it out with their teacher. The most important thing your child needs to know is that a difficult teacher is not their fault and it doesn't mean anything about them as a human being, unless of course they are deliberately acting out and causing problems.

If this is the case then you must be honest with your child and tell them how they are creating the situation and that it is their responsibility to themselves to know that they are creating the problem. If it is truly the teacher that is the problem then it is your job as their parent to support your child. Let your child know that you are behind them if is not of their own doing. Do not be afraid to go into the school and speak to the people necessary in order to resolve this for your child. Keep your child informed as to what you have done and what the results were.

HOMEWORK

Parents often try to convince their children that they must do their homework so that they will do well in school. But this doing well is based on the parents' perspective, not the child's. Keep in mind that your child is a child and may need to learn through trial and error. Experience is the best teacher.

> *Love your child enough to educate*
> *them about their choices.*
> *Then love them enough to allow*
> *them to make their own choices.*

Yes, it is your job as a parent to guide your child and prepare your child for the world. But it is not your responsibility to make the child's choices for them. All too often, parents decide what their child should do or be and do not leave this up to the child to discover for themselves. In the long run, this approach creates a dependent person who is not a freethinking, self-governing individual and commonly a child who does the complete opposite.

Providing careful guidance and detailed instruction is definitely part of your job as a parent. However, when it comes to homework, it is the child's decision and decision-making skills that are being discovered and explored. You must allow the child to explore these decisions and results. Your fear of whether or not your child will be successful or get good grades is not their fear, so do not make it theirs. This is quite difficult for many parents.

You can manipulate children into getting good grades
But is the sacrifice of their heart worth it?

The best thing you can do is allow your child to make choices, even if the choices lead to perceived failure. As long as you are sure that the child understands the situations, options, alternatives and the process, decision-making should be allowed to become theirs. The only time that this should be different is if you know your child has some type of Invisible Challenge™ and needs more detailed direction or professional help.

Homework should never be a battle between you and your child. Fighting with your child over homework is a lose/lose situation. This is not to say let them do whatever they want. After you educate them on how it benefits them it is sometimes beneficial or necessary to put a little "parental pressure" on them.

Your values are not their values

Assuming your child knows the rules and responsibilities regarding homework, try the following tips. Remember, if you baby your child and do not allow opportunities for decision-making and potential failure, they will grow up to be a baby in an adult body who often fails or fails to discover their own happiness.

TEN PARENTING HOMEWORK TIPS

1. Ask the child questions so that you are sure they clearly understand the rules and results of their choices. If they do not, make this information clear and have them re-explain it to you.

2. Once the child understands, inform them that it is their choice to do it or not.

3. Be sure to let the child know that if they are having any problems or difficulties in doing the homework and would like help, you are always available to assist.

4. As a courtesy, remind the child to do their homework if they are still having difficulties.

5. Once the child has made their choice, allow the child to experience the results. This may include poor grades, detentions and in extreme cases, failure.

6. Once you have stated your position and have empowered your child to make their own choices, do not allow for any complaining or whining about grades or experienced results. Simply say, "It's your choice to do your homework or not and you must experience the results." Do not engage in any pity parties or arguing. If you must, walk away from the situation and tell them they know what to do.

7. This one is an absolute must to be successful in this process — keep your issues and feelings out of the conversations! Do not get emotional and do not yell!

8. Find a process or a way to assist you in dealing with your emotions or feelings that come up in regards to doing homework, being successful and getting good grades. In particular look to your past and see where the same feelings and challenges are relevant to your own experiences and traumas.

9. Remind your child that you love them no matter what their grades or choices are.

10. Be sure not to punish the child emotionally, silently or with any subtle remarks made about the child's homework or decisions. And never bring up the past or compare them to other children.

You can lead a child to the books but you cannot make them learn!

THEIR OWN RESULTS

Do not do their homework for them even if they do not complete it. Assist them in understanding their homework but require them to finish it. Many parents do homework or projects for their children, fearing that their child will fail. If they are old enough to choose they are old enough to do it or not. This type of parenting may prevent the child from failing this time but will assure that the child fails later in life because they have not learned the skills or experienced the repercussions of not staying with their work and remaining committed to the end.

If they choose not to do their school work allow them to have the experience of what happens when they make that choice. Then have a conversation with them about the choice and its results. But do not try to influence them to do what you want. Please do not mistake what we are saying here to mean just let your child do whatever they can and allow them to fail without any help. By all means use logic here. If the child is struggling to understand assist them in understanding and do everything possible. If the child is struggling because they just don't feel like it or make excuses that it's too hard then allow the child to experience the results.

Do not judge what happens to your child in the school or grade setting. Love them for who they are and know that you are teaching them a greater lesson. Sometimes a child will make this more difficult because they have become accustomed or addicted to the drama or the caretaking that occurs when there is conflict or difficulty in completing their work. They have realized that some level that this drama gets them attention. It may take quite a while until they actually change, so you must be patient and remain consistent.

Many parents worry; "My child must get into college and what will happen to them if they don't?" Rest assured they will survive and figure it out. Yes, college has become quite a large business and has worked its way into the everyday world creating the belief that everyone must get into college and have good grades in order to succeed in life. This is completely false! There are many billionaires and millionaires that have never gone to college. This is not to say that if your child wants to go to college you would not encourage it but it is to say don't base your child's life or success on college. Remember college is a big business it makes billions of dollars every year and pays many millions of dollars to those who run it. If college was pure in its nature, education would be offered for free.

CAREERS

Are you one of those parents who insist your child goes to college? Have you pushed them toward a particular field that you felt would make the most money or had the greatest opportunities? Understand that this is a form of programming.

Things like these that are done by parents are often well intended but commonly have detrimental effects on the child and their sense of self direction. Of course it's okay to suggest to your child but never to push them towards something. You must allow your child's destiny to unfold. If you have taught them to be self-directed, self-maintaining, self-sustaining and freethinking your child will naturally gravitate to what makes their heart sing.

If you have not taught them the skills then they will struggle to make decisions and with the direction of their life. Children are commonly expected to know what they want to be when they grow up at too young of an age. Quite often a person does not know what they want to do or be until they are in their 20s maybe even 30s. Do not worry if your child seems to be drifting from job to job or career to career; this may be their adventure in life that will lead them to what they ultimately love. At the same time if you have a child that knows the direction they want to go by all means encourage them and provide them with every opportunity to attain that experience.

But, never do it for them. Always allow them to go through the process and perform whatever tasks or communications that are necessary for them to attain it. This allows them to be the creators of their life rather than you creating the situation for them. This is called empowerment. By teaching your child to do the things that are necessary in their life for themselves you empower them for the rest of their lives.

There is so much to understand and explain about programming that this alone would take another book just to explain. So hopefully you have a taste so that you can begin your journey into conscious parenting.

CHAPTER EIGHT
CHILDREN AND FEELINGS

Every experience you have has a feeling to it. Feeling is the experience. Human beings are feeling beings. Feeling defined by our previous definition, not emotions. Without feeling you cannot exist. Your biology is created to experience feeling. It is an antenna for feeling. It is impossible not to feel and when you deny your feeling, you are denying your experience. When you deny your experience, you create resistance.

From a physics perspective all feeling is energy or frequency. Based upon this scientific fact we would like to say that all experiences are energetic in their nature. Therefore all human beings feel energy.

The most beautiful thing in all of creation is to feel. The problem most people have with feeling is accurate interpretation. It isn't actually the feeling that is painful or unpleasant — it is the interpretation or judgment of the feeling. It is your judgment of the experience that makes it pleasant or unpleasant. That judgment stems from a belief system.

In truth, feeling is simply that: just feeling. Feeling is a benign experience that everyone makes their own meaning about based upon their belief systems. To feel is to be alive!

Children often do not have the capability or the skill to deal with, express or understand their feelings. Their primary skills are developed by watching, mimicking and making up a reason why people behave the way they do. Most adults are still in the same boat, and that's why their lives often do not running smoothly. This is why it is imperative that you explain to a child what feelings are, what emotions are, how to cope with them and the appropriate words to use when expressing them.

If you really think about it, there are times when you know why someone does something without ever asking. You have assumed your story about their behavior to be true. This may or may not be accurate. The reason people do this is because at one time they saw someone do or say something, found a common denominator in their circumstances and then decided that this is why people behave in a particular way when certain things happen. Then, for the rest of their lives they've use this as a marker for judging and determining behaviors. This becomes true for the person judging even if it is not true for the person they are judging.

Almost everyone defines or judges events in the present by their experience of events of the past. Simply said, the past determines the present experience. Most people lost the ability to be in the present moment at an early age. This state of being present is referred to as the innocence of a child. Innocence to most people means they are naïve and open to be hurt. The phrase "the innocence of a child" simply means that each experience is like a new discovery. With this perspective on life your speculation about why someone is doing something will be more accurate. You will be more factual and neutral in your interpretation

If you understand the following definition of hurt you will find it is not possible to be hurt by anyone but yourself: hurt is not getting what you want. Teach the child to understand and define their feelings so they can actually cope on their own or change their perceptions to make their life more enjoyable.

WHAT A CHILD NEEDS TO LEARN FROM

THEIR PARENTS ABOUT FEELINGS

- What they are feeling and the words that are used to describe the feeling
- How feelings affect the body
- Why they feel these things — how beliefs create feelings
- How to cope with, interpret and express feelings
- The difference between emotions, sensate feelings and gut/ intuitive feelings
- How to respond to the expressed feelings and actions of others
- How to integrate — but not conform — mentally, emotionally and socially
- That feelings are energy and scientifically provable

Feelings and emotions are often confusing, because when people refer to feelings they generally are thinking about emotions. But feelings are actually a sensate experience. Emotions are a belief system-based response to an event. These are two completely different things, though people tend to use the same words for both.

EMOTIONS

Emotions are an experience your mind and body are having. We give them labels like happiness and sadness so that we can describe and communicate these experiences to ourselves and others. We use them to define our relationships with others, too, "I love her" or "She makes me so angry." For each person, emotions are determined by their belief systems and judgments of an experience. Once someone has an experience their sensate feelings trigger their mental beliefs and judgments that create a response to that experience which is then expressed as an emotion.

People experience emotions physically as well as mentally, but this differs from person to person. The physical feeling occurs after a perception and belief system is triggered thereby creating a chemical reaction within the body. The inward feeling as well as the outward expression is unique from person to person. When some people feel anger it may be like a burning in their heart area. Others experience anger in their solar plexus. Some people feel a pain in their abdomen. Some people cry when they are angry. Some people cry when they are sad. Some people smile when they are talking about something sad. Our inner experience and outer display is expressed in different ways and this can cause communication problems if we don't tell others what label we have put on what we are experiencing. For example, difficulties may occur if I cry when I get mad on someone interprets that I am sad.

WHAT INFLUENCES EMOTIONS

This map shows what influences human emotions. First, there are the labels that we use to communicate the emotions that we are experiencing internally. These are the words that we use to understand what we are experiencing and what others are experiencing. These labels also impact

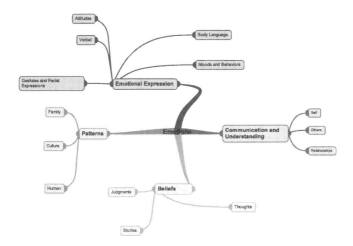

our relationships. This can be especially difficult when two people have two vastly different ways of expressing the same emotion. For example, a woman may cry when she is angry, but the man cries when he is sad. A woman may smile when she disagrees and a man may have no expression when he disagrees.

Humans have many different ways of expressing emotions. This varies by individual, gender, mood and upbringing — the way your family reacted or emoted. There are also cultural expression, verbal and facial expression and body language. Each area is an opportunity for misunderstanding and miscommunication. This is why when you are in a relationship you must educate the other person on how you express as well as understand their form of expression. By doing this you will eliminate many misinterpretations.

Your behavior and belief patterning also adds to this complexity of emotions. Patterns are learned behaviors, ways of thinking or believing where you unconsciously respond in the same way even if that response does not benefit you. You learn these patterns from your family, culture and the collective consciousness of humanity. All of these factors feed into and determine our emotional experiences as well as our judgments and opinions.

Finally, our personal beliefs influence our emotions. These beliefs consist of judgments both positive and negative, our thoughts about events and situations and the stories we make up. For example, "I always cry at weddings." or "When x happens, I experience y emotion." The crying is a programmed emotion. The belief is that crying is what I do in this particular situation. Two simple examples are, "I don't like this so now I am sad." or "I enjoyed the sound of that so now I am happy."

Beliefs are assumed truths based on past experiences. Stories are when you project how you would feel or what you would do in a given situation onto another person, even though you factually do not know that they would feel the same way.

For example, "I would be embarrassed in that situation." So you assume that everyone else would be embarrassed too, even when this is not a fact. Your emotions are about you. Anything that bothers you or distresses you is about you. Assuming everyone, especially your child, experiences emotions like you can guarantee miscommunication and misunderstanding. How you experience something is about you — it is never about the other person.

People have misconceptions about children. They believe that children think and feel like adults, that they give the same meaning to things that adults do, that they see things in the same way as adults. These are all misconceptions. Don't project your feelings and experiences onto the child. Find out instead what the child is experiencing by asking them. Never tell them what they are feeling, always ask. If they are having trouble with the verbiage, educate them on the proper language to use to describe what they are saying.

No emotions are bad. All emotions are equal in the human experience, yet most of us grew up hearing things like, "Nice girls don't get angry." "Men never cry." "Don't be sad." "Be happy." and "Smile!"

In fact, emotions are just an experience and phrases like these invalidate what we are feeling and teach us to act in ways other than the way we feel, rather than allowing us to learn to experience and deal with our feelings uniquely. As an adult, it is important that you also feel what you feel without judgment and express it appropriately. For your children this is an opportunity to watch and learn about emotions and how to appropriately express them.

Emotions are unconscious reactions to beliefs about the way you perceive your world.

HOW EMOTIONS ARE LEARNED

We are taught emotions unconsciously. For example, if you spilled your milk when you were three and your mom yelled at you for being clumsy, you may have responded by thinking, "I am clumsy. I am bad." This is never questioned or discussed. As an adult, you spill something and you feel embarrassed or wrong. You may never think, "It was just an accident." Then you pass these judgments and experiences on to your children in very subtle and unconscious words and behaviors.

WHY CHILDREN ARE DISRESPECTFUL

The answer to this depends on the age group you are talking about. For the purpose of this book, we will address this in general terms.

Children do not know how to deal with their feelings and often do not even know what they are or why they have them. Because of this, children will revert to behaviors observed in the people around them when similar circumstances have occurred. They will also use these behaviors to imitate what they have observed in order to find out what will either get them what they want or allow them to be accepted.

For example, when a child has seen someone in the family — usually mom or dad — drop and break something, then respond with an outburst or by swearing or being silently upset, the child has just learned what to do when they drop and break something.

The child has now unconsciously recorded these behaviors. In the future, when the child drops something and it breaks, they will respond with an outburst or by swearing or being silently upset. Oftentimes it comes out of the blue and you will think, "I don't know where they got that behavior!"

As an adult, you often automatically react to things in ways that you're not even aware of, but your child records everything you do and will eventually use some version of what they experienced. At some random age, your child will draw upon these unconscious memories and react to the situation with the behaviors they have witnessed, often to the surprise of the parents. The child may put their own personal spin on those behaviors; causing the behaviors they are exhibiting to be unrecognizable by the parents.

For example, your two-year-old child does something you dislike and you respond by suppressing your anger and talking through your teeth firmly yet appearing not to yell. You have just silently yelled at your child. For the sake of this example, we will assume that you continue the same behavior for the next several years.

When your child is 10 and you have done something that has displeased them, they yell, "I hate you, Mom!" or "Mom, how can you be so stupid?" The typical parent would be surprised and offended that their child was yelling at them. The parent may think, "I never yell at my child or treat them that way."

However when the child displeased the parent, the parent let them know with feeling but without yelling and the parent assumed that the child did not notice the same communication. All that has happened is that the child has taken the suppressed displeasure and verbalized it. All too often the child is then punished for using the invisible behaviors they were taught. The moral to this story is that you reap what you sow.

In other words, the way you behave and the feelings you convey are intuitively and cognitively understood and felt by your child. These were the examples and frames of reference of how to behave and react in any given situation that you have taught your child and they are simply repeating them.

Children do not invent behaviors. They simply imitate and modify behaviors. Parents need to be aware of their behaviors and feelings. Parents must be conscious that they convey feelings and behaviors even if they are invisible and that someday their children will mirror them back. If you are aware of this, you will know where their behaviors have come from. If you are a self-aware parent, you hopefully will have corrected your inappropriate or unkind behaviors and feelings and you will be able to instruct your child on how to change theirs. Loving care of yourself will make you a loving, caring and most of all wise parent.

SENSATE FEELINGS

Children are hyper sensitive to energy or what we might call a sensate feeling. We are not talking about an emotional feeling. Have you ever felt someone was staring at you, then turned around and saw that is exactly what's occurring? Have you ever sensed that someone was angry or sad without them expressing it? This is a simple way of describing what a sensate feeling is like.

Children need to be taught about sensate feelings and given a clear method of describing and responding to those feelings. To be a well-balanced human being, you have to have very clear communication at all levels.

When children are very young, you will notice that they are surprised by sudden sounds, voices and entrances by people, even if there is no sound. It is not because they are scared, like most people think. It is because they are startled by the energy. They feel the vibration/energy of what is happening and it startles them. They don't know what it is. It is like being electrocuted. If you can imagine that all of the sudden movements, gestures, loud voices and intensities are like electrical vibrations zapping the child, then you can understand why they feel shocked and jump or cry. It is the energy or the vibrations of the person or the things that the person does that may affect the child.

You may see an infant react adversely to an adult who has done nothing or cry when a particular adult holds them. In this case the adult is carrying some vibration or energy that doesn't feel good to the child's sensate system and the only way the child has to express themselves is by crying. Honoring your child and removing them from the adult's arms is to reinforce your child's intuitive nature and build trust. Even if the child is not cognitively understanding what you are doing they intuitively know.

You can experiment with this by trying to put your awareness out and touch them in your mind before you are in their presence. By extending your awareness out to them, they'll feel you before you get there. This will be less startling. By being aware of this, you have a great start to understanding sensory experiences.

UNDERSTANDING SENSATE FEELINGS

Define the difference between an emotional feeling and a sensate feeling for the child. Examples of sensate feelings are when you walk into a room of people and you sense tension or excitement or when you stand close to a wall with your eyes closed and you feel the presence of the wall or when there is a loud noise and you feel it in your body. These are sensate feelings.

When you can't come up with words or definition for a feeling, that's when you have to look at the sensate feelings. Sensate feelings are feelings without emotion that you can feel with your eyes open and/or closed.

ASK YOUR CHILD HOW THEY FEEL

Don't assume you know what a child is feeling. Know that it's not helpful to tell the child what you think they are feeling. Oftentimes we assume something makes them sad but we really don't know until we ask the child. When you do ask, you cannot imply that they are sad nor expect them to be sad because you would be. The moment you say, "Does that make you sad?" you are implying that sad is the correct answer. A child typically wants their parent's acceptance and approval. So they will assume the implied answer is correct and say, "Yes, it makes me sad."

The child will start to label things sad when what they feel has nothing to do with sadness. The child might be 14 and say, "That makes me sad." and the subject will actually be making them angry or breaking their heart. A broken heart or being angry feels different than being sad, so you have to be careful about the way you speak to the child and exactly what you imply. You really have to speak to the child neutrally.

This is a whole skill in itself. In learning to speak to your child neutrally, you learn that anything you interject will turn the child into a preprogrammed responder. Saying things like, "That is bad." "That is wrong." "Don't do that." and "You will get hurt." tells the child what's going to happen. Phrases like "That really bothered you didn't it?" "That looked awful." "That must've been hurtful." or "You must be really happy." all imply the answer and do not allow the child to self-reflect and self-discover. With these cases the child has not found out on their own or decided for themselves and will most likely comply with the implied answer, mainly because you are the authority from their limited perspective of the world.

When asking your child how they feel use the following steps.

- "Please describe to me what happened."
- "How do you feel about it?"
- "What does it mean to you?"
- "What words would you use to describe the feeling?"
- "What feelings do you have in your body and where are they?"

Once you have ascertained this information then attempt to discern what words you would use to describe what they have said to you. After you have decided what words would be appropriate share them with the child and remind them about their beliefs and their choices. Empathize with your child only from the perspective that you have compassion for them going through the experience not because you agree with or are reinforcing the belief system associated with these feelings. Confirm your child's feelings, if you happen to agree, only as a form of validation of their experience.

When they are describing to you what they feel and they don't have a word for it say something like, "When you are feeling what you are describing to me, most people call that anger or frustration."

When it comes to anger and frustration as well is hurt and sadness you are going to have to determine through questions if they are feeling frustration or anger. They look very much the same and everybody lumps them into one category but they are absolutely not the same. If you treat a frustrated person like they are angry, you'll make them angry because that is not what they are feeling. This is why describing the feeling is important. Ask questions until you have an accurate idea of what they are feeling.

The other thing to do, especially with younger children, is actually instruct them as to what those feelings are. You have to listen carefully to what they are saying and say, "Oh, that's frustration. You look angry, but this is frustration and that's anger. See how they are a little bit different?" Describing the nuances between emotions is extremely important. You may be surprised at how they don't know what many words mean that you normally assume they do understand.

At times you may have to ask a child, "Do you understand what that word means?" and if they don't know, stop and explain before you move on talking about subject. All this is required to assist your child in truly understanding and being able to express what they feel. Your time and patience invisibly reflects to your child the love you have for them.

UNDERSTANDING AND COPING WITH EMOTIONS

All emotions are equal whether happy or sad, angry or depressed, apathetic, guilty, shameful or prideful. The only reason that we think of them as good or bad is because people have judged them that way. This is understandable but this does not change the fact that all emotions are just emotions in theory.

You want your child to question. "Why do I have this feeling? What caused this feeling? Why do people have these feelings? What should I do with this feeling? Can you help me understand how this feeling affects my body? My body gets hot when I am angry. It gets cold when I am ashamed. My muscles get tense when I am afraid."

While going through this process what you want is for your child to be able to relax no matter what emotion they might be having. You can do simple techniques like breathing. Guide them through relaxing their muscles. "Okay, now relax the muscles in your arms and in your neck. Keep feeling what you're feeling but relax your muscles. Okay, put your shoulders down." You can even touch them. Put your hand on their shoulders. Say, "Relax your shoulders and feel your body relax but still pay attention to your emotion. See where you're feeling it in your body and relax that area of your body. You are allowed to have that emotion. Now tell me about what you are feeling." If you can get them to relax their body it allows for the emotion to pass through quicker and allows them to observe it rather than get lost in.

Steps for children to understand their emotions

1. First have them feel the emotion and how it feels in their body, then have them identify that feeling through some description, no matter how rough or vague it is. It could be kinesthetic, words, colors, etc. Help them identify the experience that created these emotions and then

proceed to the next step.

2. Give them a word or phrase to describe the emotion so they can relate a word to the kinesthetic feeling within their body. The words describe what we call emotions. Teach them to understand what the words mean and to express the appropriate words associated with the feelings they are experiencing.

3. Then ask, "Do you want that emotion? Here are your options and here's how you can process it appropriately." If you get them to relax their bodies, you will find that the emotions will often begin to dissipate. The tension in their body holds their emotions and recycles the process of the feeling.

4. Now speak to them calmly. The tone of your voice and the feeling within your body should be relaxed. Even if the child is freaking out and you have to fake it, pretend to be relaxed. Remember, children are sensate/intuitive beings and will feel you being tense, which will cause them to remain tense.

Emotions are not to be controlled or eliminated Emotions are to be understood and redirected

Do not expect or try to control the child's emotions. You are not trying to eliminate their emotions. You want them to feel, discover and understand them. When you sense the 'negative' emotions, your job is to teach the child how to work through them — choosing whether or not they want them, giving them the options and letting them process them the way they have decided to process them. You want them to become consciously aware human beings.

This will give them the tools for their future. When they leave home they will have a foundation for life and be able to direct themselves and decide what to do with their emotions. You cannot control their environment when they are not with you. They will encounter all types of emotional patterns in their school and neighborhood. You want to teach them to consciously make choices about how they feel and give them some tools to use when you are not there.

EMOTIONAL AWARENESS TECHNIQUE

This technique facilitates the child's awareness of themselves and their own decision making ability about what they want to do with their emotions. It also teaches them that it is perfectly okay for them to have any emotion they choose. It gives the child permission to be themselves without judgment.

It's okay to feel your feelings. It's not always okay to act out on them. As your child feels things, you teach them what the appropriate responses and behaviors are. You can't just say, "I know how you're feeling but you can't do that." This doesn't give them any understanding. For example, it's perfectly okay to feel angry. It is not socially appropriate to hit a playmate in response to that feeling.

Have children learn the following technique and they will live life more enjoyably. This technique can assist you in teaching the child the tools and options for how to appropriately express themselves.

The six steps of the emotional awareness technique

1. "Tell me what you are feeling."

2. "Do you want to feel this way?"

3. Give them options of what they can feel instead.

4. Explain an appropriate way to express their feelings.

5. Teach potential outcomes of various ways of expressing this emotion.

6. Have child work through the scenario again using the skills and language they just learned or just allow child to process the information.

Step 1. "Tell me what you are feeling."

When you speak to the child, let them know that you just want to understand what is going on or what happened. Explain that you are not upset and that they are not in trouble. Be calm, neutral and responsive. Ask open-ended questions. Guide the child to express what they are feeling.

Keep your own issues aside. Ask questions. Don't assume you know what's going on. Find out all the facts before making a judgment when guiding children.

An example of miscommunication because questions were not asked is: a five-year-old boy was looking up a five-year-old girl's skirt. The boy was punished by the teacher for this act but the child was confused as to why. The teacher failed to realize that she had asked the little girl in front of the class if she had shorts on under her skirt and this question prompted the boy who was standing next to her to look. The boy does need to be taught that this is inappropriate, but the teacher projected her own meaning of the boy's actions and acted according to her meaning. A better approach would have been to ask the boy why he did this and then explain that that was not appropriate.

If the child is very upset, have the child center themselves first. Your goal here is to teach the child to do this themselves so they can do it for themselves when you're not there. You are simply facilitating the acquisition of this skill. Use a relaxation technique such as the ones above or have them close their eyes, breathe and relax their muscles, starting at head and going down.

Ask questions so that you can discover what they are feeling.

Step 2. Ask, "Do you want to feel this way?"

Ask them this question and then accept their answer whether it is yes or no. It's okay for them to have any emotion they choose. Allow the child to feel whatever it is that they are feeling. This fosters self-acceptance and self-confidence.

Step 3. Ask the child, "What could you feel instead?" (This question is used if they choose not to stay in the feeling or emotion they are in.)

First have them give you all the options they can think of. You would like them to give you at least two different options. Then give them multiple choices with at least three options. For very young children, they may need some help with this. After seeing if they come up with anything, you can give the young child options of what to feel instead:

"You could choose to have fun."

"You could choose to go play."

"You could choose_____."

Step 4. Explain appropriate ways to express the emotion.

If the child chooses to feel differently, you could respond with "Okay, go have fun," and the situation would be over. If the child chooses to stay with the emotion, ask the child how they could express it appropriately or differently. Offer examples and language if necessary. "Instead of screaming because Billy took your toy, what else could you do?" Your child could tell Billy that it's not okay to take the toy and ask for it back. If he chooses not to give it back, they could let an adult know the situation and help settle it or choose to play with another toy.

Step 5. Teach potential outcomes

Give potential outcomes based upon age-appropriate situations and understandings.

"If you choose to cry and run away, Tommy may think you don't want to play with him or he may not want to play with you. If you choose to tell him you want to play he may invite you to play again."

"If you choose to hit Tommy, he may hit you back or not want to be your friend.

"If you choose to talk negatively about Susie to your friends Susie may talk negatively about you to your friends, she might hit you when she finds out or she may ask you why you did that."

Step 6. Have the child work through the scenario again using the skills and language you just taught them or just allow them to process the information.

Teach the social courtesies of apologizing and how to ask for what they want or need in a socially appropriate way. Your child should never apologize because they feel bad. You should never encourage a child to feel bad about something they have done or said. Guilt and shame are very damaging weapons to use on a child. Apologies are not delivered because of guilt, but because it is the socially appropriate thing to do. For example, if Emily hit Susie because she wanted her toy, have Emily go back to Susie, apologize as a social courtesy, then ask to play with the toy. Of course you have to make sure that your child understands the purpose of the apology and the inappropriateness of their original action. You can always find out if they understand by having them repeat it back to you.

What to do with your emotions

At some point after the interaction, you need to process the emotions that you put aside while addressing this situation. Never stuff your own emotions and don't judge yourself for having them. Address your emotions by using the same process through self-reflection. The steps are the same, except for you as an adult you add one more question. You can process them internally or by journaling. Practicing this technique on yourself makes it second nature when you're using it with your child.

1. What was the feeling?
2. Do you want to continue to feel that way?

3. What are your options?

4. What is the appropriate expression?

5. What are the possible outcomes?

6. Work through the situation again or process what happened.

7. What beliefs are childhood memories were behind your feelings?

To truly change emotions you must change your beliefs

SENSING ENERGY

It's important for a child to be aware of how it feels in different environments. In environments where there are a lot of people, there will be many different feelings, emotions, thoughts and anxieties. As you sit in the middle of them, it is like sitting in a pool of water with a lot of fish swimming around. You can feel the waves move around under the water even though you cannot see them on the top and after a while, you will start to feel your body move around in the water with the waves.

It is much like this with the emotions, feelings or thoughts of other people. Sometimes their teacher may be sad or the person sitting next to them may be very angry or their sister and brother may feel stressed.

Those feelings are under the surface and no one can see them, but they are constantly occurring. A sensitive person feels these unexplainable things that aren't seen by anyone and it's hard to believe that they actually exist. Yet they are being affected by them. They can affect the sensitive child's behaviors and the decisions they make.

Encourage the child to be aware of the differences between what they feel at school, when they are at home and when they're outside playing. These all will feel quite different. While they are learning how it feels in these different environments, attempt to teach them not to confuse the feeling with the events that are going on and what people are doing. How the environment feels at school or anywhere else is more important than what is actually happening in it. Because when they learn to pay attention to how things feel or how their environment feels, they will begin to understand themselves more easily and not be so confused or distracted by other people's behaviors or what's going on inside other people.

As the child becomes aware and learns to feel and sense their environment as well as themselves, they will be able to deal more easily with the environments of school, crowds and other places without reacting to them or being disturbed by them. They'll know that it is their choice and their behaviors that they need to deal with. They will actually be more self-centered and balanced.

If they do not learn these things or learn to adjust to these different feelings in their environments, they will simply be a ping pong ball bouncing around from one feeling to another, one behavior to another, without any real idea of how to direct their feelings and behaviors to experience life the way they choose.

Most adults are not experienced with being aware of these different feelings and senses either. This can be a learning and exploration for both of you. This will not only be growth for both of you but will strengthen your relationship as well.

SENSATE AND ENERGETIC AWARENESS EXERCISES

Sensate awareness is a process used to ground the child and make them more aware and conscious of their physical body as well as their environment.

Environmental awareness

The purpose of this exercise is to teach the child environmental energetic and spatial sensate awareness.

 Have the child move close to objects with their eyes closed to sense the objects near them. Once the child has sensed the objects, move the child random distances to and from the objects so they can sense the differences. These objects can be walls, posts, shelving, trees, etc.

Body awareness

The idea here is for the child to create a conscious awareness of and connection to their physical body. Most people unconsciously use their body to do things and are seldom aware of how their body feels.

Have a child wiggle their toes, feel their feet and scan their body with their awareness. Have them tell you what it feels like in their body. Have them become aware of random body parts such as hands, legs, feet, knees, stomach, etc. and have them describe to you what they feel like. Encourage them to use adjectives and descriptive sentences that relate to temperature, feeling and sensations. You may also address the five senses at this time.

When finishing this process, always return to the feet. Have them feel and describe the sensations in their feet to keep them connected to the ground and knowing that their whole body is present. You may also introduce textures and materials such as sandpaper, dirt, sand, water, ice, tree bark, etc. to stimulate sensations in their body. Getting a child into nature is also extremely helpful. There are lots of scents, textures, sounds and feelings that also ground the child. Always review and discuss their experiences in order to complete the circuitry in the brain.

Speaking

This develops a sense of how their voice feels and sounds.

Have the child speak while doing the body awareness activity. This means hold a conversation with the child about other things while they are paying attention to body parts randomly. This integrates left and right hemispheres as well as creating new neural netting that will accommodate and make permanent the child's new functional abilities.

Have the child pay attention to their voice volume and the vibration of their voice in their body. Optimally, take a child into a bathroom or small room where the echo is quite substantial. Have them talk with their eyes closed and tell them to feel and experience the sound of their voice echoing off the walls. Then have them talk at a normal volume that would be socially appropriate and have them feel and sense that sound bouncing off the walls.

Then you do the same. Speak very loudly in the confined area, feeling the vibrations bounce while they listen. Then change the volume of your voice to a normal speaking level and have them feel and experience that. Then once again have them speak at varying volumes and then take them to a socially acceptable volume and have them feel the vibrations in their body and associate the feeling of the volume in their body with the sound in the room. This allows the child to kinesthetically feel and hear their own voice simultaneously. Next if you can place a set of headphones over their ears to reduce or eliminate the auditory functions and have them speak at different volumes and intensity asking them to be aware of how the sound feels in their body.

Sensing others

Ask your child to close their eyes. Hold your hands close to their head then have them sense the heat of your hands and the feeling of your hands close to their skin. Randomly move your hands further and closer to all areas of their head, including the top of their head, side of their head, back of their head and facial areas. All this is done without touching them. Ask them to guess how far your hands are from them.

You may also have the child walk closely to a wall while blindfolded. Guide them carefully so they don't hurt themselves and tell them to let you know what they are feeling or when they are feeling it and give you a description of what they are feeling. You can use different sized walls or objects so they have a sense of different feelings. This allows them to use their body's sensate system.

PARENTS AND HOW THEY FEEL

AROUND THEIR CHILDREN

Parents need to be aware of how they feel internally around and emotionally about their child. Children are quite sensitive and pick up on feelings they aren't even consciously aware of. It's your job to help them sort what's yours and what's theirs so they can discern this when they are with other people or in other environments.

You can't stop all the stuff you are going through, but you can learn how to tell them, "Yes, this is mine and this is what I'm feeling. This is not about you."

If you're feeling something, don't deny it and say that you're not. If they say you're feeling something don't deny it. If you are unaware of it, tell them you're not aware of it at this moment. Their sensitivity may be picking up something you're ignoring, avoiding or aren't conscious of.

If they're accurate say, "You're right, I am feeling ___ today. You don't have to do anything about it. I am having an off day. It has nothing to do with you." Make sure they know this and confirm their feelings. This validates their sensitivity and creates a trust in their own intuitive nature.

THE ENERGY AND INFLUENCE OF OTHER

PEOPLE AND THEIR THOUGHTS

All children must be taught to discern between their thoughts and feelings and the thoughts and feelings of others. They must learn how to check on their own thoughts and discern the difference between what they are thinking and feeling and what seems to just pop into their head.

The thoughts and feelings of others energetically/intuitively influence everyone. The child must be taught to understand this. They should be given exercises to discern the difference between their own thoughts and feelings and those of others. Otherwise the child will tend to believe and respond to things that are not actually theirs.

Sensitive children and adults are affected by thoughts and feelings of others and often assume those thoughts and feelings are theirs. They then respond to those thoughts and feelings, which can unnecessarily complicate their own lives.

The sensitivity and lack of conscious awareness of what is theirs and what is not can and will create a dependency on the outside world for their own identity and they will not have the ability to discern what their own experiences truly are. Because they never learn to differentiate their own thoughts of who they really are or what their own inner experiences are, they tend to assume they are their environment. This becomes an unconscious assumed identity — whatever energies, thoughts or feelings are in their environment are who they are and that those experiences are actually theirs. They never know who they really are inside and always depend on other people or external circumstances for validation and identification.

Because of this confusion when sensitive people have a feeling or inkling of wanting to be themselves there will be conflict within them and/or with others, their environment or circumstances. Because they do not have this discernment skill and really do not know who they are, as well as don't have the appropriate skills to handle the situation, they will either fight or withdraw from the outside world in an attempt to find their own identity.

This is an attempt to gain their own emotional and mental freedom so that they can establish their own identity. From this limited perspective, conflict and resistance are the only way to establish their freedom or own individual identity and in most cases has probably been all that has been modeled for them. They must be taught that their own identity or freedom comes from within them, not by following or resisting others or the world.

The child must be given exercises and taught skills to be able to identify and feel the difference between their thoughts and feelings and those of others or their environment in order for them to establish a real sense of identity. Otherwise they are merely puppets, responders, parrots or pawns to the energetic, emotional and mental circumstances of their environment.

This will leave the child feeling powerless, useless, not good enough, helpless, etc. because they can never meet the expectations of other people's thoughts or feelings, no matter how hard they try. Without the skills to discern these things, they will be constantly trying to meet the unspoken emotional and mental expectations of others or society. At best, if they give up seeking their own identity, they will be able to mimic the behaviors that other people expect them to have. In the meantime they must surrender their own inner self to the outside world and its expectations, which will always leave them feeling empty and dissatisfied.

A child must be taught to focus on who they are inside. The time must be taken to allow them to experience and discern what they are feeling and what they desire. This is done by teaching them not to focus on everything they have heard, been told or thought they were supposed to be. You must teach them to focus on what they feel and then integrate that into appropriate human social skills so that they may accomplish what they really want through socially acceptable means and/or sometimes by going outside of that box.

CHAPTER NINE

FREEDOM AND RESPONSIBILITY

The New Discipline

FREEDOM AND RESPONSIBILITY

Freedom for the child is when they can self-reflect without feeling bad about themselves and without the fear of disapproval, rejection, punishment or not being loved. Now of course not every child is ready for this type of freedom. If this is taught from birth it will be easy for them. But if introduced after patterns and beliefs are created then it will take some preparation for them to handle it maturely.

Responsibility can only come with freedom. Freedom is about self-direction, independence, choices, free will and lack of restrictions. Freedom for a child is about making mistakes and then feeling safe enough and confident enough to reflect on those mistakes and decide whether to repeat those mistakes or not.

Responsible: *being conscious of being the primary cause of something and to accept accountability for being the primary cause without judgment whether that something is perceived positive or negative*

Freedom: *the power or right to act, speak, or think as one wants without hindrance or restraint*

The ideal situation for a child is to experience freedom at home. Home should be a safe environment where a child can be free to make choices and at the same time be responsible for consequences that may occur.

A framework should be provided for the child to live in and this will be the structure that they will know and can then modify to fit their needs in different stages of life. A parent will direct and guide when necessary in order to maintain the framework as a steppingstone to each child's unique life experience.

In the past, "discipline" has been a term used in regards to raising your children. Discipline is defined as the practice of training people to obey rules or a code of behavior, using punishment to correct disobedience. Our definition is as follows:

Discipline: *a system of rules governing conduct or activity, field of study, branch of knowledge or specialty, orderly or prescribed conduct or pattern of behavior*

Today's children are quite different in the fact that they do not respond well to discipline, at least by the old definition relating to punishment. Hopefully today's adults are of a different mindset than in the old days, because if you treat your children in this fashion you can typically expect one of two things.

1. They will become good little robots, giving up their creativity and following your orders. If they go this route, they are absolutely set up to fail. They become sheep instead of creators and, as the old phrase goes, the sheep will be led to the slaughter.

2. You can anticipate that they will become rebellious, oppositional, and will distance themselves in order to find their own freedom so that they may create their own life without limitations or restrictions. Whatever you decide to do as a parent will determine

the qualities of and influence the next generation.

It is up to you to decide what you would like to experience. Ask yourself, "Which child would I like to have:

- The passive little robot and well behaved sheep?
- The rebellious oppositional child?
- The freethinking, creative individual?"

If you raise your child with choices, freedom and responsibility, you give the child the opportunity to be a freethinking, creative individual without the need to rebel and fight you. You also give them the ability to be self-directed in life.

The new definition of discipline is setting boundaries to educate and establish skill sets to prepare your child for life, then reinforcing those boundaries to establish a conscious skill set for your child to choose from and use as an adult.

These boundaries and skill sets must be logical, reasonable, rational and functional. They provide your child with adult skills to create a life experience for themselves that is relative to the culture of their time. This means that the parents must be progressive and see current trends in order to educate their child with these new skill sets. The reinforcement and education of these boundaries and skill sets is done logically, reasonably and rationally. An in-depth explanation of why you are reinforcing these and how they serve the child is required. Repeating the explanations of how and why you are doing what you are doing constantly reinforces the idea until the child exhibits an understanding and displays behaviors that match the understandings.

As a parent you must be open-minded and accepting of change.

Answer the following questions:

- Do you love your child enough to allow them to be who they are and who they have come to this earth to be?
- Do you love yourself enough to become the most loving and conscious parent/person possible?
- Do you want to control your child or love and direct your child?
- Do you desire to have the best human experience possible?
- Are you willing to do whatever it takes to create the life you want?

Your answers to these questions will determine the type of child and experience you have as a parent. The choice is simple: loving direction or control and out dated discipline. We suggest that you raise your children from the consciousness of freedom and responsibility.

Most parents want their children to be responsible. Personal responsibility can only come with the freedom to make decisions and accept the outcomes of your decisions.

The old mentality defines responsibility as such: *having an obligation to do something; caring for someone as a part of one's job or role, doing things under pressure from an authority*

In this definition, freedom is not possible. To be responsible in this fashion creates obligation in the sense that one is being controlled. There is often a sense of burden and limitation. Try to remember a time when you were told as a child that you were responsible for something. Was it ever used with the sense of freedom, openness and the ability to choose?

Typically not!

Responsibility was used as a way to control you; to get you to conform or do as you were told. There was rarely a choice involved that resulted in anything other than a negative outcome.

Let's redefine responsibility and freedom for today's parenting and for your own personal experience.

Responsible - *being 'response able', having the ability to respond in an appropriate and functional manner, accepting the results of your response*

Freedom - *being free from limitations, having the ability to exercise your free will, accepting the outcome of your choices; being a self-directed, freethinking, self-mentoring, self-reflecting, self-sustaining, self-monitoring human being.*

Remember that your job as a parent is to prepare your child for their future and to give them the skills to become a functional human being. Your child is not a possession or something that you own. Your child is your gift of love to the world, and by preparing them for an enjoyable life and giving them the skills they'll need, you show how much you love. Keep in mind that your child still has the option to use what you have taught them or not. You are simply giving them the tools — it is up to them to use them or not.

Your child is a separate human being with their own free will and direction in life. If you treat your child as though they are a possession, make the child follow rules and the only choice you provide is between following rules (reward) and not following rules (punishment), that's not freedom. You create victims. You create people who feel trapped and limited and definitely not creative. Often you create people who feel hopeless. Under these conditions no matter what choice the child then makes, they are either a victim of their choices or a victim of those who make the rules. If you create this mentality of following rules at all costs with your children, you have created human beings that cannot think for themselves and who must have others tell them what to do because they have not learned critical thinking and self-direction.

To send a child that has been taught this out into the world on their own is to abandon the child in a world of tigers. If you see that your child is struggling or barely surviving, it may be because they never had the opportunity to survive on their own in a safe place with freedom. The only thing they know is to go from this rule to that rule and try to decide which rule is less painful.

Typically people who parent their children with rules which must be followed, whether they make sense or not, are parents who want their children to do what they want them to do because they either have no patience or tolerance as a parent or because they themselves are victims. These parents do not see their child as an individual with their own important opinions.

These parents are often so self-involved in their own issues that they cannot see the beautiful soul of the child. This is a reflection of when the parent lost touch with their own beautiful soul and surrendered to the will of others and the ways of the world. So if this happens to be you or even your parents have great compassion; for the disconnection from your own beautiful soul is a very painful experience. Keep in mind though this connection can be regained. Nurture your child's soul and spirit so that they can live and lead the full life many people on the planet do not have the opportunity to experience.

Conversely there are parents who give little or no rules to their children. This is equally difficult for the child. Sometimes parents think by doing this they are flexible and fun-loving parents. In actuality they are neglectful in their parenting. Often times this type of parent is afraid to 'put their foot down.' This is commonly because it either happened to them or they are afraid of being disliked by their child. If you are afraid of being disliked by your child it may be a sign that you are too attached and dependent on them loving you and to give you some self-worth and value. This type of dependency begets dependency from your child.

With this type of parenting the child suffers because they don't know how to appropriately interact with the world, or be self-directed and it creates a very fearful person. This fear may be internal or expressed. This is one reason many children stay at home into their late 20s or even their 30s. The child has so much fear about going into the world and being responsible on their own that they are in a sense, frozen.

Just because the child is in a bigger body and is intelligent it doesn't mean they have the proper skills. Often when the child is in a young adult body and is intelligent it is assumed that they are emotionally ready to go out into the world. This in fact may not be true. They may have never developed the emotional intelligence or confidence to be able to do so.

If you didn't teach them or give them the appropriate skills or experiences in their early years — if they never made enough choices and experienced consequences or found solutions on their own — they won't have the skills or the emotional confidence to be independent. This lack of emotional confidence may be hidden under their intellect and rational justification; so don't be deceived by this use of intelligence.

Teach your children to question rules not oppose them. If the rules are not logical, reasonable, and rational then those rules do not need to be followed. This includes your parenting rules. If and when your child questions your rules you must be able to explain them. You must recognize that if you cannot explain them clearly and they don't make sense then your rules are either invalid or obsolete. By teaching your child to ask questions, you give them the skill of discernment and encourage wonderment. It's important to remember that you are not only teaching them the skills — you are modeling them. Your child watches and feels everything you do. All of your decisions, responses, communications, explanations, reactions, emotions, fears, hesitations, loving or unloving actions and more are recorded in their psyche to be used and referred to in their own personal life.

Freedom to question rules without repercussion creates an independent freethinking child

If you do not teach a child freedom, they will always be dependent in some way on others and they will fear freedom. The fear of freedom is the fear of being independent and the fear of knowing your own inner self. A child who is free within their own being has greater wisdom and discernment when participating or socializing with others and more often makes healthy choices.

Children can learn skills if they are given the opportunity. You must give them every opportunity you can. When you teach them freedom — the ability to make choices and experience the results — the child will have learned the skills and it will then be up to them to use them. Part of the learning of these skills is learning when and how to use the skills they have developed.

Your child unconsciously assimilates every message you send whether you are conscious of those messages or not. Children are like sponges and they absorb everything they see, feel and experience. All of these experiences then go into the subconscious as part of their behavioral patterning and belief system. These messages, verbal and nonverbal alike, are received every day.

Non-verbal or hidden messages are probably the most important and potentially the most lethal. The message you send consciously, unconsciously, verbally and nonverbally will come across loud and clear regardless of how it appears. If your child feels you saying one thing and feeling something different they will sense the dishonesty.

Basically, what we are saying is that you must be a conscious parent. Being aware of your inner motives and your outer expression allows you to communicate honestly with your child. Your child will feel that integrity and an unexplainable trust will be developed. Keep in mind that most of the things your child feels and interprets about you happen intuitively.

Children must be free to be responsible.
In that freedom they will know your love.

Let's go back over a few things. First, freedom and responsibility; you cannot be responsible without freedom. A truly free person is spiritually, emotionally, mentally, physically, and socially free. Anything else is enslavement of some sort. This limits a person's ability to be responsible. When a person is not truly free, there is a structure for them to be dependent and for an authority to take care of things. This can be seen in society as well is in parenting.

When this lack of freedom is in your parenting style, there is a tendency for the child to be lazy and wait for someone to take care of them. When a parent takes the attitude that they need to make their child do things, it's still a form of taking care of them. It's not suggested that you let your child do anything they want, but this is a reference to another form of dependence.

Please be patient we will get to new concepts and ideas shortly. We are attempting to cover many of the common attitudes and challenges of parenting first.

When you tell your child what they should or shouldn't do on a regular basis, you're not allowing for freedom of choice or independence. No one can become responsible if they are told what to do and how to do it. There is a difference between authority and facilitation. You are not an authority. You are the loving guide facilitating their human skills and self-discovery. As a facilitator you instruct and model for them, then you allow them to explore and discover. Instruction is required until the child has learned the skill or at least understands how they work and how to apply the skills in society.

It is expected culturally that governments, schools, books, religions, and professionals tell people the "shoulds" and "shouldn'ts" while providing the illusion that the people are free. The fact is people are not free — they are governed. Being governed does not equal freedom. It can only give the appearance of freedom. People are expected to be "responsible", but it is not true responsibility or freedom. It is compliance based on rules created by someone in perceived authority. This compliance is usually due to the fear of punishment in some form rather than conscious choice.

Love yourself enough to be your own authority
Love your child enough to teach them to be their own authority

Commonly children are taught at an early age that governments, school systems, religions and the professionals are the authorities. This needs to be changed. Children should be taught that people in these positions are simply people like them in those positions. People in those positions are no better or more intelligent than the child. The child should be taught to discern if people in perceived authority positions are accurate, factual or are operating from their heart.

This directly relates to parenting and parenting styles. In this type of parenting, the thinking is that children will comply with the standards set by those in charge. Usually if one is responsible in this way, then they are perceived as responsible people. This is not responsibility and in this there is no freedom. This is simply following the rules and being good sheep. Don't teach your children to be sheep. Instead, teach your children to be shepherds of their own life who cooperate with others for the greater good of the whole. Teach them that the greater good of the whole does not mean sacrificing themselves but instead means cooperative experiences leading to mutual satisfaction.

Love yourself enough to see the facts and the truth
Love your child enough to teach them the facts and
the truth

REWARDS AND PUNISHMENT

Positive and negative reinforcement are two of the most common methods used in parenting. Let's look at them and relate them to belief systems and patterned behaviors that they create and that drive them.

Positive and negative reinforcements are attitudes. These attitudes are usually ways that parents or authority figures attempt to get the children to conform. Neither is an optimal parenting technique. Positive reinforcement in its typical model is giving the child a reward for something they have done. Negative reinforcement is punishment, or taking something away because the child has not conformed. If you examine both of these models closely, you will find that the intention of both is to manipulate a child into doing what is desired by those in charge. This manipulation may be either well or ill intended. Typically it is done by those in authority for their own agendas. It may be as simple as the parent is trying to get the child to do something because it benefits the parent or the parent perceives that it benefits the child.

Positive reinforcement = bribery

Negative reinforcement = punishment

In the long run, both of these methods teach the children to manipulate others in order to get what they want. Children also learn that they must sacrifice or give up some aspect of themselves in order to please others; so they do not have to suffer or so that they may feel good. Both of these methods have long-term adverse effects. They potentially teach the child to:

- Manipulate others in order to get what they want.
- Do what others want no matter what they feel in their heart.
- Conform to others in order to avoid a perceived negative experience.
- Conform to others to receive false and temporary acceptance
- Depend on other people's reactions to determine if the experience is right for them
- Look to others for self-worth and value based upon positive or negative responses
- Disconnect from their own beautiful soul
- Become a slave to those in authority

In the long run, you have taught the child to give up their own inner guidance and self-direction and depend upon the actions and reactions of others to determine their direction in life. The child then loses the willingness or the ability to create their own life and is subject to the will of others. In very simple terms, you have taught your child to become a sheep and follow the will of others at the sacrifice of their own heart. This isn't the original intent of any parent, but it is the long term effect these methods have on a child's psyche.

Rather than rewards and punishments, it is choice, freedom and responsibility that produce healthy, freethinking, self-directed individuals. By giving the child choices and teaching them that they are responsible for their own experiences and not responsible for the actions, responses or behaviors of others, you free your child and allow them to become whoever they will become. There is no greater love than this.

You are not responsible for how or what other people feel
You are responsible for what you do, say and intend

By coming from the perspective of choice and responsibility, you are teaching the child that they govern their own life and that they must become functional in the world in which they live. If they choose otherwise it is their own creation. They are the owners of their own creations and responsible for them.

Choice is absolute freedom

Parents should understand this for themselves as well. Your thoughts, beliefs, attitudes and behaviors create the life you experience. By you understanding this and making this your way of life, you will have children that will far exceed any expectations you ever had. By empowering your child with the status of sovereign creator, as opposed to sheep or follower, you have assisted in the creation of a magnificent human being that will far surpass the human beings of past times.

Choice and responsibility are an attitude and perspective. When you come from the perspective of choice and responsibility you see the world through the eyes of a creator. When you see through the eyes of a creator, your children will learn, model and intuitively absorb these attitudes. What you say to your child may sound the same as it always did, but the words will come from a different attitude and perspective.

A sovereign creator lovingly interacts with all of life

Examples of choice:

1. Your child is spending too much time playing video games and is not getting their homework done or is often emotionally miserable after they finish playing. You know these video games are not optimal for your child's growth, mood or behaviors. In this example, you may make the same statement as you would in positive or negative reinforcement but with a completely different attitude and intention.

"Suzy, you may only play video games for 15 minutes because you usually do not complete any of your other tasks and you're often grumpy if you play longer than that."

This is a parental directive. At times, you must be the director of the situation because you are the parent, the child's guide and have full authority to make decisions that you know in your heart are in your child's best interest. In this case, you are not making the statement to punish the child. You are simply telling the child that they are responsible for their behaviors and for completing their tasks; and because you have seen and are acknowledging that they have not followed through in the past. By doing this you are assisting them in learning self-direction and self-reflection skills. As the parent and guide it is your duty to make parent directives where necessary with loving firmness so as to prepare your child for life.

2. Your child is watching TV instead of doing their assigned chores or homework.

"Brendon, you are allowed to watch TV, but I did tell you that you were to complete your tasks before watching TV. You now have a choice: If you continue to watch TV and do not complete your task now, you will not be able to watch TV for three days. Or you can do your tasks now and be able to watch TV as always. The choice is yours and you are responsible for the results of your choices. I have explained to you what your options are and the results will be based upon which choice you make. Feel free to decide which one you would like to experience."

You don't want to bribe your child with money, candy, food, toys, TV or games. Bribery is not a motivation; and offering a reward to finish or complete something that they must complete anyway does not teach them to be self-sufficient or to do what needs to be done. This type of parenting teaches the child how to be manipulated and how to manipulate others for a temporary outcome. In the long term, this creates great hardship for the child throughout life. They will use these same skills to manipulate their spouses, partners, bosses, employees and others.

RESULTS NOT PUNISHMENT

The words "punishment" and "discipline" often have negative connotations. The word "results" simply suggests the outcome of an action. So along with choices and responsibility, begin to educate your child about results or cause and effect. These are very simply defined and easily understood. Results are what occur based upon the choices you make. Cause and effect is about how your choices affect your experiences — when you do something, something happens. If you can explain this to the child, it makes it easier for them to make choices now and when they are older. You may also explain how making choices and cause-and-effect affect and empower them.

An easily understood example that you can explain is: If you place your hand in a door and you close the door on your hand, your hand will hurt. The pressure of the door closing on your hand causes the pain that you feel. If you choose to do this, it is okay because it is you creating your experience and you are free to choose the experiences you wish to have. In life you have options. The options that you choose have results. There is no good or bad. There is simply choice and result. You are free to make any choice that you wish. It is however wise to know the potential results before you make your choice.

By using these methods — choice, responsibility, and cause and effect — you ultimately teach your child to become a creator of their own life experience. They are not dependent on other people's behaviors, judgments or reactions and they are free to choose and experiment. Even choices that you may not agree with and experiments that you may find unpleasant to watch can be great lessons that teach wonderful skills to your child about the world and how to live more fruitfully in it.

RESULTS VERSUS PUNISHMENT — THE SUBTLETIES

You need to be emotionally detached, and your results-oriented experience needs to be based on logical, reasonable and rational facts and potentials that are relative to their experience in life. Keep your agendas and subtle manipulations out of the results. Be factually based not emotionally based in presenting results or potentials. This is very difficult for many parents because they want their child to succeed or avoid pain. Failure and perceived pain often teach the greatest lessons and bring about the greatest changes.

Factual probabilities and results: It is just simply logical, reasonable and rational that if you drive on the wrong side of the road the possibility to crash, hurt or kill someone else or yourself is greater. That is a factual probability and/or result of your choice not because it's good or bad, not because you are emotionally attached when explaining it, but simply because it's a logical result.

Do your best not to be emotionally attached or to project your ideas of right or wrong, good or bad on the results of the child's choices. Allow them to have the experience and decide for themselves. If you're emotionally charged while enforcing the results you should be aware that it's your issue as the parent not the child causing you to have a feeling. You should then seek to discover what is driving you or that feeling. Avoid focusing or directing your emotions or your energy on the child because they will feel that and they are not the source of your feelings. They are simply the trigger that has set off something inside of you. And in your role as their model you must now self-reflect and address them appropriately.

When you are emotionally charged while enforcing results, it's no longer a benign, neutral system of choice and result. It's now superimposed with an emotion that also implies, "You have to do what I say in order to be liked, loved or appreciated and if you don't, this is your punishment."

The punishment, which comes from an emotional place, is contradictory to the choice process. "The punishment is that you will be battered emotionally by my verbal tone or inferences." You have now created a conflict, an inconsistency and have lost integrity. You have modeled 'do as I say not as I do.'

Allow the child to make their own choices. Allow the child to have their results without your emotions, verbal or emotional badgering. This allows them to learn, discover and develop their own way in life and find out what works and what doesn't without being told or forced into something because of your needs or desires. This is true choice — anything less is a sham and the child feels it and knows it. This also builds trust and models loving acceptance.

It is very easy to mix your good intentions with your old patterns and be blinded to what is actually happening. Because in your mind you are thinking, "I am doing the right thing." and yet emotionally you are accessing unconscious old patterning and belief systems that drive you to behave in the conflicting fashion. Be patient with yourself, this will take time to find the balance and make the changes in your parenting style. Keep in mind that it is your belief system and patterned behaviors that will be your biggest challenges. Changing the way you think, believe and behave is the key to being the optimal parent.

EMOTIONAL PUNISHMENT - THE INVISIBLE PUNISHMENT

Almost everyone people has been emotionally punished or disciplined at some time by their parents or other people.

This one is tricky because this punishment is not visible. It is an attitude, a sound, a feeling, a look, a gesture, a lack of response, being less kind or loving, an emotional disconnection, an invisible wall, a harsher or more firm touch among other things. You probably have seen it or felt it as a child or even done it as an adult.

Whatever you do, never do this to your children!

In most cases the person doing it can either justify it as a misunderstanding or misinterpretation. They may say "I did not do that. You imagined that." It is easy to blow it off because there is no visible proof anything occurred. Therefore it can be dismissed. But, everyone knows what really occurred. Everyone felt what happened. But now it is a secret world of communication that can be denied or used like a secret weapon!

Secrets like these destroy relationships at the root and never are a wise choice. This type of behavior usually stems from some internal belief system about being hurt, disappointed or abandoned. The behavior that results from using this technique is spiteful and based in fear. It does nothing except to separate and divide a relationship. For the child it makes a statement about their worth and value, whether they are lovable or not and most of all begins to destroy their trust in you. At this point the child must decide survival or sacrifice. "Do I sacrifice my own heart for my parents approval?" becomes the question within.

Fortunately or unfortunately the child is always seeking the parents love even if the parent is unkind. This puts the child in a very precarious position. This position leaves them open to constantly having to please the parent, sacrifice themselves or separate emotionally from the situation and people involved. In the long term it creates a situation where it is difficult or impossible for the child as an adult to have an intimate loving relationship.

Honesty and truthfulness are acts of love both towards yourself and others.

If you are hurt and disappointed by your child, know that it is not your child that is disappointing you. It is your memories of when you were disappointed as a child or where you may have disappointed others by doing something similar. Never emotionally distance yourself or punish your child by these subtle gestures and unseen communications.

If you were hurt or disappointed at least be honest and truthful. Express to them what you felt and why you responded the way you did. Then most importantly tell them that it was not their fault and it was something from your past that got triggered and caused you to respond that way. You must let them know that they are not responsible for your feelings as a model that you are not responsible for their feelings. This creates the opportunity for everyone to become emotionally sovereign. You might want to list or review all the way and areas of your life that you use this 'secret weapon.' Awareness is the first step to the elimination of this in your life. Please don't judge yourself for it. Most people do this unconsciously because it was a family pattern. Love yourself and your child enough to say, "It stops here and now!"

CHAPTER TEN
CHOICE PARENTING

Many people did not feel or believe they had many choices when they were children. Because of this many people feel that their children do not have choices or the ability to make them. Sometimes you might even hear a parent say, "Because I'm the parent, that's why!" This is the ultimate power trip and conveys to the child that they do not have choices.

Choice parenting is a lifestyle not a process. It is a way of being. If you choose choice parenting as your preferred style then you cannot drag all of your old parenting styles along with it. To do so will create conflict and confusion for both you and your child. It will cause you to be wishy-washy and inconsistent.

It is common for it to take some time until you have adjusted to the new parenting style as a way of being. So you can expect that at times you will fall back into your old style and the type of parenting you were raised in. This new way will just take some practice and adjustments. You will typically find that when you fall back into your old style or the way you were raised it is because you have issues, patterns and belief systems attached. What you should know is that every time you fall back in to your old way of parenting it is because there is some memory of an unfulfilled emotional need and or habitual behavior that has occurred unconsciously. Being conscious and aware as much as possible will minimize the amount of times you fall backwards into the old style. Consciousness cures everything.

CHILDREN AND CHOICE

Choice parenting is based upon your genuine inner intent. Your intent must be, to allow the child to make choices and accept the results of their choices in all situations. Present to them the options that they have to choose from without leading them to one choice or another. Always project three to five choices or possible outcomes for them to select from. To give them only two choices is to in fact very subtly direct them. This is not going to allow them to develop healthy discernment and critical thinking skills. With only one or two choices they will know one is good and one is bad. With multiple choices and knowing potential outcomes the child can decide for themselves what each choice means and how they want to experience their life. This creates self-directed critical thinking as well as reasonable, rational and logical thinking skills. Your child will be able to make decisions based upon facts, not emotions and from their heart.

Choice: *an act of selecting or making a decision when faced with two or more possibilities*

Of course in the beginning you have to teach your child about choices: what they mean, what they are, and the possibilities surrounding them. Go into detail. The greater detail you give them the more prepared they are and the easier for you it will be. Too many parents don't like to give too much detail or aren't very good at explanations. This is your opportunity to change all that. This opportunity will also help you in other areas of your life, so you get to benefit from this new experience too.

You have to explain what choices are and what happens when you make the choices. "Here are the options: if you stick your hand in the door and slam it shut, it hurts. If you take your hand out of the door before it closes, it doesn't hurt." That's the way you explain all of their choices until they start to get it. "You want watch TV? Sometimes when you watch TV, you watch violent shows and you get really nasty or difficult afterward. So you can choose to watch TV and be aware of your emotions and be able to continue watching them or as a result of that nasty or difficult behavior you won't be allowed to watch those types of shows or TV at all for a while." This explanation is results and choice based. As opposed to: "every time you watch those kinds of shows you get miserable so now you aren't going to be able to watch TV." This explanation is a command based in emotions and authority.

Practice, practice, practice, change of any sort takes practice and application. Almost everything that is new is awkward. If you're patient and consistent you will find that the changes will begin to naturally occur. Depending on how old your children are and how consistently you apply these changes may not show up for anywhere from three months to a year.

We have found in our experience that parents with older children (10+) may not see noticeable change for anywhere from one to two years. But when they do occur things change quickly. So know that this is a long-term process and don't give up before you see the results even though sometimes it can be frustrating and almost disappointing when you have expectations of change.

5 STEPS OF CHOICE

1. Identify what's going on.

2. How do you feel inside?

3. What choices do you have?

4. What are the possible results of those choices?

5. What is the best way to carry out the choices you have made?

You must outline basic house rules and guidelines along with choices and results prior to the choice process. These house rules must remain the same and only be adjusted for age appropriateness. These house rules and guidelines will include and are not limited to:

- household duties
- appropriate communication
- appropriate treatment of others
- appropriate care of family and individual property
- personal boundaries
- social conduct outside of the home

Evaluate each step before moving onto the next. Find the words and feelings that clearly describe what choices must be made to reach the potential results of each choice. Finally, choose the most appropriate way to carry out and express the choices that have been made.

Example:

1. Identify what's going on - Johnny doesn't want to do his homework.

2. How does Johnny feel inside – 'I feel angry and I would rather go

play."

3. "Well, there are three different choices that I can see - You can do your homework and go outside and play, you can not do your homework at all, or you can go out and play and do your homework afterwards.'

4. "If you do your homework now - then you can play the rest of the night. If you don't do your homework - then you will probably get a failing grade at school. If you go out and play right now - then you might have to do homework and not watch TV.'

5. What would you like to do based upon those options?"

Use this process for each situation and do not be attached to the outcomes or results. The results are up to your child to deal with not you. Yes, sometimes parents say I have to deal with my child's emotions about their choices. Well, now you don't. If you teach your child the same choice process with their emotions they get to choose what they want to experience. For example:

"Well Susie, you made the decision that created the results and now you must deal with own your emotions. They are not mine and you can't take them out on me. I have already taught you how to handle your emotions so you may choose to go up to your room and do what you need to do, you may choose to stop talking to me like that right now or if you stay here and yell at me you will then choose to lose a privilege. You may choose whichever you prefer."

In this example it is assumed that some of the basics have already been outlined. You must also remain pure in your intent. In this model your intent is to completely allow them to make choices not manipulate them into making the choice you prefer. Remaining unemotional or without a charge is a sign that you are pure in your intent.

You have to take the time to explain the results of choices so that the child gets it. Every child needs a different form of explanation so tailor your explanations toward each child's specific needs. It's going to take you a few years to train the child (and maybe you, too!) in this style of understanding. The child is not good or bad in their choices, their choices simply have results. Also teach the child that they can make out-of-the-box choices that nobody ever thought of that may have either have really cool results or might not work. It doesn't matter how it turns out — that's the fun of discovering how to communicate more clearly, understanding your child and making your life run more smoothly. Your own outlook and perceptions are also a choice. How you perceive parenting is all about you.

When you limit your perceptions you limit both you and your child.

Too many people see limited choices and results because they themselves are limited. It just happens to be all that they are consciously aware of at any given moment. Just because you have limited perceptions with which you limit your choices it is no reason to judge yourself. Everybody does this in their own unique way.

But what if there were other possibilities? What possibilities haven't you thought of? What if I choose this? I never thought of that! This type of thinking could be extremely freeing for yourself and your child. Tell your child, "Hey, if I don't have the answer to that, and if you don't like these choices, you give me another choice and explain the potential results. I'm listening."

Don't let your parental fears encumber your child's discoveries. When you have fears about your child's experiences, understand that this is your issue and in order to be a healthy parent you must resolve your issues in regards to your fears. Your child's discoveries must not be influenced by your fears or judgments. Of course, we are not referring to physical safety. Physical safety is of course a primary objective in regards to parenting your child.

Take the time to clearly educate your child on the choices, personal responsibility, and results method. Once this understanding has been established, the implementation of this process begins. The key to this is that your attitude as a parent must come from the perspective that there is no punishment and there is no wrong. There is only self-discovery and parental direction. With this attitude you change the energy behind your parenting from one of an authoritative or manipulative perspective to that of a cooperative, educational, loving non-judgmental perspective. In the end, this will teach your child that they are loved no matter what their choices are, but most of all that they are the creators of their own life experience and thus you have given them true freedom.

CHOICES, AN UNDERSTANDING

Your ultimate job as a parent is really to assist the child in becoming a functionally responsible human being. If the results you create for the choices are too lenient or too harsh, it doesn't teach them to make responsible choices. It simply teaches them to manipulate the situation.

The result then is that when they leave your care, they are most likely going to have a hard time in life.

You can create results that are so polar opposite or absurd that they have to see the difference. With the choices being so polar opposite they will be able to see the difference logically even without an explanation. This is not to manipulate them into making the choice you want. The purpose of this would be so that they can plainly see the difference and then still choose what they want. You should not be vested in their choice. Your real intent should be attempting to force them to use their discernment skills.

There are typically transition issues for parents when they move into the choice parenting style. It is all too easy to take the concept of choices and put it into command and demand parenting. For example, in the beginning a common way of blending these two parenting styles is when parents say, "Okay, you chose that. Now go to your room." This is changing choice into command while giving the illusion that the child had a choice. By blending the two it is often a sign that you really are either having a difficult time or don't want to put forth the effort. Well, the choice is yours. Just like your child, you have choices to make. None are good or bad they simply have results associated with them.

Commonly when making the switchover it is a lot of work to explain and layout options. Many parents don't want to take the time or energy to do this and others try it for a short time and get tired of it. It can get exhausting in the beginning. But relate this to exercise. If you start exercising your muscles will be sore and if you stop exercising when your muscles get sore you will never get into condition. However if you continue to exercise through the soreness you will eventually be in condition and can do more than you ever thought you could. It is the same in parenting. Push through it and you will get to the other side.

Most people didn't either realize or think about how much work it is to be a parent. You may have thought, "Wow, it would be wonderful to have a child." or "Ooops. I guess I'm a parent now." In case you need a reminder or haven't noticed, parenting is often hard work and takes a lot of effort. However, if you have excellent parenting skills and have worked on changing your patterns and beliefs, parenting will have rewards far greater than you ever expected. One of the most unexpected rewards is that you yourself will grow as a human being.

PARENTAL REQUIREMENTS

Your requirements as a parent are to provide your child with food, shelter and clothing. That doesn't mean designer clothing but enough clothing to protect their body from the weather, enough food so they are healthy and a place to sleep. That is all that is required of you. Anything and everything else is an option. Okay, it may not be an option to you because of your beliefs but factually that is all that is required of a responsible parent. Many parents believe they have to give their child what everyone else does or what society says you should. These things are not only untrue but they are also unhealthy. If you could afford nothing other than food, shelter and clothing you would be a functional parent. If you added real unconditional love you are a superb parent.

As an example, imagine that your child has decided to 'forget' to do the chores that were agreed upon. In the beginning, the consequence may be that they don't watch TV until chores are done. Continued 'forgetting' may result in the loss of games or electronics for longer and longer lengths of time. The choices are still the same but the results escalate. It's just like in real life — if you don't pay the electric bill the first time you get a notice. If you continue not to pay it, you're without power.

You have to be on your game all the time in order to get the child on their game. This is where many parents have a difficult time as being on your game all the time can sometimes be tiring. When the child does what they need to do without you monitoring then it becomes easier. But if you as the parent are slacking on your duties of upholding the system then the child will slack.

Remember the child not only sees your model but intuitively feels it. It's not really hard for them to figure it out by using the trial and error method, "Oh, I tried this. It didn't work. I tried this. It worked! Okay, I'll just do this until it doesn't work anymore, then I'll try this one." There's no effort.

Parenting is the same way. If you say, "You didn't clean up after yourself, so go to your room," your child may think, "I'll go into my room and hang out. That's not such a big deal." But if you say, "Oh you didn't clean up? Well, now you have to clean up, do the dishes, do the laundry and scrub the floor." eventually they will figure out that the list keeps getting longer because they are not keeping their end of the deal.

As a way to drive this home you can keep getting more and more absurd until they finally decide just to clean it up. "If you would have just cleaned up the little spilled milk then it would have been over. Instead, your choices and actions tell me that you want to change the tires, clean the car, sweep the floor, and rake the leaves and a few other things." Should they complain your responses simply; "I'm just upholding the rules that we agreed upon and you are making the choices, so I am supporting you in your choices" without emotion or any other intent than to uphold the rules.

When upholding the rules you must speak and act lovingly, firmly and confidently. You cannot sound or feel wimpy or passive. This next sentence is extremely important. The way you feel and the energy you project must be firm and feel unchangeable while feeling the love in your heart for your child. This may be very challenging at first because most people get emotional when upholding rules that are not being followed. If you remain unemotional and lovingly firm your child will know that you mean business and feel that you love them.

You do not want to break a child's spirit.
You want to teach them to direct from their spirit.

A loving parent will develop a loving child. Too often, a loving parent is understood to be the kind of parent who isn't too difficult with their child, doesn't push them too hard and is really gentle with them. That is incorrect and inaccurate! Sometimes as a loving parent you need to be hard and push them. Loving parents are simply parents with a kind heart who have the skills to do anything it takes to teach their child how to be a healthy human being. You don't need to be an authoritative or a permissive parent. You just need to be a loving parent with a kind heart who has the human skills to teach their child how to be a personally responsible, humane person.

When parenting keep in mind:

- Love is not wimpy

- Love is not passive

- Love is not aggressive

- Love is not mean

- Love is not always gentle

- Love is not always liked

TEACHING SELF-DIRECTION

It's a parent's job to set guidelines, not to be in the business of behavioral management. You want to teach and instill in the child their own self behavioral management skills. Your child should know how to handle situations involving themselves and/or the behaviors of others. (Obviously this is taught in an ongoing basis and at age appropriate situational skills) At the same time, you want to ensure their physical safety and that they know what is emotionally appropriate. Within the guideline there should be a lot of space for the child to make mistakes and experiment in order to figure things out for themselves.

If you manage their behaviors, then they become "dependent responders" — they will not be freethinking self-directed individuals who can make wise conscious choices. Your child will not be able to appropriately discern if they have no experience and are not taught how to self-direct.

When you choose to manage their behaviors you place them in an emotional and psychic box. A child typically tends to respond to this "boxing in" and will often emotionally spin, react, bounce, rebel or withdraw based upon their own inner impulses and patterns they have already developed. Typically a child will either fight or give in to this parental control. This may not show up until later in life in the 'horrible teenage years.'

Because of their own unresolved issues from their childhood parents often want their children to have the life that they didn't have, which means they don't allow the children to have their own lives. At some stage, usually as a teenager, the child rebels because they have never been given the freedom to make their own choices. Unfortunately, having never been given the freedom, they also didn't develop the skills. They often don't know how to make appropriate or wise choices, figure out options or find solutions. So they find others to tell them what to do. They turn to a friend or a group of friends, a wife or a husband, a teacher or a boss in order to have the same relationship they at some level wished they had with their parents.

Children are never too young to begin learning this way of being. Even before the age of five when they are not yet cognitively developed they are assimilating intuitively the information and the way of being that you are modeling for them. Know that you are planting the foundational seeds for these lifelong skills. Eventually when the child becomes more fully cognitive and aware of the understandings they will practice using what you have taught them.

You are always available as their advisor but never the "answer person." Whenever your child comes to you with the problem always ask them what they think should be done or what is an appropriate response. If they are on target you confirm them. If they are off target then you give them two or three suggestions of possible responses and allow them to choose. For some parents it is going to be difficult to allow their child to make their own choices. It is common for parents to want their children's to make the right choices, so to speak, and give them the "right answer."

Love your child enough to allow them to experience their choices.

CHAPTER ELEVEN
RULES AS GUIDELINES

Let's talk about rules.

There are two types of rules:

1. Rules that are mandates - these are rules that you are required to live by that are usually unyielding and unchangeable.

2. Rules that are functional guidelines — these are rules that serve a purpose; that can be questioned and are changeable if they prove to be illogical, irrational or unreasonable. These rules are used as outlines to create a functional situation and can be modified if it improves the experience of individuals or the whole without detriment.

For the purposes of this information when we use the word rules we are using definition number two, rules that are functional guidelines. Children need rules that are functional guidelines not rules that are mandates. Children need parents to put rules into place so that they may become healthy individuals in society. These rules assist the child in having an enjoyable experience of life. Children use rules to bounce off of, to test their limits. Rules are simply concepts or ideas that are set into place so that a child can stay within certain boundaries while they are discovering self in a social experience.

Rules are put into place by families, communities, cultures, countries, etc. Often, these rules are mandates and simply a way of controlling individuals. The need for that control is determined by the individuals who perceive they are in authority. As a parent you are required to create and enforce rules that are functional guidelines to assist your child.

Some people might say that rules are needed to follow so there isn't chaos. If you had truly free people (as defined above), they would automatically be responsible and rules would not be necessary. This is not, however, the current condition of humanity today.

One of the main reasons we do not have truly free, self-directed people is that we have authority figures setting rules and restricting freedom. These people set rules to benefit themselves either financially or for a sense of power. Because this has been occurring over thousands of years, people today do not have the skills required to be truly free.

You have the opportunity to teach the next generation true freedom. This freedom is defined as being free from limitations — spiritually, emotionally, mentally, physically, and socially. It means exercising free

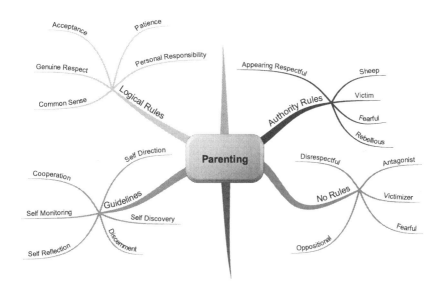

will and accepting the outcome of choices. It means being a self-directed, freethinking, self-mentoring, self-reflecting, self-sustaining, self-monitoring, self-maintaining human being. When we refer to spiritually free, we are not talking about the freedom to worship or religion. We are speaking about the innate essence of every individual to be accepted and revealed to the world. Religion and its rules are directly related to control, power and authority. This topic is however too complex to discuss in this book.

Human skills and inner-connectedness are absolutely required to be responsible and to be free. Without these skills and inner-connectedness, the individual will do things that are inappropriate and dysfunctional. The inner-connectedness creates a higher level of consciousness. This consciousness is required to become truly free.

Human beings must be taught these things so that upon becoming free, they will be responsible and won't need rules. This responsibility comes from conscious choice and the experience of what it is like to be free. Once a person has learned the order of things, they will naturally have their own rules that will coincide with, or interface with, other people's rules. This is social freedom. Everything else is based upon control. Trying to control a person's behavior, trying to control the way they think, trying to control the child — all these things are set under the same paradigm of control.

Most parents believe that they are setting good boundaries by providing rules for their children, but often they are not. If the rules were simply guidelines, like training wheels on a bicycle that are removed once the child is able to ride, this would be an excellent process. But in this case, in humanity in general, rules are set and made to be kept. Law and order is the foundation of this society. In a higher functioning society, law and order would not be necessary because of freedom. Freedom would bring about the personal responsibility that wouldn't need the rules and people would not need to be controlled.

Look at where this is true in your life and how you've done this to yourself. How have you accepted these rules and this control in every aspect of your life however subtly? Where do you follow the rules of society because you supposed to, or because you will be punished if you don't? This is the same training that you got when you were a child from your parents. For some of you, it's the same training you have given to your children. When will freedom actually occur? When will true freedom finally be allowed to the children of the world? And when will the adults of the world take back their freedom? If you begin today you set the new standards for future generations, the choice to begin is yours.

GUIDELINE RULES - SETTING THE STANDARD

When you make rules, explain to the child that you are the parent and these are the rules. Begin this at a very early age. You can still do this even if your child is over the age of six but understand that it will be a little bit more challenging. You make the rules because you are the guide, protector and instructor for their life. You make these rules so that they can have a healthy and enjoyable life. They may not like the rules now but they are still the rules.

When they do xyz, the rules state that there is a result of abc. It is up to them to decide if they want to do xyz and to understand that should they do xyz, abc will occur because of their choice — not because you are a mean, punishing disciplinarian. Of course, use age-appropriate words when explaining this to your child. For example, if they choose to fight with their siblings, the result may be that they must go to their room.

By constantly saying, "Don't" "Stop" "No" "You can't" and such phrases you inadvertently teach a child to develop an oppositional defiant or rebellious attitude. This is where the child takes a stand, saying, "No, you can't make me do it." They learn to resent authority, for they see authority as controlling and taking away their rights and personal power. When you simply use different words, change the feelings behind them and use the choices style parenting, the child will learn to be more co-operative. This does not mean they will not test you — you can be assured they will.

Correcting and redirecting the child who is misbehaving is different than disciplining them. When you correct a child, you must never attempt to break their spirit. You must love them even when you are frustrated. You do not have to like their behaviors, but remember: *Children are not their behaviors!* Differentiate between the two. Children must not surrender to their parents, yet they need to come to an understanding and agreement even when they do not like it.

As a parent you need to be logical, reasonable, and rational in your correction of your children. Take the time to teach your child to know and understand their feelings and be able to verbalize them. Then teach them and have examples of appropriate behaviors to express those feelings. Do not forget that they may be either too young or immature to fully understand all you would like them to know or change.

You must also look at why you want them to change. Is it for your convenience or comfort, or purely functional for their experience? If it is for anything except the latter, you have issues standing in the way of your parenting.

You should know, however, that if you have not prepared your child from a very young age then correcting and guiding them will feel like a lot of work. After the age of six the ease of educating your child becomes more complex. Remember, your child has your behavior patterns and belief systems, so when your child seems difficult, know they learned most of what they do from you!

When the child wants to pit themselves against you and they don't want to do what you tell them to do, it is advisable for you to know that their pitting themselves against you is just them remembering their inner strength and trying to establish it in their life.

But the outside world doesn't respond well to that type of behavior so they have to understand that there are these differences. Your job is to make them do enough so that they are functional yet not push so much that they start to feel powerless, because when they get older they can't or won't do things for themselves or be able to do what they want.

Your child will be the greatest teacher you will ever have. They will teach you all about your patterns and belief systems while giving you the opportunity to change them. Love and treat them as they need to be loved and treated in order to reach their heart. Never love your child the way you would like to be loved. Love your child the way they want to be loved. If you reach their heart, their mind will naturally follow. Connect with them from your heart, not your mind, and their heart will be more accessible. Even when you are utterly baffled or frustrated, love them and speak from the heart. Remember you are the model and if they see you love from an open heart and they will do the same.

SETTING RULES

It is advisable that either both parents or you alone if you are a single parent, sit down and write a list of rules that you would like to have for your family that will make your situation pleasant. Some people might say that it's a little ridiculous to write a list. But we would say, this avoids many problems and complications later on and makes for very clear rules for both the child and the parents. This also makes communication with your partner very clear and simple and there can be no arguments over what the rules are. Ultimately doing this little exercise makes life easier.

This does not mean writing, "Take out the trash every Wednesday at two o'clock or you will be punished." It simply means establishing general rules.

For example:

- There will be no disregarding of another person's feelings.
- No yelling or screaming.
- Treat each other with kindness even if you are angry; express your anger without hurting or harming another person emotionally, verbally or physically.
- You may communicate what you have to say or feel inside

without repercussions.

- I may only listen when I am in a good space or I may not listen to you when I am in a bad space and unable to understand you clearly without my issues getting in the way. If this is the case, I will listen when I am able.
- You may ask any questions that you have pertaining to any subject.
- Your choices and your behaviors will determine the results you experience based on the rules of a household.

These are just a few examples.

When you have decided on a rule stick to it no matter what, especially when children are young. Be firm (not rigid) and do not give in under pressure. Be consistent. When you are wishy-washy they learn not to respect your words or you.

Unless there are unusual circumstances, you should never change your mind. If necessary, you can make adjustments the next time that situation occurs. Sticking to the rules you have decided upon is keeping your commitment, which teaches your child about commitment by example. If you continually change your mind and are too flexible, your child will not have any boundaries or rules that they are sure of. They will not be very functional, they will not be able to stand up for themselves and what they need, and they will have a higher potential of being taken advantage of because they do not know how to commit and remain firm.

Too flexible of a parenting style also teaches your children that you can be manipulated. This will eventually create many conflicts and arguments. Once the child knows that you can be manipulated, because you have manipulated them or been too lenient, they will not respect you or the rules.

A child will continue to push for something as long as they feel the inconsistency of your mental, emotional and psychic boundaries. If you are wavering or not firm inside yourself, they will know. They will intuitively feel this inconsistency. When they are pushing boundaries and you feel it as a challenge, you must look inside at your own areas of inconsistency or wavering and correct that. In this way you can remain loving yet firm with the boundaries you have set for them. Set your rules mentally, emotionally, physically and verbally. Be consistent on all levels because once they are set, they do not change! You may set and reset the rules with each topic but never change them once they are set unless you sit down together and renegotiate.

You do not want to break a child's spirit; you want to train them to direct their spirit.

If you haven't set up rules before, or if you are changing or adding new rules and holding to them, the child may react more strongly than usual to see if you are really changing. Sometimes it may be worse before it gets better. You must be committed to the change and remember you are doing these things to prepare the child for their experiences in the world.

This is when you say, "Look, I am putting the rules in place because I am your parent. I know these rules are going to help you even if you don't believe it or like them. I know what it will be like when you are older and I know what you need out there when you leave the house. These rules are being established so that you can function when you leave here. Otherwise you're going to bump into teachers, employers or fellow employees and they're not going to take this stuff. That's going to be really hard for you. I realize that I haven't done this before and that was my mistake. If I had known better, I would have taught you this a long time ago. But I didn't, so now I have to do some catch up time."

Tell them, "As I learn, I am teaching you. I know you don't like it and I know it's a change because we both got away with things. It's just going to be different now. You may not like it, but as you figure this out you'll see that things will run smoother, which is the objective here. We are supposed to be in the house because we love each other, not just because I am the authority and you are the rebel. We are here together in this and as I do my part and you do your part we get to live a lot more comfortably and a lot more enjoyably. This is the goal I am after."

Don't barrel down on them, just talk to them, even when it is a monologue. They'll look out the window or act like they're not listening, but they hear you. Remain neutral and tell them anyway. They do get it. What they do with it, you can't do anything about.

Sometimes parents want an immediate answer. We want to know they got it now. There is no answer. There are tips and tools that assist the child in getting it themselves. It is not about fighting the child. That's not to say they won't fight you, because they will. Be aware if you have the need for power or to be bigger and stronger than your child. You instead need to be in the energy of love because you care about you, your child and their well-being. Show them! Be the example.

SAYING 'NO'

Children hear 'no' about twenty times more than yes. They are taught to say 'no' as an instant response. Parents say 'no' when the child is doing something the parents don't want them to do or don't like. What parents don't realize is that they are teaching their children to say 'no' to them when the children are able.

As they get older, children begin to form opinions and make choices. When a parent asks them to do something that the child doesn't like or want to do, they often say 'no'. When this happens, the parent often sees it as disobedience and disrespect and views the child as bad. But isn't this what the parent taught — to say 'no' if you do not want to do something? How is it that the child is bad but the parent is not if both say 'no' for the same reason? Is it any wonder the child argues or is confused? If you say 'no' when you don't want to do something, why can't they? Be aware of how often you say 'no." Before saying it, check and see if there is another choice.

POWER AND CONTROL

Many parents want to be the power. This is the way they were raised. Power is about wanting to control and be the authority. It carries the energy of a rigid response to things. This does not come from a space of love and neutrality so it carries a different feel to the child. The child can feel the control energy as you, the parent, are not centered inside with yourself. When you get to the space inside yourself where you really know yourself and love yourself, then you will have a consistent energy that the child knows and feels intuitively and there is no fight. When you carry the power/control/authority energy, it evokes the fight or resistance energy and they will react. You must do your own inner work in clearing and releasing the authority issues you may have from your own family patterning.

You have to realize that once you get into it with phrases like "Why? Because I said so." and "Do as I say, not as I do." you're into power and control. You're teaching them that they need to control or be controlled.

Now when the parent gets into a control contest with their child what is actually coming up is their inner child or their childhood memories. The parent remembers how they were powerless, angry and frustrated. Now they are confronted with children who are smaller and weaker than they are, so they enforce their power and pass on powerless memories to their own children. This creates the perception that adults are more powerful than the child is. Then when you create your perspective as an adult, you are still powerless because you see other people as adults and not yourself.

If, on the other hand, you have been a pushover, what have you taught them? You can be pushed around. This is a double-whammy: When you step up for the power, they already know you don't have any. Now they are going to push and test to see how little you have. That's the example you give them inadvertently.

That is why you have to be consistent. You have to be clear as you are saying, "This is not about power. I am doing it because I am the parent. While you live with me, these are the rules. These rules make sense. These rules are for you, not for me, because I have already done this.

My job is to prepare you for life and that is all I am doing. Up until now, maybe I didn't do such a good job." Owning your mistakes is really important.

SO WHAT IF YOU REALIZE YOU MADE
A MISTAKE IN YOUR DECISION OR RULES?

Even if you make a mistake, be consistent through your mistake, then go back and explain the error. Say, "Hey, you know what? I really told you to do this, but probably this other thing would have been the better choice." You don't want to change in the middle, because then you become wishy-washy and they will work that every time. Follow through with the mistake, as long as it isn't extreme. Of course, change it if it is.

If you should happen to realize it's an extreme mistake, say, "Hmm, let me reconsider this. I think this is a better option." If it's a minor mistake, you say, "You know what? I really meant to say that but I shouldn't have yelled at you. I should have said it in a firm voice, but because you weren't listening any other way and I was frustrated, I yelled a little bit. Even though I make mistakes, you still have to do what I say. My making a mistake doesn't allow you to get away with stuff, let's just make that clear." In this way you clearly inform the child.

If you haven't owned your mistakes and you override them, your child will do the same thing to you. They are just modeling your behaviors. There is no instant fix or instant cure. There is just you laying the foundation for the child, brick by brick.

TECHNIQUES CHILDREN USE TO GET THEIR WAY

Children train you the way you have trained them. They will use the behaviors you have taught them for testing these patterns to see how and where they work. Every parent should know that loving your child is not letting them do whatever they want, giving them everything and being their best friend. Many parents mistake being a good parent for being their child's friend and are afraid to tell their child 'no.'

Children will use anything that you have done to them to try and see it will work on you. Some common behaviors that parents teach their children are anger, the use of fear, guilt tripping and the old divide and conquer.

Your child may use guilt trips to make you feel bad about your parenting. The older they get, the more complex they get at doing it. They will find your weaknesses and use them to get what they want.

Understand that their manipulations or trying to get their way is not a bad thing — it is simply their experimentation in finding out how the world works. Most people think this is negative because it is not something you want. What you have to understand is that it's not about getting what you want. It's about allowing a child to grow, experiment, and be who they are with guidelines as to what is appropriate in a human society.

It is wise if you are tolerant of their experimental behaviors. It is also wise if you understand that everything they experiment with they have seen. They didn't just come up with this. They have seen you do it, or have seen someone else do it, and are testing to see how these things work, which ones work for them, and what modifications they have to use.

If you grew up with any of these or other manipulations, you have likely taught them to your children. If you were brought up with guilt, you can rest assured that they will find your guilt button or that you have used that button in front of them.

The thing that most parents don't understand is that the way you manipulate your world provides an example to the child on how to manipulate theirs. Manipulation is often thought of as bad, but in this book, manipulation simply means doing something to get something. It's that simple. It is not good or bad, nor is it positive or negative. It is simply an attempt at trying to meet needs or desires. If you have parented with anger, you may find that your child will use hostility or acting out behaviors to try and manipulate their world and get what they want.

They may try to use fear. The fear may be in a statement something like, "I am going to hurt myself. I want to kill myself." These are usually the bottom line or the last ditch effort to try and make their world work. You have to pay close attention. Is this truly a serious condition or is it simply a manipulation? Treat it according to whichever you determine it is because you know your child best. When a child uses the "I am going to kill myself" line, there's not necessarily a need to run them off to therapy. Sometimes this can do more harm than good. Other times, when it is a serious condition, it is wise to send your child to therapy. Discerning the difference here is very important! We highly suggest that if you are unsure, you seek assistance for clarification.

Fear can also be used by threatening you, a family pet, or a sibling. They may even attack their siblings in an effort to manipulate you — it may have nothing to do with the sibling that they attack. They just know that if they attack the sibling, you will respond in some way. Maybe they only want a response just to know that they matter, or maybe they want a particular response from you. These are the things that you have to understand your child to know.

The divide and conquer technique is where a child uses the parents against each other, the siblings against the parents, or the parents against the siblings. This is sometimes an attempt to get out of the limelight. It puts the onus on you and gets one of you to agree to their position. Once they find the weak spot in your relationship, it is a guarantee that they will work this as long as they as they can.

It is optimal for parents to be in union with each other when it comes to raising the child or disciplining the child. The parents should stand together as a unit, which means something said to one parent will get the same response from the other parent, whether they're asked separately or together.

You can believe that they will test this. Again, they are not being defiant, they are being children. They are seeking to learn how to work their world. How does it operate? How do I get around? How do I meet my needs? Too many parents perceive these behaviors as negative. When you are united in your parenting, the child cannot use this method. When you see any of these manipulative techniques being used, it is advisable that you explain the technique to your child. Explain what is being done, how it works, and why it will no longer work in the family.

It is best if both parents sit together and talk with the child if this is at all possible. In some cases it may not be possible for both parents to sit together, such as in separations, divorces, or where there is hostility between parents. Single parents should stand as a wall also. You act in union with your truth, with what you know is the best for the child. When you sit with the child and explain the different techniques they are using, you explain that you understand them. You explain what they are, how they work, how most human beings try to do this and experiment with these. They are not bad techniques, but they are not very useful. They are not healthy and they are not acceptable in your household. Explain that should they decide to try to use these, their behavior will have results.

CHILDREN, PARENTING, LOVE AND TRANSPARENCY

A child is never too young to hear your words, but you also have to remember that your energy must match your words. The energy in your feeling, the energy in your attitudes must match your touch and your words. When that energy is congruent, as the child gets older their cognitive abilities expand, then the explanation matches everything that they felt and a complete understanding is achieved. Whether they agree with it or like it is not the issue. The purpose here is not to have them like it, it's to have them understand and feel what you are teaching them. That's why what you do when you do these things must be done with love.

Love doesn't mean wimpy.

Sometimes love is a little strong, sometimes love is intense, sometimes love is gentle, but with that love it's always congruent with the words and touch that match.

Sometimes you do have to push the child to the edge of their tolerance so they can see clearly what they are actually doing and learn from it, but you must do your best not to push them too far over that edge. Pushing your child requires you to be emotionally and spiritually connected to them. Assuming this is true you will be able to feel their emotions before they surface. Whenever they are being unreasonable or illogical, you can push them to see the facts and to see if what they are doing makes sense. You take them to the edge of emotion and then ease up while explaining the situation.

Warning: *You must be loving, kind and conscious while doing this. This practice described above should not be practiced without training or intuitive connection. The unskilled may cause more harm than good.*

When you are pushing them, you continue to tell them why you are doing what you are doing and what it means. They also must be taught that they can lighten up and that they don't have to choose to be in an off mood — they can choose the mood they want to be in. They must know that whatever they choose is alright, but that there may be repercussions from their choices, either positive or negative.

When you are teaching them, you must never try to influence them either directly or covertly. This allows them to feel their own strength and not yield to the parent or others. What you are trying to do by pushing them to the edge of their tolerance is show them that this mood is a choice. This is a potential opportunity for them to decide what they want to do and what they want to experience. In a strange way, it is actually empowering to them because you are teaching them that they have the power of choice over their experience. Even though they may not understand this at the time, you must remember that you are not looking for immediate results.

Remember that you chose to have your child and with that choice comes the requirement for you to grow, change, be less self-centered, and nurture your child's heart — not suppress it. Often, you must learn to temper your desires and issues.

Everything that you are reading about what to do with children is what you can do as an adult. These techniques will not only help you understand your children or grandchildren, they will also help you understand yourself as a child and ways you were programmed. It's not just the mental programming or the assumptions you made, it's the kinesthetic and emotional programming as well.

Be aware of yourself and those around you, because everyone has the same basic sensate system. However developed or underdeveloped, they still have those sensate systems and respond to them. A child is a pure sensate system. They are a clean slate. As an adult, you have a sensate system with a 99.9% chance of a dysfunctional mental system. A sensate system paired with a highly dysfunctional mental system means that the interpretation of the sensate system is going to be misunderstood nine out of ten times. If it's not completely misunderstood, it will at least be misunderstood to a great degree because your own programs, beliefs, and experiences are filtering those sensate experiences.

This is why everyone's perception is different, and why no two human beings experience the same sensate event in the exact same way, even though energetically the experience is the same. After the interpretation, your unique response system kicks in. You now have this sensate event, the interpretation of it, and a response system. In each individual, that combination is completely different and thereby changes the same event to a different experience. You can see how important it is to assist the child in not having as many of these programs as possible.

KEEP IT LIGHT

It is absolutely necessary to keep humor and an air of lightness in your parenting style. Humor does many things. It can make it easier for the child to listen to you, it can be a way to show your child not to take life or their emotions too seriously and it can create a deep inner trust and bond with your child.

All too often when you are in the routines of daily life it is easy to forget and see the humor in everything you experience and how silly human behavior can be sometimes. Humor also shows your child that you are light of heart. Never use humor with sarcasm or in any way that is demeaning or emotionally damaging. However you can make fun of or light of your own behaviors and do it in a lighthearted jovial fashion as they are behaviors that make no sense. Do the same with your partner and this will model for the child a lighthearted loving interaction with a partner.

Sometimes human behavior is quite comical and totally illogical, find the humor in this. Never take your own illogical, irrational behavior personally. Your behaviors are not you. Find the humor in your own behavior and you teach the child self-acceptance and awareness.

THE BILL OF RIGHTS

Parent's rights

1. The right to like your child or not
2. The right to your own life without the children
3. The right to have an enjoyable relationship with your partner
4. The right to not sacrifice for your child
5. The right to your own space (physical, emotional and psychic)
6. The right to say no for the purpose educating and preparing your child
7. The right to express yourself
8. The right to your own feelings
9. The right to your opinion while not imposing that opinion on the child
10. The right to make decisions in everyone's best interests and safety as the guardian

Children's rights

1. The right to be loved and unconditionally accepted
2. The right to be what their heart calls them to be
3. The right to be treated age appropriately equal
4. The right to not take care of their parents physical or emotional needs or desires
5. The right to their own space (physical, emotional and psychic)
6. The right to choose

7. The right to be heard

8. The right to express themselves

9. The right to their own opinion

10. The right to their own feelings

To honor yourself and your child is to be the loving model that your child can emulate. To teach the child to honor themselves and others while being sovereign is to give them the gift of loving wisdom.

CHAPTER TWELVE
THE GOOD AND BAD CHILD
The Pain and Pleasure Program

The pain and pleasure program is probably one of the core programs all children learn. They must decide if being 'good' (pleasure) or being 'bad' (pain) is going to work best in their world as they see it. People train children to be pain and pleasure responders. People also train them as to what pain and pleasure are. Then they use these systems to manipulate them, as children and as adults. These children turn into adults who train their children in the same programmed behavior and beliefs. The choice between being a good or bad child and the pain or pleasure model are commonly the only choices an innocent child has.

The child selects a pain or pleasure model based on that which gets most of their needs met and that which they witnessed being modeled by their parents. Around the age of two they begin to test these programs, otherwise known as the 'Terrible Twos.' The question is, terrible for whom? It's terrible for the adults who want to control them and have them behave in a particular way. It's also terrible for the child who is punished, coaxed, taught and manipulated by the parents who cannot cope or want to control them. Maybe this should be called the 'terrible for the two-year-old' stage instead.

Another aspect of the 'terrible twos' is that they are in a purely exploratory phase that has nothing to do with the rules or what you as a parent wants. They are so adventurous and in wonderment of their world that they do things often without awareness. Their pure innocent discovery of their world is the beauty of this age.

What happens is simply because of the lack of consciousness and the abundance of parental issues. The parents have made judgments about life and created issues. These issues are then imposed on the children unconsciously (and occasionally consciously) by the parents. Around age six, the child is at a stage where they want to try something else and experiment with the patterns and beliefs they were given. If the parents are not conscious they will often punish the child and tell them things are not acceptable if they don't fit into the parent's paradigm. For the conscious parent they will see the child's innocent beauty and allow them to discover.

At approximately ages 10 to 13 and then again around 16 the child is in the exploratory stages. Some physicians, psychiatrists, guidance counselors may say these actions are due to their hormones. Hormones are not the sole cause. Hormones only complicate and often worsen the natural process that is already occurring. A child learns at each of these stages whether it is alright for them to be who they are or not. Then they make a choice either consciously or unconsciously if they will conform to the authorities in their life or go for creating their own life. If they choose their own life, it's often seen as going against authority — it is not. It is only choosing their own life over the expectations of others. When children are forced to conform, parents often wonder why the child has no will of their own. Silly, huh?

This does not mean that a child should not learn to interface with others smoothly, as this is quite different. A child must be taught the difference between the calling of their heart and the calling of their personal desires. The calling of the heart is the interconnectedness to their soul. The calling of their personal desires is the belief systems and patterns of the mind. They must be taught the skills to interface their heart's desire with their mind and to be socially appropriate with other people and society so they face the least amount of resistance possible in creating and achieving their own soul's calling.

On the negative side what a child often learns through these trials and tribulations is:

- It is not okay for me to do what I want.
- There are painful results from doing what my heart calls me to do.
- I never get what I want.
- I can never have what I want.
- I cannot make decisions that go against the grain.
- If I do what I want I will suffer.
- I must do what others want.
- If I don't do what others want, they will make my life miserable.
- Life is pain or pleasure, based on other peoples' desires and rules.
- I must fight or suffer to do what I want.

These beliefs are often the source of Oppositional Defiance Disorder (ODD). After being forced to fight or conform, those who have decided to have what they want and not to give up their dreams often resort to ODD-like behavior because they feel there is no other choice. Once they decide to take this path they unconsciously operate this way and are seen as being difficult, which then creates the need for another type of compensating behavior. After this initial behavioral training of pain and pleasure, everything in a person's life is the creation of some sort of behavioral compensation in order to fulfill the paradigm. At least until a person is taught to break it.

The good child conforms. They become the people pleaser and do everything everybody likes. Whether they love it or hate it, they're going to do it because of what they get out of people-pleasing.

'Good' children get things by pleasing. They are nursemaids and caretakers. As a rule, good children rarely grow up to be entrepreneurs. They become great employees, service people or managers because they know how to take care of things and do the right thing.

Thinking outside the box is very difficult for them to do. To go beyond pleasing or fulfilling the needs of others would be out of their comfort zone. This is not to say that they can't change. It is however often difficult for the good child to say they are going to be different because their whole life has revolved around doing what others want and getting rewarded for being a conformist.

'Good' children are at best conforming creators, and really don't create something that has never been done before because they unconsciously do what is necessary to avoid pain, please others and be seen as worthy by others. They do not always do what they love and they avoid going against the grain. Sometimes they believe they are doing what they love when in truth they are actually doing what boosts their perceived self-worth and they interpret that as doing what they love. In this particular case they are not doing what their soul is calling them to do. The reason for this is rooted in the good/bad, pain/pleasure principle.

Conforming children are capable of real creativity, but it's stifled in this type of programming. It is instilled in them before they can think for themselves. The child can be set free from this trap but they must be taught that pain and or pleasure is not required. They must then be taught how to think, feel and create for themselves. This will take them out of the unconscious good child syndrome.

A summary of the good child program is this: "If I am good, I have value. If I am good for others and do what they want, I have value. If others are pleased with me I am pleased with myself."

The summary of a bad child program is simply the opposite of the good child program. "If I create pain, disharmony and disruption, then I have value." This may not be the program they prefer, but it's the one that they've found works in their life or that they have been forced into. This program rewards the child with some sort of perceived pleasure, of getting attention for being bad.

They fight to stay bad because they make an identity of being wrong or bad. They escape by emotionally checking out. This identity is however painful to them and they always struggle with worth and value. They often attempt to use this "bad identity" to feel good about themselves and are even prideful of who they are in this identity.

'Bad' children are seen as oppositional because when they don't like something, they simply resist —going against following the rules like the good child. In most cases it is not actually oppositional. They're just digging their heels in and saying, "This is the way I'm going to be." Adults perceive them as oppositional because the child is not conforming to their wishes, demands or commands.

Unlike a good child, who becomes a conformist even if they hate it, the bad child will do what they want in spite of the repercussions. A bad child is often seen as a bad employee because they don't do what they are told to do or are nonconformist. The bad child questions authority, whereas the good child usually adheres to authority. The difference is simply that because there are more people in authority who do not like the bad child's behavior, these children will have a more difficult time in society. But they are often better survivors in adverse conditions.

There's also a third type: the middle child.

The middle child is both a good and bad child who can change back and forth and knows how to use whichever model works in any particular situation. This child is extremely adaptable and probably the most creative of all. This child is fairly balanced. They have seen both the good and bad programs and have decided that both can work. This child can be an excellent employee, manager or entrepreneur.

Everyone fluctuates in between the three types; this information just gives a black and white understanding to start with. Children must be trained to make decisions based on their heart and integrate those decisions with their human life and environment.

What a child needs to know is that the good child style is too passive and the bad child style is too hostile. They need to know that both of these styles used alone make life hard or difficult. The good style makes for obedient, frustrated experiences and the bad style make for hostile, frustrated experiences. Neither style works for the individual in a healthy way when interacting with those in authority positions in society.

Examples of those in authority positions are teachers are teachers, bosses, parents, government, doctors, lawyers, judges, principals, coaches, famous people, etc. The problem is that from a very early age, people believe that those who have jobs that require decision making or delegating are in charge. They are not! They are simply doing their job. They are no better or worse. Everyone is equal because every person has one main common denominator — they are human. Their job does not make them more powerful, better or give them any greater value than anyone else.

The other challenge to this 'authorities with titles' situation is that society has bought into this concept and therefore believes that is natural to reward those in these positions with higher salaries and notoriety. This whole system was created by those in power seeking to remain in that place. Please let your child know that none of this is true and it is all merely a belief system, that they can have equal notoriety or income whether they have a title or not. Teach them that every human being is equal and the only thing different is that every soul is unique and the human profession they take is different, not better or more valuable. The day when everyone is seen as equally valuable, no matter what their position is the day the world will be an even more beautiful place to live.

You must keep in mind that once a child has decided which program is theirs you are dealing with an identity, not just behavior. An identity is much harder to change than a behavior. The child has come to believe that they are this identity and will have no idea of who they are or how to behave if you try to make them change. They must be taught how to behave and respond all over again or it will be too terrifying for them. You must be patient and deliberate in your instruction of new behaviors, thoughts and feelings. Change is possible but it is a large undertaking that is well worth it, although it may not seem so during the process. Remember that you are their mentor. It is your job to see that they have the tools to succeed in life. This is a very noble and honorable job, probably one of the most honorable jobs one can have as a human being. In essence you are planting the seeds for the future of humanity by being a parent.

We are not condoning bad behavior, middle or good behavior — we are simply describing generalizations of these types. Each child as an individual may have a combination of any of these three types. These types are simply for reference and understanding purposes yet hold a lot of truth.

Understanding alone cannot create change. But through understanding, change may begin. If a belief system is programmed in the precognitive stages of development then it's more than likely a lifelong program unless the parents consciously address it as soon as possible. Precognitive belief systems are the hardest to change. For these you have to change the feeling/energy of them as well as have the understanding. Psychology alone cannot change precognitive programming.

Precognitive – *before the set of all mental abilities are developed i.e. processes related to knowledge: attention, memory and working memory, judgment and evaluation, reasoning and "computation", problem solving and decision making, comprehension and production of language, etc.*

If you can alter precognitive programming in preschoolers, you will change their lives in a huge way. The older they get, the less the degree of change. Other than beginning with the parents at conception, relatives and preschool hold the greatest potential for the greatest amount of change in the child's life. Understanding, teaching and treating the child differently only goes so far and does not make real change, but it does provide wonderful coping skills. However good the coping skills are, a child will still perceive the world from those original programs. These programs will continue to interfere with and wreak havoc on their lives. Making true change at this level should be one of your most important goals in helping and teaching your child become all that they can be.

Don't expect that you will be able to change everything for them. You will never get to all of their programming. You can however get to many of them and teach the child the skills of how to deprogram themselves. As you do this understand that you are trying to make a major change. You may not see this change until the child becomes an adult, if at all. You are planting the seeds of change that you may never see come to fruition. You must not look for results but stay focused on the mission of supplying the children with ways to make change in their precognitive and cognitive programs.

One of the biggest problems in raising children is that parents, with all the stress that are going on in their lives, don't have the extra energy to do real parenting. When they're in a good space, they can be wonderful parents. When they are in a stressed space, they want the child to shut up, sit down and behave.

What does "behave" mean? Behave typically means "Do what I want you to do, when I want you to do it." Whether you believe it or not you do not want behaved children, you want conscious children who know when and how to behave in the appropriate situations through conscious awareness and choice.

This is one thing you have to teach the children: how to discern appropriate behavior at appropriate times by taking them out of the pain/ pleasure principle. Teach them, "You're not doing it for pain or pleasure. You are doing it because you've chosen to do so, because you are the creator of your life." Of course one has to always use age-appropriate language.

So you are really giving them the gift of autonomy. You're not just talking about it, and we don't mean autonomy where your children can dress themself. We mean internal conscious autonomy with the proper discernment skills, accurate understandings of what the choices are, how to use their skills and what results their choices will bring about.

By eliminating the pain and pleasure programming you create the potential for autonomous, sovereign human beings. Journal about where you are and are not autonomous and sovereign, whether it is mental, emotional, physical, social or spiritual. This will give you an awareness of the programs that you have most likely passed on to your own child and the programs that may be interfering with your own personal happiness.

Chapter Thirteen
The Magic of Touch
Children, Touch, and Sensate Training

Touch is one of the most important topics in raising a child and in maintaining a healthy personal relationship. Touch is an extremely important form of non-verbal communication. A child feels your mood. If you are tense or calm, the child will feel and react. How you touch the child is a vibrational/energetic communication. Touch is also an excellent form of grounding. Being touched by another person awakens you to the sensate aspect of your being and assists a child or adult in feeling alive.

Beginning with infancy, touch the baby all over (not the genitals or private parts but the rest of the body, only because there are too many personal and societal issues in regards to this area the body). Lightly massage and move the baby's limbs when they are tight. Stretch them out, limber them up, move them around and move the joints and limbs in circles.

What does this do? It moves the energy in the body that is being blocked by tension or pain. This is a way to release it. It also brings your child's awareness into the body and assists them in beginning to relate to their physicality. To put it simply it grounds them into their body.

Massage, soothe, coo and talk to your child but most of all feel the love flow through your hands as you touch them. On deeper levels your child will feel the love and nurturing in their sensate system which will eventually be understood once they develop their cognitive skills.

As your loving touch awakens their sensate body/system your child develops a deeper soulful connection to their human existence.

While touching your child you will usually find the infant becoming much more relaxed over a period of time. If not, the child is still having some kind of emotional need that they cannot express or they are simply having difficulty relating to their physical body. Until you figure it out or they adjust, they will probably remain distressed. Remember, the child feels your energy intuitively and getting upset or stressed by the child's crying will only intensify their distress, so stay calm.

Keep in mind you do not have to fix it for your child or make them stop crying. Sometimes the crying is a way for them to channel off the energy in their environment or excess energy from their developing physical body. Therefore crying is a good thing. If you get emotionally involved and feel that you have to stop your child's crying then you are too involved. This may be reflective of your own patterning of fixing things for others; that your inner child is crying or that the child is not happy with you and therefore their crying holds meaning for you based on some perceived trauma or patterning from your childhood.

When you hold the baby to your chest, they can hear your heartbeat, just like what they heard in the womb. They are also feeling the vibration. This is another way of soothing them.

Parents are often aware of their touching the child when they're playing with the baby, yet become unconscious of their touch when taking care of or doing physical maintenance, such as changing their diaper, washing them, etc.

Changing a diaper, washing, dressing and brushing hair are also forms of touch. Let's just use wiping as an example. Whether it is done to the face or the bottom, wiping is often done simply to be efficient, with no thought to how it feels for the child or an awareness of how the child reacts. You've seen people wipe a child's mouth almost as though they were sandpapering their lips to get the food off. This simple gesture sends a message to the child. Maybe that message is your body doesn't matter, or the parent has control over their body or something else.

Wiping a child's bottom is often done with a cold wipe that a parent wouldn't use on their own backside. Yet the baby's much more sensitive bottom gets wiped quickly, sometimes roughly back and forth with this cold wipe and you may wonder why the baby fusses. The parent gets frustrated and can't figure out why the baby fusses and gets fidgety when it's time to get changed. Imagine your legs up in the air, being wiped with sandpaper and ice cubes. Do you get an idea of what the baby may experience? What would your reaction be if someone did that to you right now? Imagine yourself with your legs up in the air, no pants on and your partner taking a piece of sandpaper out of the freezer and scrubbing your bottom.

When this happens the child can't do anything. The adult has them pinned down and is focused on getting the job done, not the feelings of the child. So what is the child learning? Powerlessness? Hopelessness? Apathy? That their feelings don't matter? Victimhood? Big people are in control. It's futile to do anything. Fight or give in. Fighting will cause more pain, so give in and accept the pain. In this way, another very subtle program gets installed unbeknownst to the parents.

We are not saying don't wipe your child's bottom. What we are saying is be consciously aware of how your child feels and get the job done in the kindest way possible. Know that your child is a conscious, sensate, intuitive being that records every experience.

Then we can look at the patterns of the parents that get triggered, too. There's the parent who is going to control the child, "I'm the parent and you are going to sit the way I told you to sit!" or "I'm in control and you will do what needs to be done because I said so." Even wiping a baby's bottom can be a power struggle. Then there is the kinder parent, "Oh honey, would you just hold still? I'm trying to wipe as quickly as I can. I will be as gentle as possible." These are two different patterns the child is now learning.

From birth, the child is being programmed for the experience of life, trying to figure out this new sensory organ their soul is now sitting inside. Before birth, the only sense they had was fluid on their skin. Once they leave the womb they are in contact with humans and different energy systems. You need to be consciously in the love with your child when you touch them.

Every touch communicates a message and if you touch every part of the child's skin on a regular basis with a loving hand, the child learns the sensation of love. That child will tend to love to be touched and will know touch as a loving act, because their senses have been programmed with love through the touch of another human being. You should touch the child as little as possible if there is not love in your hands or heart. This is aside from basic disciplines to move them or keep them safe. We're talking about simply touching their skin. Touch is an intimate experience and speaks to the child's soul.

Children can and should be trained about how to interpret touch. So they should be touched everywhere, especially if they don't want to be touched. If they love to be touched, you do it just because they love it. If they don't want to be touched, you're doing it because they do not love it, and so they can acclimate to touch and learn to love it. You touch every part, except the genitalia, which you touch only for maintenance. This allows them to be sensately connected to their world.

Every single chance you get you must touch your child, even when they are a teen. You touch the head, the toes, the feet, the legs, the arms, the armpits, the back, the neck, the nose, the face. All this is teaching the body to record the sensations of touch — what it means, how it feels, that it's okay, that it's neutral, benign or pleasurable. Later you teach them the intellectual skills to discern the intents of others as well as whether they prefer to be touched or don't prefer it. Then teach them how to distinguish between their issues about being touched which is a mental program, versus the feeling of the touch.

Just a note here: children on the autistic spectrum often do not like to be touched. They should be touched in spite of their desire to shy away from it. It is important because they need to turn on their sensate body and become more connected to their physical body.

As you are teaching the child when you are touching them while they are very small, there should be love in your hands. If there is not love in your hands, you should not be touching the child, because the child will intuitively understand the feeling of love or repulsion or if you have an agenda.

If you are touching your child to soothe them, that's one thing. If you are touching your child to manipulate them into being quiet because they are irritating to you, a whole different message is being delivered. Your child will grow up with an unconscious belief about what touches mean and will respond to them through their patterns.

If you have ill intent or if your mind is on a different subject — let's say you are fighting with your partner — and you are touching the child, you're sending a mixed message. They feel your vibration of anger, hostility or discontent while you are touching their skin.

Besides physical touch, voices and sound can touch the child, too. Voices and sounds are not only heard by the ears, they are felt by the skin and sensate system/body, which sends signals to the nervous system, which translates to the brain's interpretations of those experiences.

APPROPRIATE AND INAPPROPRIATE TOUCHING

Touch can be sensual, sexual, friendly, nurturing, aggressive, business, neutral, etc.

Appropriate touching is touching your child with love. It doesn't matter if you are giving them a verbal message. It just means that you love them.

Inappropriate touching is touching your kids with an agenda that is not loving or with a negative attitude. It doesn't have to be sexual. Do you have an agenda to manipulate your child? Do you rub them on the neck and say, "Hey, are you going to take care of this?" That is inappropriate touching. You are putting thought and energy into your child that is conditional and not loving. That is inappropriate touching. You can give them a message, love them and touch them, or you can have an agenda and touch them in order to manipulate them. However you can give them a loving touch and deliver a message they do not want to hear.

An example of an inappropriate touch is angrily holding somebody's hand. If you are angry, don't hold their hand. That energy goes from you into them directly through their hands (a conduit right into their brain), through their nervous system and sensate body. They get exactly what is going on. If they are picking it up in the room and you're not touching them, what do you think they get when you are plugged into them? It is like shot with a taser gun, thousands of volts of energy running through the body all intuitively felt.

Your child knows when you're upset and most likely dreads being touched by you then. If you do it anyway, they may get freaked out or pull away because every time you touch them they feel an unpleasant jolt go through their system. Children are sensitive psychic beings — they feel almost everything you are going through.

Sometimes parents try to emotionally involve their children in their personal opinions and experiences. When a parent is not in balance within themselves they will often try to get the child to side with them in opinions, arguments or debates within the family, with friends or acquaintances. This is a form of emotional manipulation. Let's be clear that attempting to get your child to be on your side is emotional manipulation.

This really confuses a child. They must choose between being loyal to their parents or not. This choice unconsciously produces the question,

"Will they love me if I choose differently?" It also puts them in a situation of having to make decisions about topics they have no real knowledge about. If the child agrees it teaches them blind loyalty. If they do not want to agree they risk not being loved or some adverse response. This puts the child in a tough bind. It doesn't help you in any way and they don't know if in the future you are going to side for them or against them. Manipulation breaks down conscious or unconscious trust in your relationship with your child.

To truly be a loving parent, all of your love and intent must be congruent. You cannot touch someone lovingly with an angry voice if you are really angry, but you can touch someone lovingly using an angry voice while you are still feeling the love. Feeling anger and touching someone is not congruent. Saying I love you when you really feel disdain for someone is not congruent. We think you get the picture, don't you?

There are two types of communication: the visible and the invisible. Be conscious of both!

When you truly get that human skills are both internal (feeling/intention) and external (displayed/expressed) you will know and hopefully use your skills appropriately and always with love. You can express to a child in an angry, firm-sounding tone while you touch them lovingly, while still in the energy of loving them. What you are conveying to them with touch is, "I love you." With your verbal skills, you're communicating that this is an unacceptable behavior. This way, even though you are addressing the behavior with an intense, firm voice that may be interpreted as angry, you are still simultaneously communicating to their senses and inner knowing that you love them. Internally you are conveying love and externally you are expressig or conveying dissatisfaction with a behavior. You can actually communicate on multiple levels while always conveying the message of love.

However, if internally you are in the energy of the expression you are conveying (e.g. angry) it changes the vibration that comes through your voice and your body which goes to the child as a communication of anger, hostility, frustration or judgment and there is no love felt. Contrary to popular belief; love can be felt while expressing what appears to be non-loving communication. Often times what a person thinks is non-loving expression is simply something they do not want to hear or feel.

Many parents try to do the opposite because they think it is better than letting the child know they are angry. They will be extremely angry or frustrated with their child and they will try to speak to them lovingly, "No dear, you shouldn't really do that." But the vibration coming from their voice and body says, "You little brat, if you don't straighten up and fly right, you're in deep trouble." The child feels that information while you are talking to them. It was all conveyed energetically through the voice and the body.

What you are feeling is energetically felt

They get a very confusing message, because you are not really addressing the behaviors or your feelings. You are being very gentle with the child because that's the way you want to appear on the outside, while inside you are saying to the child, "You are frustrating the heck out of me and I just want to tape your mouth shut and put you in the closet!" The child gets that feeling but it doesn't match the words, so they don't understand. This mixed message alone will leave the child with an inability to communicate clearly. In this style of parenting what the child learns is: lie, suppress your feelings, parents can't be trusted, things are not ever what you think or see, to be confused about what they feel versus what they see and hear, this is the way to communicate and more.

With the gentle voice and the angry feeling transmitted through your body, you are completely incongruent. It's not clear in the child's mind. Their body is receiving a message that is completely different from what their mind is receiving. They will not be able to communicate their own feelings when they get older because you were not honest, truthful and congruently loving.

On the other hand, if you are still communicating with love but using intense words with your voice, you explain to the child why you are using the intense voice and what you were trying to correct or adjust or that you are just trying to get their attention and make sure it's all completely understood.

There is no hidden agenda or mixed message it's a very clear message: "I am raising my voice and talking to you in a firm way because you weren't listening and I was not able to get your attention in any other way. This wasn't safe or appropriate and I need to get you to know this. I needed to get your attention with my loud voice but I still love you." The vibration of love still comes through the intensity of the body and the voice. You may also have to check your voice levels, maybe you are too loud. There is a difference between loud and firm. Many children turn off to loud voices very quickly. Loud voices are a verbal spanking. If you get to loud apologize for the loudness but state "I meant what I said but should not have yelled."

There are variants of these combinations, but you get the general idea and understand that you convey information to a child through your voice, your vibration and your body. Scientifically it is known that your body emits vibrational frequencies based upon your mood changes, emotions and your mental state. Those vibrational frequencies are what is being transmitted from your body to the child's physical and sensate body. They will pick up the frequencies that are congruent or incongruent with the words you are using and these will teach the child to lie, be honest, be consistently clear or be unclear in their communication, based upon the training and modeling you have presented to them.

Now pull this information into your own adult world. All this is why you are who you are today. This is why you have the difficulties, challenges or successes that you have today. You have received these messages, these congruencies or incongruences, to some greater or lesser degree and in any combination. You may be able to clearly communicate sometimes, clearly communicate all the time or never clearly communicate. You feel or don't feel things, you may mix up your interpretations, not know what you are feeling or thinking. All this relates to touch and feeling in relationships of all types, whether it's an intimate or partner relationship, or whether it's a friendship.

Your ability to communicate, connect, understand, or feel the other person, and how you interpret them is mostly based on this type of training and understanding — or lack of understanding — from you parents. Your entire body interprets the frequencies, vibrations, feelings, sounds from your environment from birth on, then your mind interprets this using the beliefs and patterning's you have acquired in order to make sense of your current world. If you were deprived of the education provided here as a child, you either remain dysfunctional or must learn something new as an adult in order to change what is not working in your life.

Even though most people think their mind is the major part of their life it is actually only a small part. Your mind is your human decipherer, your interpreter. Your body is the receiver of all of your sensate experiences in the human world. So many people address the mind, but it's just a small part of your receiving system. The mind simply helps you understand and interpret the world in order to function and communicate with your human world. The mind is highly overrated. The heart and soul of a person is highly underrated, mostly due to its invisible nature.

Within the body is what many call 'the heart of the person' but this is not the physical human heart. The heart we speak of now is that connection with your soul/spirit and your physical body. That is the actual receiver of all of your human experience. It is what really makes you tick. It is your intuitiveness/gut feeling and your life source. It is the truth interpreter of your body's sensate system and it cannot be fooled by the mind, appearances or fancy talk. Without your soul/spirit, the body would be dead. Without a mind, there would be no interpretation or understanding of your life. Both the head (mind) and the heart (soul/spirit) must be in balance for you to live a balanced life. This concept is not intended to be religious or spiritual but simply a concept that addresses both the visible and invisible aspects of life.

We hope that you understand this idea that your whole body is a sensate organ that receives all of the frequencies in your environment, both seen and unseen and your mind interprets those feeling based on the beliefs you have created or acquired. And that you communicate with your whole being which in turn creates responses and experiences that you find displeasing or pleasing. Then you pass this on to your child consciously, unconsciously, visibly and invisibly.

Now you might be able to have a different perspective on how you experience your world and your life and understand why feeling is the key to life, not emotions.

Emotions are a mental process

They are a response to a mental judgment of an experience based on a belief system. Life is about feeling. Hopefully with this new perspective you can conceive of how important it is for you to be conscious around all children. Not just your child, not just your best friend's child, not just a niece or a nephew, but all children.

Touch is both physical and non-physical. Your energy/vibration touches everyone you encounter. Touch your child vibrationally/energetically and physically with the love all human beings deserve. This changes the world.

CHILDREN TOUCHING THEMSELVES

Children touch their genitals. Expect it. Some do it more than others. It is about self-discovery, so please do not project your beliefs onto your child's behaviors. You must learn and discern when to respond to it, when to respect it and when not to be afraid of doing what is necessary, because some parents are freaked out by their children touching their genitals when they are little. Some parents get over it, some parents don't care.

Understand that in the beginning they are just babies and it is just a body part. It only becomes something other than a body part when you turn it into a sex organ in your head. Your child doesn't know it is a sex organ until they are somewhere around 10 or 12 years old. Until then, you teach them what they need to know about other people touching them and what to do. The moment you start thinking, "Oh, that's a sex organ, I can't or they shouldn't touch that." they have already picked that up in your feelings and now they begin to form judgments which interferes with healthy sexuality. It is just a foot, it is just an arm, it is just a penis, it is just a vagina and it means nothing unless it means it in your head. This is what people really have to understand.

When a child begins to touch their genitals, they rub or fondle them at first because it sends sensations through their body and it feels good. In the beginning it just feels good. They have no idea of sexuality. Later as they are subject to television, the internet, peers and you, not to mention their active hormones, they begin to develop beliefs about sexuality.

If touch has been a loving experience for them, this is something they enjoy with themselves. If they are told touching themselves is wrong, bad or dirty, they probably do it anyway in secret and then judge themselves as wrong, bad or dirty and experience guilt about themselves or their sexuality.

If they are taught to believe it is wrong to touch themselves in that way, and that they will be judged for it, it is likely the sex will be an issue when they begin having intimate relationships. There is also the possibility that if it is seen as bad or wrong they will desire the 'forbidden fruit' more.

You can teach them that certain times and places are not appropriate for that behavior, but never teach them that the behavior itself is wrong.

So your son is playing with his penis on the couch in the living room. You explain to him, "This is not something we do in public." We're rewording this for children, but the essence of what you want to say is, "It is not socially acceptable because it is something you do with yourself privately. I'm teaching you what is appropriate behavior with other people and what is not. Touching your penis or vagina (call it a penis or vagina, don't use baby or slang terms) in front of other people is not appropriate. Doing it with your partner when you're older (and you wouldn't tell this to a very young child) while you're loving and enjoying each other is a beautiful thing. But doing it in public or in front people you are not intimate with is not acceptable."

You have to teach children that the reason we have certain rules is for social circumstances, not because these behaviors are wrong or bad. You have to say, "Today, in this world, people don't walk around naked or touching themselves. People make judgments about naked bodies and most people have certain feelings about penises and vaginas that make them feel very uncomfortable. That's just the way it is at this time. In order not to cause problems for other people and yourself, you need to have and learn what we call socially acceptable or socially appropriate behaviors. That's really why we're teaching you this.

"If everyone in the world was naked, no one would notice you had a penis or vagina in any way other than the way they notice you have two hands. And it wouldn't mean much of anything. But that's not the world in which we live, so I've got to teach you how it is out there in the world."

At this point touching themselves sometimes is important to establish. You don't want them create an addiction to touching their genitals. Sometime children touch themselves to release stress and if this is allowed all the time it becomes a precognitive habit pattern. So use your intuition in determining when it is too much.

Masturbation and fondling triggers chemistry in the brain which allows them to feel a certain euphoric state, that's one reason they do it. So anytime they get stressed out, anytime they get anxious, anytime they feel bad about themselves, they may fondle themselves or masturbate. This is not necessarily the program you want them to install and leads to addictive and intimacy challenges.

When they want to know why, say, "Well, because when people do that a lot when they're little they tend to want to do that a lot when they're an adult and it's not appropriate, and it's often a way to escape the feelings you do not like and that is not healthy."

You don't want to explain too much. You don't want to say that they do it when they're stressed out, because then they may start to do it when they're stressed out. You just want to tell them somehow that people who tend to do it too much when they're little tend to do it too much when they're adults and it creates problems for them.

"And when you're older, I'll explain it to you more clearly, but you have to be about 14 before I can explain it. For right now, just understand that I'm telling you the truth and I'm trying to help you out so that it's not hard for you to be in the world. Why don't you do something else?" Then redirect them.

"Here, why don't we paint? Want me to massage your back? You want to be touched? Here, honey, I'll rub your arm, I'll tickle your arm." Touch their back, their buttocks, their legs, their feet, their head and their face. Touch them everywhere except for their penis or vagina. Now they can associate that touch is good all over. You want to rub them so that it feels nice and they can associate pleasure all over their skin.

CHILDREN'S REACTION TO TOUCH

Some children have areas on their body they don't want you to touch. "Don't touch my hair."

At first you respect and avoid these certain areas. You touch their skin, you get them used to the feel of your skin and then you can even work on their hair. It depends how strong you want to be. "You don't like it, I'm touching it. Not because I am power tripping you but because I want you to be comfortable with and in your body." It is funny how things change if you do it lovingly and not aggressively. They may intensely resist but they will respond over time. Be patient.

Real life example: There was a child who really hated their hair touched and the parent purposely touched their hair whenever they saw them. Every single time the parent saw them, they said "Hey, how are you doing today?" and touched their hair, and the child would give them that face.

Sometimes the parent would just touch the end of their hair where they could hardly feel it and just rub the end of their hair. Just enough so the child knew their hand was there. After a while the parent would move up and stroke their head. Later the parent would touch their head while hugging them and after a time they didn't even care if their hair was touched.

So you want to purposely, kindly and gently do that with whatever the area of the body they have difficulty with. Touch your children for their sake. If you happen to have difficulty or issues with touching your child you need to reflect inward and discover where and when you found touch and or your body repulsive. Help your child learn to enjoy being touched. Put cream on them; rub their arms, do whatever you can that is touch related. Just do it. If it freaks them out, do it anyway. They will resist you, but know that if you don't do it now this is their program for life. "Don't touch me, get off me." What kind of sexual relationship are they going to have, just a genital one? They are not going to have a loving one because you can't touch, you can't massage, and you can't caress. What kind of children are they going to have? What are they going to do to their children?

So you have to purposely start at a place that they feel safe or comfortable. If they like their feet touched or their back touched or even if it is on their clothes first, fine. Rub whatever and where ever you can, slip your hand under their shirt once in a while and let them get irritated, take your hand out and do it on the shirt. But whatever it is, break them in with the touch. Touch should not be aggressive and some children will put up a fight. If they do resist, do it anyway. Not enough to make them angry but just to the edge.

Touch is more important than most people can imagine. There are so many things that happen to their psyche because you touch their skin. The appropriate or inappropriate touch is telling them unconsciously whether they are loved or not. If you touch them when you are not in a loving space then they won't want you to touch them. Then even if you touch them when you are loving they are going to expect you to not be loving and will resist you. Many parents get their feelings hurt when their child repels them. Know that it is not about you (unless you have been unloving or manipulative in your touch. Honestly be who you are at the moment. Touch them with love or don't touch them at all if you are going to touch them without it.

If sometimes you have to grab them and say "Hey, knock that off," or if you need to restrain them from hurting a sibling, that's different. We are talking about touching them and getting them used to it. Just lovingly touch them like you were caressing them. If they don't like it too light, touch harder to see if they like hard touch, pressing them more like a massage. If they like it very light and don't like the deep try both and then reverse them. Tune them into feeling deep, shallow, light, gentle, firm and they are all okay. This teaches them to be aware of sensate system/body and of their environment.

It also allows them to have intimate relationships with other people, and not just sexually intimate relationships. It may be a best friend who just likes to rub their arm or a spouse that likes to cuddle. With this touch acclimation they are not going to freak out when touched because they will know what a loving touch is and what is not. They will find touch pleasing and be able to more deeply connect with others and themselves. Teaching them this touch thing is crucial for them as human beings, and if you are having touch difficulties you need to work on your own too.

Parents need to have the skill of touch. If you have trouble touching somebody else then there is some definition about what touch means when you do it or receive it. Maybe you're hung up on the traditional stuff like if the person is male/female it means you're initiating sex. If that is the issue and the other person is responding that way, then you have to understand that they were programmed to think that way or that the only time they get touched and the only time they can have that feeling is when sex is involved. So you both would have to work that out.

If you don't like being touched then it may be something about receiving. What does it mean if you receive? What does it mean when someone touches you? Maybe some place along the line someone touched you inappropriately. And now when anybody touches you it brings up that memory somewhere (consciously or unconsciously) and you just feel gross or dirty or like you can't or don't deserve to receive somebody actually loving you; someone actually just touching you because they want to. You think, "I'm not good enough for that; you know that I can take care of you, but oh, don't touch me." There are just so many possibilities.

You have to work out those issues and teach your children these things. If you start to have any kind of thoughts about it being inappropriate, you need to look at why you are thinking that. We hear so much paranoia about perverted parents because there are child molesters, but then people become paranoid and they just can't love.

You can love without having to be sexual and if you've got that switched in your brain, you have to figure that out. Realize that love, touch and sex are three different things. None of them are the same. They can all be intermingled, but they are not the same. If you can't separate them you can't teach your children or really experience touch yourself. Learn about it and teach your children loving touch versus inappropriate touch. You can even talk to them about how they are inappropriately touching each other and don't limit inappropriate touch to sex. This is where most people go and it is not about sex.

Lovingly touch them so that they can be comfortable with their skin, and do it on purpose regularly. Say they are in a bad mood and you don't want to touch them then. Touch them anyway. You want to teach them not to be isolated because they are in a certain space. You should be able to theoretically touch them no matter what mood they are in. Angry, happy, sad, it doesn't matter. Rub them on the neck or the back — they should respond exactly the same as they would if you were not even touching them. When they are at that stage they are comfortable with touch. When they respond, "Get off me …. Just leave me alone," you respect that appropriately, but you also know these are markers to say how close to comfortable they are with just being touched.

Lovingly being touched sets them up for a life of enjoyable touch because if they don't get this straightened out by the time they are a teenager, typically almost everything in regards to touch is going to be about sex whether you are aware of it or not. You have to admit many teenagers have sex on their brain a lot.

What do they promote on TV all of the time? You see this topic advertised everywhere. The sexual programming in this current society is overwhelming sometimes to a forming child and to adults as well. They program women to dress sexually and men to look at them that way. With this constant barrage on a child's senses it is easy for them to distort the lines between sex, intimacy and loving touch. So you must teach your child appropriate touch and sexual attitudes.

Do your best. You won't be perfect in all this, but you are going to set a good foundation.

SEXUAL VERSUS SENSUAL

Many people confuse or blend these two. Here we want to delineate the difference between sexual and sensual. When your child is of the appropriate age begin to educate them on their sensuality. Then again when your child is of the appropriate age educate them on sexuality. Only you can determine what is the appropriate age for your child because this includes mental, physical and emotional maturity.

Sexual - *activities connected with physical attraction or intimate physical contact between individuals.*

Sensual - *that which is pleasing to the senses*

Sensual is quite commonly used in reference to sex. But for our definition here we are defining it as that which is pleasing to the senses for the purpose of understanding that human beings are not sexual beings but they are sensate beings. Simply meaning that human beings are feeling beings. Within those feelings sexual experiences are included but are not limited to that. Human beings feel so much more than just sexual experiences.

Take the five senses for example. Then add into it the sixth sense of what we were calling earlier the sensate or invisible feelings. Touch is a sensual experience in it does not have to be sexual. When educating your child please do not confuse the two, clearly delineate the difference. If you have these confused in your mind and your belief system it would be wise for you to reevaluate and re-understand what these two words mean.

Being sensual activates the sensate system. This allows a person to sense their environment and savor the experience. Every human being is sensate. Learning how to interpret your sensual/sensate experience accurately is of the utmost importance. Once you have this clear in your own mind then teach your child to interpret sensual experiences as sensate experiences and assign appropriate meanings to what those experiences are. Advise them that they can be sensual and sexual but that's sensual is a different experience than actually having sex.

When it comes to the education of your child on sex please educate them on the physical act, their personal responsibilities and care, safe sex, their emotional responsibilities, their own emotions versus their physical sensations and emotional intimacy. Let them know that their own pleasure is equally as important as their partners. All too often people get caught up in self-gratification, the gratification of others or confusing the chemical changes that occur in the body and their own emotions or emotional state.

Make it clear that sex is sex and that love is love. Educate them that the two are separate and can be combined. Some people may disagree with this. We would say that it is possible to have sex just for the sake of having sex with no love involved and it is possible to have sex to express your love. Teach your child that using sex to express your love is the highest form of the experience.

Many uneducated children grow up to be adults who use sex for power, manipulation or release without any concern of their partner and what this type of attitude does to relationships. They are all too often caught up in their own personal needs, belief systems or pattern behaviors to self-reflect enough to use their sexual experience wisely. Teach your child to be wise and while doing so hone the wisdom of your own sexuality and sensuality. Also teach your child the markers of potential unhealthy partners as a form of wisdom so that they may choose wisely when considering sexual or life partners.

Of course teach them in your own style and with your own moral values whatever they may be. We suggest that you keep them balanced, clear and honest as your child will intuitively feel and eventually know the difference if you have taught them too rigidly or too liberally. Teach them to see sex as a part of everyday life, not something taboo, forbidden or naughty. Be careful that you are not giving them mixed messages. For example: telling them that sex is a natural part of life and then acting prudish. Or telling them be careful and wise when having sex and then allowing them to dress overtly sexual or suggestive. Keep in mind that today's culture encourages women to exposed body parts either through revealing or tight clothing, which is all sexually suggestive to those who are attracted to women.

Don't be afraid to address the topic of sex and sensuality or your child's developing sexual nature. Your open honesty will teach the child that it is not something to be ashamed of or hide. This sets the foundation for your child to be able to have a healthy sexual relationship with their partner. During these times many parents have their own sexual issues arise, due to the age or gender of their child. If you should happen to run into this don't worry, you are normal. It is a common thing and is easily overcome as long as you are willing to face it and understand your own sexual programming and sensual nature.

If you are still confused or combine sex and sensual when your child is going through this, please do your own inner work and shift your perspective so that your child can feel what a healthy human being feels like. This may include working intimately with your partner on topics that you may be struggling with. Keep in mind however, that your partner may be having their own issues in regards to this topic and may or may not be able to talk about it. If they have difficulty please be patient and work toward a resolution amicably so as to not cause your partner fear and thereby they push you away.

Sex and sexuality will be experimented with by your child, from masturbation to the interaction with other people. Whatever you do; do not judge or emotionally react your child or their behaviors. Even if it freaks you out, act calm and collected while discussing this topic unemotionally. Remember if you are freaking out then you have conscious or unconscious sexual or sensual issues. Changing your perspective on sex and sensuality will change the way your child responds and you react.

Educate your child on loving intimacy. When having sexual relations with someone they should know that if they are intending to be that close with someone that, loving intimacy is extremely important. This does not mean that you must be "in love" or that they are your partner for life, it simply means being loving during the sexual experience. If they are a long-term partner then educate them on how opening your heart and being intimate while connecting soul to soul while sharing the physical sexual experience is one of the most beautiful things a human being may experience.

Chapter Fourteen
RELATIONSHIPS
Family, Partners, Children and Self Relationships Explained

In this chapter you'll find a new way of looking at what relationships are and what they are not. This information may also stretch your paradigms and open you up to a new way of looking at relationships of all kinds. Everyone has grown up with rules and roles about relationships and has bought into them as 'This is the way it is.' Then they use these rules and roles as a way to manage all of their relationships.

In order to become free of these limited perspectives and fully enjoy your relationships while creating the experience you want rather than the experience you must have based on these rules and roles, you must first question everything you believe and perceive about what relationships mean to you. Then decide what is working, what is not and make adjustments to suit your desire.

RELATIONSHIPS DEFINED

Many people are searching for meaningful relationships. They may be doing it to complete themselves, to feel fulfilled, to place their love onto someone, to be loved by someone, etc. These are but a few common reasons for people getting into relationships.

*What most people don't understand
is that you cannot have a full, rich, meaningful
relationship with any other human being until you have or
begin to have a meaningful relationship with yourself.*

What does a relationship with you look like? It is when you are connected to the essence of who you are, when you are connected to your heart (inner heart). You are connected to your true feelings and intuition, not your beliefs or programs. You have taken the time to reflect inward to discover what you want and what you feel in your heart and are not driven by passed on belief systems and patterns. You know what you feel your direction is and you are not wavering on your course, yet you are adaptable. You are sure and confident about the decisions you make and the directions you are heading in because you have felt, discovered and discerned them for yourself. It feels right. You know it to be your truth and you follow that direction. With that surety and confidence, you can share your life experience with someone else and have a human relationship.

This unwavering yet adaptable direction enables you to fully experience life without looking to the outside or to someone else for some sort of validation, response or feedback. Of course generally you live with respect and cooperating with others as much as possible, but overall you know you are on the direction and course you are supposed to be on or have chosen and nothing else matters. This state of being allows for you to now consciously choose a relationship with someone else.

We should mention here conscious choice is not about mental decisions, it does however include them. It is about the feeling of your inner heart along with your awareness of who the other person is, their personality, the heart connection you have together and what you enjoy together etc. It is choice with a conscious heart and mind.

Choosing with a conscious heart requires going on an inner journey of self-discovery. In this process the objective is to learn about your patterned behaviors and belief systems that contribute to any or all challenges you have had in the past and may still have when it comes to having relationships with other human beings.

Five steps to a meaningful relationship:

1. **Self-discovery** - inner exploration of your beliefs, patterned behaviors and attitudes towards other people.

2. **Change** - being adaptable, flexible and finding processes that assist you in making changes in your behaviors, beliefs and attitudes.

3. **Unconditional acceptance of yourself** - once you have discovered some of your behaviors, beliefs and attitudes in regards to relationships, accept them. Know that these are just programs that can be changed. Change the ones that don't work in regard having meaningful relationships and keep the ones that do.

4. **Unconditional acceptance of you partner** – accept your partner as they are without judgment or the desire to change them. Be able to discuss openly and neutrally with them what is not working or working and mutually agree on ways to make this easy for both parties.

5. **Learn to love yourself** - learning to love/unconditionally accept yourself and being happy with who you are is required for you to have a meaningful relationship with someone else.

The priorities of your earthly loves are to:

Love yourself first

Then your partner

Then your children

Then everyone else

Many people would disagree with this and may also say, "Where is God in this equation?" In order to understand why this order is so you must know a few things.

- You cannot truly love anyone else more than you love yourself. Thereby loving yourself opens you up to a whole new experience of loving others.

- Your partner will be with you after the children leave home. So loving your partner second allows for you to have a long-term relationship without being interrupted during the child raising years.

- Your children are priority but they will eventually leave home. When they leave it will be you and you and your partner.

- And finally to the question, "Where is God in this equation?" Here we will refer to God as Source. You were birthed from Source therefore you are a part of Source. Based on this information if you love yourself first then you love Source first.

Relationships with Others

Many times on a deep subconscious level relationships are sought out because you are seeking a part of yourself that you are not connected to or has never been developed fully, and there is a perception that another person can provide you with the opportunity to find or complete something for yourself. You see reflections of yourself in what others say and do. What they do for you is a great service and yet it is rarely seen that way. People abuse each other for that service when they get mad or mistreat others for reflecting to them the things they don't want to see about themselves.

The person who reflects yourself to you is not just a partner they are a divine gift. You will find that your friendships, your family members and yes, your children, will also show you things about yourself you may not have otherwise seen; that is if you are paying attention. Remember, *people are your mirrors and teachers* and everyone you come into contact with will provide you with a learning opportunity. Children especially show you all the areas in which you need to grow whether you enjoy it or not. Parenting is quite the self-education. All of your relationships with others are about YOU! Yes everything you experience with others will tell you something about you, positive and negative.

It Begins With Love

In the first chapter we talked about modeling self-love for the child — loving yourself and showing the child how to love themselves. A mistake people often make is that they want to make someone else happy. They believe they will be happy if someone else is happy. PROGRAMMING ERROR! ERROR IN THE PROGRAM!

At best all you can do is do things that temporarily please others. It is not your job nor do you have the ability or capability to make anyone else happy, ever. You are simply to love. End of conversation. You are to make you happy. In your happiness and the love shared with others, happiness exists. The process of living to make others happy is living outside of yourself. So, if you are living outside of yourself to make another happy, you will always feel abandoned, left out and like you never quite get enough of them or from them. This occurs partially because you are trying to use their love or responses to feel your own self-love. No matter what you do or how often you do it, it will never be satisfactory or enough because you have not taken the time to truly love yourself.

Most people take care of other people believing consciously or unconsciously that it will make the other person love them back and if you do it in the way that they want then you will get the love that you want. If they don't love you back or in the way you want them to then there is disappointment, blame and heartache. And often the thoughts that they don't care, you can never do enough, you did everything you could do, if I only would have, could have done more etc. This type of love is always disappointing. Because you never get what you want and are constantly sacrificing for others. If you love in this way you should know: it will never work or be satisfactory because you are ultimately abandoning your own love/the love of self.

If you take the time to get centered within yourself, however, and change a lot of these dysfunctional, misguided programs and love yourself first, your life as well as your child's will improve. Your life experience and your child's will begin to change just because you have changed. You will see that it's a very practical, logical and hands-on process and seems to happen naturally once you have begun the change. As with many other things we have spoken about be patient with yourself and you will see results.

Too much emphasis is made on loving behaviors and has created an entire mindset that has overlooked what love truly is. Love is a feeling, not a behavior. Behaviors are included with the feeling but because of the feeling behaviors will naturally occur not the other way around. It's how it feels when you are together, not how you act when you are together. If you feel loving, you will automatically act loving. If you act loving, you will not necessarily feel loving. And your child, being a psychic sponge, will unconsciously and intuitively respond to the lack of love you have for yourself, to your bad programing or software. It's guaranteed that your child will know the difference between whether you feel loving or are just acting loving. The same holds true for other people as well.

You should know that your child will treat you exactly as you have treated them. They will go through the teenager years and try many things with their behaviors, but when push comes to shove in your real relationship, your child will treat you exactly how you treated them. Some children act very loving and do all the right things — coming home on Sundays for dinner in some traditions or buying you Father's Day or Mother's Day gifts — but they don't really feel it and the love feels empty. In fact, they may still be angry with you for something they perceived was done to them as a child. Think about your life, maybe you have experienced something like this yourself.

Traditionally people have been taught that the expression and display of love is the most important way to communicate it. But in truth love is a feeling, not a display or a communication. You can feel if someone loves you or not, no matter what their words are. This is especially true for children. They feel your love, no matter what you do or say.

How many times have you done things for your parents while you were angry at them and you weren't necessarily feeling loving but obligated? It comes down to this: Do you want to have a real loving relationship with your child or do you want to have one that looks loving?

Love is a feeling not a behavior.

MODELING SELF-LOVE TO YOUR CHILD

Why should 'self-love' exist? First of all, you deserve it and because your essence is love. You loved yourself/were love before you arrived on earth while you were with Source, why wouldn't you love yourself now? You are taught to love others when you should have been taught to love self. You should love yourself more than anybody because without that you don't have anything to share. Self-love is imperative as a parent. This love needs to be modeled. Imagine it like being a lifeguard; you need to learn to swim before you can help or teach others to swim.

Never forget how precious and impressionable

children's minds and spirits are.

They come into this world helpless

looking to you to be kind, loving and helpful.

Let's be clear about what love is not.

When you need a pat on the back, recognition or praise from someone else (including your child) for what you do... this is not love.

When you do thing out of obligation, feel like a martyr or you need to tell people about it ... this is not love.

When it's most important to you to be their friend, their buddy, their chum ... this is not love.

When you bend over backwards to make sure they don't experience disappointment, frustration, boredom or loneliness ... this is not love.

When what you've done is used against or to manipulate someone, that old "After all I've done for you!" trick... this is not love.

Love is doing it from your heart, because this is what you have chosen to, because you want to. Without wanting anything in return. When you don't consciously or unconsciously look for anyone to notice or validate you. When what you do or say does not make your ego 'feel good.' Pure love is when:

- You are just being the love.
- You are full.
- You are fulfilled.

- You are complete.
- There is no desire for anything.

When you give to be noticed, recognized, approved of , you are not in a state of pure love. If you disregard yourself or place others first your child recognizes the lack of love you have for yourself and will act out or imitate that example.

When this happens parents often say, "What is wrong with my child?" Well, part of it is your child's programs, part of it is your programs and part of it is your child just growing up and experimenting. Now, you have to sort out and determine which one of these it is or if it's something else. The truth is there is nothing wrong with your child. They are doing exactly what they have seen modeled for them and are doing it in their own style. Sometimes when they do it in their own style the basic pattern is not recognized in parents don't recognize it.

It is often difficult for parents to believe or even conceive that their children actually are imitating their behaviors or patterns, especially when they don't recognize them. Most parents are not even aware of their own belief systems and patterns, which is a major factor contributing to this disbelief or lack of understanding.

Change your beliefs not your child's behaviors

Of course this doesn't mean that you allow unacceptable behaviors. Remember you are the source and foundation of your child's perceptions and behaviors. Some parents might see this as burdensome or overwhelming. We would tell you that this is the joy of being human. Parents pass on belief systems and patterns that set the foundation for the next generation. You haven't done anything wrong! In fact, most of your own beliefs and behaviors aren't even yours!

If you take the time to self-reflect and change many of your dysfunctional programs your life will become easier and more joyful. Your child will begin to change just because you have changed. They will however have established many patterned behaviors of which you will be required to assist them in changing. Let's face it you just figured it out, there is no way they are going to figure it out as a child. Therefore you, with your new learning, will be able to assist them at a very young age as opposed to them having to figure it out as adults while they are raising children. What a beautiful gift!

Many people don't want to do this because they don't want to do the hands-on work. They want the child to be fixed. They want everyone else to make an effort but they don't want to do it themselves. They believe, "If everyone else is happy, I'm happy," but that's really not what happens. They often believe that other people are the cause of their misery or unhappiness.

You are the sole cause of your unhappiness whether you are conscious of it or not!

No one can make you happy except you!

You can't make your child happy. Your child can't make you happy. Your partner can't make you happy nor can you make your partner happy. No matter what they do they can't fix what's inside of you. No matter what you do you can't fix what is inside of them.

You and only you have the power to make yourself happy. This is the same for each and every person. What you can do is enjoy other people but you cannot make them happy. This is where unconditional acceptance and the realization that every person is responsible for their own happiness can completely change the way you see life.

*Doing these things for yourself is
the ultimate act of self-love.*

RELATIONSHIP WITH A PARTNER

Now let's talk about a relationship with a partner. What we are talking about here is husband/wife, boyfriend/girlfriend, girlfriend/girlfriend, boyfriend/boyfriend, lovers etc.

The first question is why do you want one?

It seems like everyone is trained from birth that this is the way it should be, and since it's the norm, it is often done without thought or even a question. So give it some thought. If you desire to have an intimate partner, then ask yourself why. What do you expect to get out of that? Is it just to fulfill some need? Is it just to fill an empty void within yourself? Please answer this question for yourself because it's important. It allows you to investigate and make a conscious choice about the way you are creating your life. It will also allow you to discover why your partnerships have turned out the way they have.

At first many people will say I just love/like them. But be forewarned that every human being has expectations about what a relationship will do for them, give them or how they should be in one.

So what is an intimate partner? You must define this for yourself. What exactly do you think an intimate partner is for and what is it an intimate partnership about? Are you avoiding having one? Maybe it isn't that you don't want to have it, it is that you are avoiding having one because of previous experiences or because maybe you don't even know how to have one. Taking the time to evaluate and discover for yourself will allow you to move forward and hopefully have an intimate relationship that you enjoy and makes your heart sing.

As long as you expect that a partner is going to supply you with something — some enjoyment, some pleasure, some pain, some whatever — then the intimate relationship is in some way doomed, or at least doomed to a lot of problems. Because when your unconscious patterns and desires are not fulfilled, your partner will somehow be blamed and the possibility of looking outside the relationship (emotionally, mentally and even physically) to fulfill those needs becomes greater. Unfulfilled needs are one of the greatest causes of relationship failures.

This is a good starting point for you to begin to understand intimate relationships. You cannot have a healthy and enjoyable intimate relationship until you don't really need one. A whole, conscious person who is balanced within themselves and truly loves themselves can create a long-lasting, enjoyable, intimate relationship with a partner. Partnerships take a lot of work. There is the coming together of two belief systems and sets of patterns that will take time to integrate in a way that all parties are happy. Be patient and diligent in regards to your own growth and the growth of the partnership.

If you have entered into a monogamous relationship and one of you is venturing off into some other satisfaction, whether it's physical, mental or emotional, it will interfere with the partnership you are trying to create. Patterns or beliefs about not being there for each other or abandonment may be triggered. One of the main reasons that people grow apart is because they are fulfilling more of their needs somewhere other than within the relationship. The challenge in a real partnership is that all of the needs of the individual be met within the individual and that all of the needs within the relationship be met within the relationship so that neither individual goes outside of the relationship to fulfill any needs that would interfere with the relationship. This is not to say you can't have outside interests. However it is to say that if you're outside interests are feeding too many inner emotional needs you will eventually create emotional distance between you and your partner.

Keep in mind that we are referring to a monogamous intimate relationship because it is the most common partner relationship that people have. It isn't because we are condoning or not condoning it. It is up to you to decide what type of relationship you want, but understand that a monogamous intimate relationship is quite difficult and yet extremely rewarding. This same type of intimacy cannot be acquired through group relationships or multiple relationships because it calls to the depths of your soul and creates an experience with one individual in such an intimate and personal way that it is not possible with groups. This is what makes one-on-one intimate relationships a little bit different. By having a one-on-one intimate relationship it holds the mirror of self so closely that you cannot avoid seeing yourself. This can be both challenging and magnificently rewarding.

How you love your partner is a direct
reflection of how you love yourself!

Conscious relationships: are you in one?

A conscious healthy relationship is two people individually working on their own issues, resolving negative behavioral patterns and developing likes or dislikes based upon their own individual preferences while sharing that with another. It is about two individuals who are comfortable in their own identity and who have a fairly healthy view of themselves so that they can come together to share the experience of life together. They have established enough trust so that they may feel safe and secure enough to be able to share life as a unit without losing their individual identities. It is teamwork!

Do you really want to be in a healthy relationship or do you want to be an individual rooming with a mother or father figure who will take care of you, fulfill your needs and give you the illusion of safety? Think about it and be sure!

Conscious relationships require absolute honesty, integrity, trust, open-mindedness, self-reflection, communication and the knowing that you are responsible for the way you perceive life.

Love for your parenting partner

If self is sacrificed for the relationship, any relationship, there will always at some point be resentment in the relationship. Self has to be addressed first so that your WHOLE healthy self is present in the relationship.

Let's go back to the beginning of your partner relationship when it was just you and your partner. You originally came together to share your love, not give yourself away to each other. Then you decided through love to create and/or parent another human being. You created this experience together. You, yourself, who is separate from your partner decided to join together with your partner to create something separate, that you could share your love with. You didn't decide to merge into your partner and lose yourself, nor did you decide to lose yourself and become the child that you created or are parenting. Hopefully you wanted to experience love for yourself, then love with another, then lovingly create and/or raise another human being together.

What you created is not yours, you are not them, they are not you — this life does not belong to you. You simply co-created this human being. If you were to paint a painting, you would not become the painting would you? It would be something separate from you. You certainly wouldn't lose yourself in your painting. If you become infatuated with that painting and stay in that painting when you finished, you would be living in the past and living an illusion. You have given up your life to live as something that is not you. Doing this would mean sacrificing everything you love, including you, for this painting and never truly experiencing the beauty of life.

If you have a partner, there needs to be a bond and unity between you two. If the partners or spouses don't have a bond, if you are picking at each other, fighting, not on the same page or not in agreement, the child that you created will see that and believe that is the way life is.

If this is modeled for the child, the child will usually make one of two conscious or unconscious assumptions. One: This is how you express love and how a family interacts. Two: The people in this family do not love each other or the child may believe that the family unit is crumbling. Then typically the child will interact with the family the same way as the model.

You must ask yourself these questions about your partnership (or of yourself if you are a single parent):

What do we want our life to look and feel like?

How are we going to partner together?

How are we going to solidify this and make it happen?

How are we going to unify and model unity for our child?

What will this look like?

Your partnership is your priority, even before the child. Make it a conscious choice. If you choose anything or anyone other than your partner as a priority after yourself, the partnership is typically all downhill from there. Some people discard their partner in many ways when the children arrive. They direct their energies towards their children and leave out the partner mentally, physically and/or emotionally. If you don't put your partner before the rest of the family, your family is in jeopardy. You and your partner are the foundation of the family. When the children grow up and they start to have a life without you, your relationship with your partner will probably be dead or near dead if you have not kept each other as a primary focus. Then you will say, "What happened to us?"

Guess what kind of a relationship you've taught your children to have with their partner someday?

You and your partner are the foundation of the family unit

If you abandon your partnership, you teach the child to abandon themselves, their partner and the family unit. As the child abandons self, this creates within the child the feeling of being abandoned, alone, never satisfied and with the need for others to fulfill them.

If one partner puts the child first, the other partner must to address it. By remaining silent you condone the choice of the children being first and destroy any chance of an equal, solid partnership. This also undermines truly effective parenting. Equal partnership, side by side, through thick and thin, with an 'us' first attitude is mandatory.

Love your child by loving your partner as your equal

How you love your partner is a reflection of how you love yourself

As partners make each other a priority they make a commitment to be one voice and unified in their parenting. Differences in parenting are discussed behind closed doors beyond the listening ears of your child. When you come out to your child you are unified. Regardless which parent the child goes to the response will be the same. Without this you have a divided household.

This simultaneously confuses the child and distorts the messages they receive. The child will then consciously or unconsciously use that division to manipulate the family in order to get what they want. It is the divide and conquer routine. They will intuitively figure out how to emotionally divide the parents to get what they want. In this scenario it is the child in charge and the parents at war with the child and each other, the ultimate power struggle where everyone loses. Unity and uniformity between the parents and their decisions will keep your partnership and the family intact while creating the opportunity for a loving environment.

Remember that children take on their parents' patterns. If parents aren't unified and the children get the divide and conquer dynamic, they develop the separate and manipulate mentality/patterning. Can you imagine the ramifications of this type of mentality? It is no wonder that there are family and relationship problems if this is what is allowed or modeled.

In today's society there are many unique households. If you happen to be a single parent raising your child on your own, you need to be unified and congruent within yourself. This is why it is so important for you to take care of your own inner world. Becoming a well-adjusted, grounded human being will show your child by example how to care for and love yourself first.

Seeing this, your child will be more likely to develop their own relationship with self. They will also see a parent with balanced male and female qualities within themselves. Seeing this, the child learns that they too have both male and female qualities, which creates a more balanced life for everyone. The child will also have a greater respect for you the balanced parent, which will often reflect in a more communicative and lovingly responsive relationship.

We understand there may be a parent not living in the household, not sharing the same ideas or ways of doing things. Don't make this a battle and demand the other parent to do what you are doing. If you stay on course with yourself you can deal with these things.

It will also be helpful for you to explain to your child the differences in parenting style without blaming the other parent. It can be explained by saying you were both raised differently and have different opinions, but these are the rules at my/our house. It may be challenging at times but remember there is a bigger picture for all involved. Whether the parent not living with you is on board or not is not really your concern, although it would be nice. You must remember, all that matters is your household. It is the only thing you can govern. There is a golden rule when it comes to this — mind your own business. Stay focused on you, not the other person.

If the child says, "Mommy/Daddy lets me do this." you must say, "Mommy/Daddy has their own rules and I have mine. My job as your parent is to show you love and guidance in order to prepare you for life; to give you the best and most balanced example I can to prepare you to have as happy and functioning a life as you can while giving you the tools to succeed at this."

Love and treat your partner as if they were the most important person in your life

Never allow the love of your child to interfere with your partner relationship

Maintaining this connection with your partner can be quite challenging as the years go by. Typically as the years go by the awareness and focus on the partnership is often allowed to slide to the background while the focusing on day-to-day life takes precedence. This often leads to complacency and distance between partners.

By always maintaining an awareness and a connection with/to your partner this "growing apart" will not happen. This connection requires conscious communication, open discussion of your feelings, needs, desires and anything that will make life easier for both of you.

Love your partner with all your
heart and consciousness awareness

DEVELOP THE SAME SKILLS

When it comes to parenting there will always be one partner more developed than the other in any particular skills. Example: One partner is good with people; the other is a better problem solver. Learn from each other and add to your skill set instead of letting one take over and the other stepping back.

When one steps back, they relinquished an opportunity to develop that skill due to their fear or low self-esteem. Once the skill is developed, you can choose to use that skill or let the other partner who is more skilled or prefers to do it take over. Growing together as parents is about learning from each other while figuring out the things you do not know and mastering them as a team.

In order for the unit to work well, it's important for each person to learn as many skills as possible both for yourself and in case one partner should be temporarily unavailable or disabled and not able to carry out those roles this would allow the family unit to still function. By learning each other's skills, the two of you become balanced, equal partners with interchangeable roles.

OPINIONS VERSUS CRITICISM

When you begin to hear each other as a critic, condemner, judge or attacker the unity in the relationship breaks down. But you should recognize when or if this occurs is that you are in some sort of childhood patterning or belief system. This feeling has nothing to do with your partner, unless they are deliberately and admittedly doing those things. If you are not sure, ask them. All too often observation and opinions can sound or feel like criticizing or judgment.

If you learn to listen to each other as sharers of information and observations then absorb the information without reservation, discern what is useful and then choose which observations and information you wish to use you will find that your relationship will flourish.

CONSCIOUS PARTNERING

As a parent you need to be aware of that from conception on your child intuitively/psychically feels everything that is in your consciousness and their environment.

Parents needs to be taught that whatever has occurred since conception, even during conception, whatever their consciousness is/was, their thoughts, their feelings, their desires, everything, all of it goes into the baby's conception as a frequency. It becomes part of the child's frequency. It may not be retained in their physical consciousness or if the parents do some conscious parenting after the baby is birthed then these frequencies can be changed. Frequency in this case is an unseen affect and is actually an aspect of consciousness in the human energy field.

Every frequency that passes through the mother's body affects the physical/biological matter of the child's body. The intuitive/psychic interpretation of all that information affects the child's programing. So now if the pregnant mother is having thoughts or flipping back and forth in polarized thinking, unable to make decisions, having fear or anxiety, repeating old programs or new programs or generally off balance. It would be beneficial for her to say to her physical body and the child within her physical body, "This is not yours, it is something mommy is feeling and learning about for herself. Not yours. Not yours. Not yours."

Three times is a nice number. "Not yours. Not yours. Not yours. I am working it out. I know you are feeling it. I am handling this. I am taking care of this, I will shift this and I will teach you differently once you come out." Feel/intend your connection to the body and soul of your child while feeling the energy of negation, if you want to call it that, run through your physical body, neutralizing the charge that was just brought through by the patterning or experience that you are going through. Visualize the unloving feeling/energy turn into particles of light and see it float out of your body.

This information is being said for your awareness in hopes that it will allow you to be a more conscious parent. Please do not become overly paranoid about what you have done in the past as this doesn't help the situation at all. Instead look at this as a great awakening and know that everything that your child has experienced from conception on has allowed them to form a personality and experience life.

All experiences no matter how positive or negative they may be perceived can be great gifts that allow an individual to understand their world. So whatever you have done that you might be regretting or you wish you had changed please realize that these were character gifts. They have assisted in developing character and wisdom for both you and your child.

It is helpful if the both partners living in the household do the same thing but it is not necessary. When you do this as a couple your statements of 'not yours' is a statement both to the child or children and to your partner. Let everyone know that this is yours, you are claiming this as your own, knowing it is yours to work through. Nobody in the household is required to retain the frequency or feelings of these charges.

If you decide to do these things and your partner chooses not to, do not become an evangelist and force these ways upon them you will only alienate them and divide the partnership!

Understand that when you go through these things that you are processing old consciousness, belief systems or patterns. The new golden age has not yet arrived and pure divine consciousness does not exist here yet. So be patient and tolerant of your experience.

Ultimately everyone and every living thing is your partner. By living on Earth everything is connected. All life, no matter what species is somehow interdependent on the others. Being conscious of how you treat the earth, plants, animals, human beings, your parenting partner, your child and most of all yourself will allow you to have a flourishing life.

> ### *Your partner reflects both the beauty of yourself and that which is asking for change.*

Remember to listen, listen and listen to your partner, they will say what you need to hear, maybe not what you want to hear. Take what they have said, verbally and non-verbally then attempt to interpret what "really" is being said by them and yourself at some unseen level of consciousness and use it for your growth.

BEGINNING A PARENT-CHILD RELATIONSHIP

Developing a parent-child relationship is optimally begun in the womb and continued after birth. When a child is conceived, connection by both the mother and the father to the growing child creates an unseen bond that will last a lifetime. Please do not assume that this is for mothers only because the child is inside her body, this connection is with and for fathers equally. The only difference is that the mother has a direct temporary biological connection. Once the child leaves the womb this biological connection ends and the connection afterwards becomes psychic and emotional.

If the father develops a psychic and intuitional connection with the child while they are in the womb bonding with the child once they come out is much easier.

As the child grows, developing and maintaining a connection with your child also grows and changes. In the infant stages, developing the bond comes through touch, sound and your presence. In the toddler stages, touch, sound, your presence and communication maintains and reinforces this connection. In the teen years, communication, intuition and feeling become the primary connection.

MOTHERS

Here we will address a few common unspoken occurrences or behaviors of a mother that interfere with or complicate their parenting and relationships. We will also address some concepts and ideas that will make it easier for mothers to accept and transition when their children leave home.

Consider that maybe sometimes the 'mother's love' that is known by most human beings is actually mother's dependency or attachment. Many dysfunctional behaviors are accepted in the name of motherhood or mother's love.

Many mothers become so attached to their children that they will not emotionally let go of them or let them grow up. Mothers who do not emotionally let go of their child often use the child as a replacement for their partner or some other lacking emotional needs. This could include the need to be loved, the need to be needed, the need to be wanted etc. Mothers who use the child for a replacement of their partner usually have distanced themselves from their partner emotionally.

They may have justified the reasons or have good reasons for doing so, but this cripples the child emotionally. If you have an emotional distance between yourself and your partner please take the time to make amends and reflect on your patterned behaviors and beliefs that have contributed to this distance. This is a wonderful gift that you could give both to your child and yourself.

Lasting relationships require that your partner comes before your child

Mothers must learn to let go of the child entirely in order to have and enjoy their partner. This is often what causes a rift in partnerships. When a child comes along it is not uncommon for the mother, through her issues, to emotionally attach to the child and abandon the husband or partner. When this happens, the partnership shifts to the mother and the child, then the partner becomes secondary. Never let your partner drift to second, this is assuming you are in the relationship for the long term.

A husband/partner will often seek other entertainment or partnerships through business, work or another relationship of some kind in order to fill the empty space in a relationship. Some don't understand why some husbands/partners drift away, but if your husband/partner is no longer the main partner, what is left for them? How are their emotional needs fulfilled? This of course could also happen the other way, but it occurs more commonly this way as the mother typically shifts attention to the child. Some of this is simply a natural tendency while adjusting to the changes, but at the longest, after the first year the mother should shift her attention back to her partner.

Many mothers unconsciously believe that by staying connected to the child she will never be abandoned, as the child will always be her child. So she allows the husband or partner to disappear because she is secure believing the child will be there, because she gave birth to it — it is part of her and there is no need for anything or anyone else at that point. Please be cautious of this type of drifting and emotional attachment to your child, it can happen so subtly and gradually that it will take you by surprise ten or twenty years later.

In the mother's mind she may want an adult partnership but may create it with the child instead of the partner. If this happens it may be because she has intimacy issues or emotional wounds from childhood. This causes great difficulty for the child because, as the child matures they create an identity of being a partner to the parent. The child may then struggle being with other people intimately. When they have to move on and be an adult they cannot let go of the mother to have a proper relationship with their own partner. Have you ever heard the phrase 'being tied to your mother's apron strings?'

If there was a dysfunctional relationship with the mother, in any way shape or form, the child will have the dysfunctional relationship with their partners in the future and the dependency needs will be transferred. This would be a result of their childhood energetic and behavioral patterning set deep within their unconscious.

Look at your family or your partner's and
See what type of 'mother' patterns you have.

If the child is a male he will seek dependency from his wife and the wife will then pass on the pattern to the child and abandon the husband so the chain goes on. If the child is a female, she will seek the dependency of the male until the male can give her a child to depend on and then abandon the male. Their conflict comes when their mind says, "I want an adult relationship with an adult, but she may not know how or why her relationship is not fulfilling.

The female child who is now the mother must make a choice. The choice is: Do I have an adult relationship with my child and corrupt the child unconsciously, or do I hold onto the child and have affairs (physical or emotional) elsewhere so that I may have the adult relationship I want and need?

In this model the mother has made her child the partner. If she chooses have an affair, emotionally and/or physically with a male (who may be her husband) but will have the partner relationship with her child. This is why husbands and wives are not necessarily always partners — the husband is an affair while the child is the relationship.

Some mothers have gender issues. Based upon childhood wounds and experiences they will prefer or shy away from a male or female child. If you have had unpleasant experiences as a child with your mother or father this will influence your response to your child. Attempt to be conscious of this influencing factor in child raising.

Ask yourself these questions:

- Did I prefer my mother or father as a young child?
- Did I dislike, hate or fear my mother or father as a child?

- Which parent did I feel more comfortable or safe with?
- Which parent was it easier to communicate with?

To break these patterns the mother must be aware of these things and release herself and the child from each other, make space for herself to break the pattern and then choose her partner for the adult relationship. This will create a different type of relationship that is unfamiliar to her, which will be very frightening and leave tendencies for her to go back to the child, but she must avoid that at all costs. She must encounter that dark night of the soul, so to speak, be with herself during these fearful times, leave her child to their own growth and yet not cling to her partner until she has established a core within herself.

This way she may be whole for her child in the proper perspective, whole for herself and for the partner of her choosing. In turn she may enjoy her partner and not depend on them thereby having a wholesome fulfilling adult life. As with many of these topics there is just so much to cover. Please try to understand that we are trying to present you with new perspectives and opportunities, not all of the answers. Look at your life, beliefs and patterns and decide if you want to make changes or if your life is working the way you would like.

Mothers are key to the child's emotional and physical health. By seeing your child as a separate entity and living being you can nurture your child in such a beautiful loving healthy way as to establish a permanent lifelong healthy emotional foundation. Your loving touch, physical care, emotional balance and heartfelt instruction will model for and educate your child on how to be a happy healthy individual.

Being conscious is an act of love!

FATHERS

Many of the thing suggested in the mother section hold true for fathers also. So fathers you may want to reread the mothers section and relate it to yourself.

Note: *this section on fathers also pertains to a partner who is not carrying the child and whichever partner assumes the role of father. Mother and father are not necessarily gender related but are more about the qualities performed by the roles they play.*

Now we are going to address a few things that interfere with or complicate the father's role. One of the first things to address here is that mothers are more connected to their children than fathers, especially at an early age. This is completely and absolutely not necessary however it is common. If the father connects with the child while in the womb through intention, intuitively and by using the sound of their voice the connection begins. Once the child then leaves the womb the father's presence, attentiveness, touch and the sound of their voice can establish an equally deep connection with their child.

Fathers should understand that the only real difference between their connection and the mother's is that the mother has a biological connection until birth. Because of this there appears to be a deeper connection. This is true while the child is in the womb because the mother is intuitively communicating with the child 24 hours a day. But once the child has been birthed there is equal opportunity for the father to bond as an equal partner with the mother.

Unfortunately, it is typical in today's society that the father's leave child development while in the womb to the mother and believe that they have nothing to do with it. This is false! The father, if they so choose can be an equal part excluding the biological connection. So fathers, don't sell yourself short. You have an equal right and opportunity to bond with the child from conception. The only question is, will you take the time and make the effort?

Many fathers have difficulty warming up to or relating to the child after birth and in the early years. Many fathers state "they are no fun until they can do things." This is all perspective and often an excuse to avoid learning how to be intimate with a new being that has no programs or belief systems that the father can relate to. Many fathers wait until the child has developed some programming and belief systems that they can then interact with them through.

Please, if you are a father and doing this open your eyes and your heart and connect with your child before they have a personality. The time before they have a personality can be the most beautiful thing you will ever experience because they are so pure. And if you look closely you will find that they actually have a personality that is more related to their essence or soul and has nothing to do with beliefs or programs which can make this one of the most intimate and magnificent experiences of your life.

While your child is young and has very little programming please do not avoid them. Spend the time to get to feel and know their essence and their beautiful open heart. Put aside your father's programming and the old family paradigm where the father simply provides and the mother nurtures the child. This is a false and delusional program. You as the father are equally responsible for the emotional nourishment and development of your child.

If you leave all of the emotional development up to the mother then in a way you are metaphorically abandoning your child, even if you provide financially. Your child intuitively feels the disconnection and will develop a closer bond to the mother. This then will give the appearance that the child is closer to the mother and mothers are more nurturing than fathers. This is an illusion and not at all true. Fathers who love their children enough to break their old patterned behaviors and belief systems will experience a unique and special relationship with their child that many professionals and families say does not exist. Be the groundbreaker in your family lineage and provide your child with the model of the 'new male.'

If you leave the emotional development of your child up to the mother you will also create a void in your relationship. As the mother spends 24 hours a day with the child and you are only there for a few moments and emotionally disconnected the mother will naturally become more connected to the child, which causes a distance between you and her. By taking the time and making the effort to do something that may be completely alien to you, you will speak volumes of love to both your partner and your child.

A father who abandons their responsibility for the emotional development of their child often will emotionally distance themselves in their partner relationships. Know that your emotional responsibility is to yourself first, then to your relationship with your partner and lastly to the emotional development of your child. All of the old paradigms of what a mother does and a father does should be totally disregarded. Use the functional, logical and reasonable paradigms from the old model and add in that both parents can be equally connected and responsible for all facets of the child's development.

In this equality the father's will teach the child about a male's role in society and the mother will teach the child about a female's role in society with the approach that both the male and the female are capable of the same tasks emotionally, mentally and energetically. The child should also know that there is a slight difference in the physical capabilities and experiences simply due to biological structure.

Many will disagree and say that the male and female brains are wired differently. We would say that in the current day and age to some degree this is true however the potential for equal brain wiring does exist and if developed the brain and emotional structure will change allowing for each gender to have equal skills.

The myth that females are more emotional than males is false. The myth that males are unemotional is false. This myth is perpetuated through daily examples. However these daily examples are never truly investigated from an energetic or belief system standpoint. We would suggest to you that these examples that people use as proof are merely thousands of years of programming and belief systems so embedded in each gender that it is assumed to be true and that it can be changed if the individual chooses to do so.

Fathers tend to take on the task of physical and worldly teaching and rarely teach the child about the inner workings or intuitive and sensate development of the child. Commonly because the father is rarely taught these skills themselves and do not have the wherewithal to teach the child these aspects of life. This is why it is important for you as the adult to look at your own inner life belief systems and patterning's in order to be able to pass this information on to your child. Never give your child lip service because you read something in a book or have been told it by some 'expert.' Teach from your experience. Then speak from your heart and your child will intuitively know when there is truth.

Fathers are equally as intuitive as mothers. Mothers do not corner the market on intuition. The only difference is that fathers must develop their intuition where mothers have already been programmed to believe that they have it. When a father develops their intuition they have the ability to become more connected to the mother and their child.

After the child is born the father must pay attention to all of the programs and issues that are stimulated by the child, the child's relationship to the mother and how the partner relationship changes. By becoming aware of this and changing your perspective you make way for a unique and beautiful experience with your partner and your child.

LOVING YOUR CHILD

Love yourself with all of your heart. By doing this you set the example for your child so that they can love themselves. You show your child that they have the right and the ability to love themselves.

Love your child in the way the child needs to be loved not the way you want to love them!

When loving your child love them gender neutrally. This means don't treat them like a girl or don't treat them like a boy. Treat them as an individual human being and allow them to become who they choose to become. Of course you will teach them the appropriate male and female behaviors that apply to the culture in which you live.

Do not judge your boy for playing with dolls or your girl for playing with balls. Do not try and redirect them but allow them to discover themselves. Every one of us has a male and female aspect within us and by allowing your child to develop these aspects you create a whole and balanced human being.

Keep in mind that your child is not yours, you do not own them and they are not beholden to you. They are on loan to you from the universe and your job is to guide them and teach them how this world operates so that they become functioning adults. You are preparing them for the world and teaching them the appropriate skills so that they can enjoy their life here on earth.

In the end, how your child watches you love or reject yourself and/or your partner will reflect to them on how to love themselves.

CHAPTER FIFTEEN
FAMILY

The Old Model

Family relationships are self-defined and you create the reality of what these relationships mean to you. Ultimately perception of family is a belief system. Many times family relationships are obligated friendships at a deeper level, especially in families where people don't like each other or don't get along. They are super glued relationships, where you have no choice as to whether you are included or not.

How many times have you personally or people you knew dreaded going to family events, seeing their siblings, parents or other family members? Just because you were birthed into a 'family' does not mean that they are really your family. They are simply human beings that allowed you the opportunity to visit earth. However many times people think just because they were birthed into a 'family' they must remain in contact with that family even if there is unloving or unkind behaviors. Hence, the obligation — this is what you perceive and have been told what family means.

From your family, from the people you grew up with and around you, you learned unspoken rules that you bought into as a truth. You did this because as a young child you had no idea that there were other options or alternatives. You unconsciously speak these rules out loud when having conversations with other people and when you're alone, you talk to yourself about them.

This makes for a very difficult life because it does not allow you just to experience life; it means everywhere you go in life there is a rule. Not only is there a rule, there is a role. With rules and roles, how can you possibly live a free choice life? Of course it's not possible. You however may live a life that appears to be free, but you can't really experience a free choice life, as you are living out all of the unconscious and conscious programming passed on to you by those in your "family". If you don't get rid of the rules you'll never get rid of the roles.

Okay, before some of you get a little freaked out about this concept please be patient. We will go over what a 'real family' means. If you can take a moment to just relax and absorb the concept we are speaking about and relate it to people you have known in your life or even yourself, you will see that this type of family and obligation occurs quite often in humanity.

What are your rules of family? It might be a good idea for you to sit down and define the rules and roles you have in your belief system about family.

For example, my rules of life may be if somebody's nice to me, I have to be nice to them. If I'm nice to them, they have to be nice to me. If it's someone is my family, I have to do what makes them happy even if I don't like it. There are plenty more, so take some time and review some more rules you may have. Think about the guilt, shame or anger that goes on in your family. These are signs of belief systems related to obligation and the dependency on other people for your value and love. Write them down and review them and you will see many of the beliefs you carry.

When we talk about these things we often referred to what people would call 'negative' perspectives. This is because the negative things are what is wrong or that you do not like. The "positive" things are things that you are going to want to keep because you like them. The concepts in this book are for you to expand your consciousness and assist you in changing things that create dysfunctional children and relationships and sometimes to remind you of the beauty that life holds.

See and relate to your children as individual human beings. If you don't like them, you don't like them. If you like them, you just like them. There is no, "I like you because you're my son or daughter." Ask yourself, if they were a stranger, would you like them? Ask that question about all your family members. If your mom, dad, aunt, uncle, sister, brother, child, son or daughter was being a jerk and they were strangers, would you hang out with them? Most people wouldn't. It is okay to admit this. Just because you don't like them doesn't mean you don't love them.

Now what you really must understand is that what you dislike about them is their behavior; not their essence or beautiful soul. People are not their behaviors. Their behaviors are choices and actions that they make from their patterns and belief systems in response to external stimuli. Behaviors in no way determine the essence of a human being but their behaviors may be likable or unlikable.

Most people cannot emotionally separate from their family and belief systems enough to acknowledge their own feelings because they feel so guilty for thinking that someone in the family is a jerk (or something worse) yet they'll talk and complain about them. They'll go to the family reunion and talk about what a pain in the neck everybody is, but they feel guilty if they say, "You're a jerk and I don't want to hang out with you." These are the rules, oaths and obligations that you have created for yourself on your own and you assume you are committed to live by them. Where did you get those rules?

FAMILY AND FAMILY SYSTEMS

The grand illusion of family is a belief that they are the answer to the question, "Where I do belong?" Originally, families were structured and used to perpetuate loyalty, which created and ensured the survival of the family, clan or group. Families are often used to support one's sense of self-esteem and identity. They are used to signify that a person has some worth or value because they belong to a group. Therefore, often the sense of belonging becomes an identity of worth and the individual is not able to be a sovereign human being.

If one's original birth family is no longer together, people commonly seek some kind of group to join. This may be a community, an organization, a sports team, a church, a debate team, a cause — anything involving more than one person, so that they may develop the same sense of belonging or worth that they have been trained to believe in.

As you can see, families are not only biological. They are groups of people seeking value for themselves through the perception of being valued by other people, the need to belong, the fear of being alone, etc. These families are usually created around a particular theme of being different or unique. This theme can be rallied around so that there is a sense of worth or a sense of belonging to a family. The same concept is used by governments and organizations to create dependency through loyalty and identity.

Most people believe that people must conform in families so that they can continue to perpetuate the family way in order to be loved, have some sort of identity or be accepted. You should not have to conform to be loved by your family. If this is a requirement then it is conditional love. You should however be able to cooperate and communicate with your family as a way to make life more pleasant and fluid.

Parents help instill this inaccurate sense of family, as they tell children that family is everything and that one's family members are the only ones who count, are more special than anyone else or will be the only ones who help in tough situations. This belief is inaccurate and false and perpetuates separation, division and in its extreme measure prejudice.

It's important not to let your pride of belonging or fears of not belonging keep you in family situations, especially unloving ones, and to teach your child the same. This is not to say that you cannot love your family or the families that you have belonged to, but that you do not need to - and should not - make your family your identity. To make your family or group your identity is to worship false idols. These false idols will never fully satisfy any human being and at some time will always feel incomplete. The only thing that you belong to and are a part of is your spirit and Source.

THE OLD FAMILY SYSTEM

Every family system is unconsciously designed to support its family patterns. That is one reason why the need of family is so great. If you sacrifice yourself, you will not question whatever patterns your family has because that is the way they believe it should be. You are supposed to stick together and protect each other so that the patterns of your family can continue to the next generation.

In times before modern society this was a very useful survival mechanism. But currently it is outdated. Keep in mind that most of these systems were designed unconsciously and that we are not suggesting that the family concept is a 'negative' thing. We are simply pointing out the unconscious belief system and energetic patterning that exists within a family and the resulting common dysfunctional causes.

Some patterns can be secret and some can be out in the open. Maybe every Sunday everyone in your family worships tomatoes. Even though you know it is silly, your family has been doing it for thirteen generations, so who are you to tell them it's silly? You may be punished or worse yet, you will be shunned by the family if you do. You can't worship on Friday, because you will be all alone. You have to stick with your family patterns and bond, so you can feel as though you belong.

You may think, "I'd never worship tomatoes!" but what holidays do you feel obligated to gather together on that you do not believe in? What does the family do when someone is ill? Do you send holiday cards or not? How about gifts? Are there certain things to serve for a holiday meal? All of these are patterns which, when done with blind obedience, are not much different than worshiping tomatoes. Some people may call these traditions. Traditions without conscious and free will choice are simply habit patterns.

There is often a larger, more subtle pattern going on beneath the surface. This pattern is the idea that you must sacrifice yourself for the family. What is being implied is in essence this: "Don't seek your own truth, live by the truth of your family. If you live by the truth of your family, you will be loved and supported. If you question your family's truth, you will be rejected and maybe even abandoned."

If you are afraid enough, you will stay with your family. If they make you angry enough, you may leave. Otherwise, you will remain within the boundaries even if you don't like what's going on within the boundaries. You might say, "Well, I'm mad at you, so I am going to distance myself for a few days, a few months, or a few years, but I'll come back because I know you are family. I really need my family ties because that is my history and my ancestry. I have to stay because that is where I am from."

Human families can be one of the most beautiful experiences in the universe but in truth the only family you are from and truly belong to is the family of Source (God).

The belief system about committing to the family creates a prison that is not real. It creates a limitation that does not actually exist. You should always treat your birth family kindly and as lovingly as possible, but you should never sacrifice yourself or your own truth for the energy or belief system of your family.

You were born into the belief system that you are in. That belief system has been passed down from generation to generation, along with the beliefs that are part of your culture, country or religion. You can enjoy your family or group and be a part of them, but it's not necessary or useful to sacrifice yourself as a person to the cause. It is the belief system you must be aware of and work with that system in the most loving and kind way as possible while maintaining your own sovereignty.

Treat the family and the family belief system with loving wisdom and exhibit the behaviors of an honorable human being.

THE FEED/FEEDER FAMILY DYSFUNCTION

The root of all dysfunctional families is what we will label the feed/ feeder energy. This feed/feeder system is energetic in its nature and is played out emotionally, verbally, mentally and physically. At its core is the belief that love and worth come from outside of you; that there is a limited amount of love and that it is something you must seek from others in order to be whole.

A dysfunctional family survives on the feed/feeder energy. In this system the perception is that there is not enough love to go around and everyone is competing for it. This concept may be either real or merely a perception. Whoever gets more is envied. This concept also contributes to a lack mentality which may also translate into financial lack. Whoever doesn't get enough or get it the way they want it often feels abandoned, alone, unlovable or not valued. Often they feel they need to attack, fight, spite or compete for what love is available. Often the 'bad' child appears to get fed less (less love) and the 'good' child gets fed more (more love). What we mean here is that the bad child tends to get less attention and the good child gets more attention as a reward or punishment for their behaviors and pleasure or displeasure of the family.

This type of system is more common than you might expect. It is quite often extremely subtle and almost invisible. In this system no matter how you hard you fight for the love everyone will starve and feel less than satisfied with the amount or type of love that they received.

In this system everyone depends on each other for the love, with a constant need for confirmation of their worth and value. This need is most commonly felt within the individual and rarely expressed. Therefore individuals within the family rarely ever know this is going on with the other individuals.

To complicate this, most individuals are running this belief and need system unconsciously. We would venture to say that this unconscious belief system and patterned behaviors (that are passed on from generation to generation) are at the source of almost all family dysfunction. The source of this pattern is the lack of self-love within the individuals of the family.

The ones being fed from are going to be drained and see the rest of the family as a burden, a lot of work or in a worst-case scenario repulsive. The ones who are feeding or needy are going to be drained because they have to spend a lot of energy trying to obtain the love they feel that they need. This system produces children who become adults that are needy and controlling either overtly or covertly. Please keep in mind that these patterns and belief systems are not your fault or your child's. These are passed on inherited belief systems. If you happen to be doing anything similar to this know that you have not done anything wrong and that you are simply repeating unconscious patterning that you inherited.

If the parents are able to hold unconditional love for the family and themselves, then there is enough love to go around to everyone and emotional feeding is not necessary. If each child in the family and the parents knew that love is the core of the family and there was love for everyone, then this feed/feeder program could not exist. This does not mean that your child will not test you or experiment with behaviors and manipulations as they grow up, but it does mean that they will not be in search of love as they will feel the love in the family even if it is unspoken.

Some examples of the feed/feeder dysfunction are people who are:
- Caretakers and those who need or desire care
- Victims and victimizers
- Controlling or needy
- Dependent or prideful
- Aggressive or hostile
- Passive or passive aggressive
- People who yell or manipulate
- Guilty or shameful

In a family with loving energy, the parents do not feed from each other or the children. They are sovereign unto themselves and share their love by conscious choice. They provide a basis of love which creates an ultimate fullness. The child knows that love exists and that there is nothing more they could need. Their human aspect might say, "I want a material or non-material thing," until a deeper understanding of love has come to fruition within the child.

When the love exists as it is, there is no feed/feeder energy. Love just is. Everyone is complete. There is no competition for time or space or attention. Everyone gets what they need as is necessary and can always count on the love to be there for them.

Once again, the source of all human familial dysfunction is being trained in and living by the feed/feeder energy system, where you require your worth and value or the false perception love to come from another or to come from giving yourself up to another in order to be appreciated. It is the sole source of dysfunction. There is no other root cause. And of course at the source of this is the lack of self-love and interconnection to your divine self.

In true unconditional love, no feed/feeder energy may exist. We are not speaking of human love, we are speaking of 'divine' love, which goes far beyond human love and is pure of heart without motive or agenda even at the subconscious level. When that exists no human could ever feel unloved or feel the need to emotionally feed.

So where are you not feeling loved? Know that when you are not feeling loved, you are in the feed/feeder energy.

When you are in the absolute love, there is no feeling of love. Instead, you are being love. Be the love. Being the love is not acting loving or about behaviors. Being the love is different. Being the love is when your entire being is the love and every action you take radiates the love that emanates from your heart effortlessly.

If you are the love you are full, fulfilled and complete.
Be the love and be fulfilled.
The irony is when you are the love there is
no need or desire for love.
Being the love shall set you free.

KEEP YOUR HEART OPEN

Know your patterned behaviors and/or your beliefs, know your triggers and know yourself. We mean really know them. Then get to know your feelings. Know why you feel the way you do and what beliefs cause those feelings. Once you know yourself (your beliefs, patterns and heart's desire) intimately you can begin to love yourself. You can only love others as much as you love yourself. You cannot give what you do not have for yourself. Once you have discovered this love for yourself you can share this love with others effortlessly and without fear.

A wise man once said:

"Know thyself."

If you do your own inner work and unconditionally accept yourself, then the more likely it is that you will be able to unconditionally accept another person. By you having the courage to look within you become the model for others. Your open heart is seen and felt by everyone. Your open heart allows your child and others to know that it can be done.

In a way, you would be the leader. Many people don't have the courage to reveal themselves or open their own hearts because of their personal fears, patterns and beliefs. All too often opening your heart is perceived of as being open to hurt. Hurt is a perception that someone or something can make you feel a certain way. This is a false perception, however common it is or however real it is experienced. Opening your heart is not letting other people in; it is allowing the love from within radiate outward.

Hurt is not getting what you want

Most people have not done the inner work necessary in order to have mastered the human skills necessary to live with an open heart. Every relationship is a work of art that takes time and dedication. All relationships take work, fortitude and commitment to a common goal no matter what or no matter how your patterns and belief systems differ. Everyone has a different journey in the relationship, but in order for the relationship to be successful there must be a common goal about how the partners would like the relationship to be experienced

A lot of people say, "You are not doing it the way I want it, so I am done," and/or say, "This relationship is not working." Well, no, it's not, it can't. Not that way. You have to do your own work, allow them to do their own, know that you are both working toward a common goal and be patient. All this builds the energy and foundation of a healthy family and/or life.

Once someone's hurt gets triggered they often start thinking negatively and tend to shut down emotionally towards the other person, which only creates a deeper separation. One of the real skills in all of this is that, no matter what, you keep your heart open. That is often quite challenging because of the perceived hurt. All of your patterns and emotional defense mechanisms say, "Shut down, get away, run for the hills!" Are you going to try to keep your heart open? Whew, what a task! If you find this quite difficult and challenging know that you are normal. This is difficult for everyone until they have awakened to greater insights about themselves and others.

It can be done, but shutting down emotionally it is a tough habit to break. Typically because somewhere in your childhood when your beautiful innocent heart was open, hurtful or perceived mean things were done or said to you and you decided that you were going to protect your heart. Again this was not your fault. As a young child not knowing any other way this seems like the only way that you could survive and is a common decision.

Keeping your head and heart open even when you are triggered by another person is challenging because it goes against everything you were taught to do. When you shut down and defended yourself, you may have even been complimented for being strong and taking a stand or some other ridiculous thing. That is the absolute opposite of what you need to do. Being strong and closing your heart are not the same. People tend to close their heart out of fear not strength. Teach your child to be open yet wise. To radiate the love from their beautiful heart and soul while having the wisdom of recognizing how people behave and why they behave that way.

You can expect your child to be hurt. When they do not get what they want, whether it is love, material things or validation from others they will typically perceive it as a hurtful experience. Even in this perception they should be taught to keep their heart open and radiate the love from within. You can do this as a visual so that they will have a coping mechanism to keep their heart open.

Keeping your heart open during adversity is the sign of a spiritually and humanly strong and sovereign individual. With human wisdom and an open heart you can remain connected to your own inner divine wisdom and radiate while being the love. In this state of being all things are possible and inner creativity is abundant.

Some people may say that this is not possible or practical and that hurt is something you must protect yourself from. They may even say that this concept is airy fairy. We would say to you,

> ### *With an open heart and an open mind anything is possible.*

SET LOVED ONES FREE

Set your family and loved ones free. Setting someone free means; releasing them from your beliefs, ideas, thoughts, demands, needs, limitations and expectations.

The old phrase that says, "If you love something let it go. If it is truly yours it will return." simply means that if you let whoever and whatever you love free from all of your ideas, beliefs or perceptions and they return you'll have the opportunity for a loving relationship with them that allows them to be who and whatever they are. They have returned freely. They are themselves and you are yourself with no attachments, designs or ideas about what or who they should be. If this occurs then you are both free, together, sharing your open hearts in a genuine loving relationship.

As you set your loved ones free something else happens. You realize you are free as well. Free to be free, to love yourself, to be the love without rules, roles or limitations — what a beautiful gift to your child.

OLD FAMILY PERCEPTION

Think about what people describe as a family. Because you were born together, and you're from the same culture and the same bloodline you're a family.

Human beings make family into something special for many reasons. The perceived family unit is a separatist idea. It's a division — it's like a country. When you place boundaries on anything your create separation. There's an illusion of family that is inaccurate, then perpetuated without thought and accepted as the norm. This is not to belittle family but it is to say the individual family as it is and has been is in fact separation by a perceived specialness. This concept is what creates conflict and war. If everyone could realize that all of humanity is your family even if they are not your bloodline then there would be a great possibility for peace on earth and the ending of war. But as long as families see themselves as special and different there will always be conflict within the human family. To be able to see all human beings as you are relations of some sort allows you to have greater compassion for everyone.

It is wise for you to be clear to your child that "families" are not what most people think. Tell them something like this, "At some point the word family doesn't matter. The fact that I love you matters. I don't need to call you my family to love you, because that would mean that my friends can't be my family and I can't love them. That would mean I can only love family members in this special unique way because we belong together. But no, that's not true. You can love everyone. However loving everyone doesn't mean you like everyone."

People believe they have to love family. There's an obligation because you're the special unit that has to be together in this way. It's not true. Many times in the old paradigm of family, family members were cruel to each other, so why would you want to stay in that type of experience?

Ask yourself :

If the people you call family were not related to you would you associate with them?

You can love/like whoever you want and you can give them whatever name you want but you are never obligated to anyone for any reason.

NEW FAMILY PARADIGM

The new family paradigm does not create the sense of belonging or create an identity for the child. The new family allows for the child to create their own identity and realize that the only true sense of belonging is when they are connected with their inner knowing, their soul or their

351

essence. In the new family the child is not valued because they belong to the family but because they are who they are with or without family. The new family system actually breaks down the old dysfunctional beliefs systems and changes behavior patterns. This is done consciously and with clear communication to all parties involved.

The child is taught that they have an innate value simply because they are and that no one can take this away or validate them, as they validate themselves. In this model there is no manipulation and/or conditional love. Love in this family is pure and unconditional even when loved ones disagree or have "negative" emotions.

Family is defined as: all of humanity. With this definition there are those family members you prefer and those who you do not prefer to be with. Love exists for everyone even when in non-preferred relationships. Love is not the old human model. Love is a soulful caring for all living beings with discernment about each individual's human ego/personality.

The new family treats everyone with love and respect. This is not to say they do not occasionally "go off" into their patterns and run a bit astray. But if they do so they always return to the place of loving kindness, own their part and honor the other person's experience even if they do not agree. This family is not 'perfect' but they strive for an overall loving relationship with all. Keep in mind that loving kindness is not all fluffy and idyllic; it can be firm, loud, stern and directing also. It is the energy and intent that is behind the words and behaviors that remains loving. The appearance may be something quite different.

When you view yourself this way you will
eventually experience life this way.
Ultimately all of life is your family.

REAL LIFE

Okay let's talk some turkey. Life is sometimes challenging and hard. Life can throw you a bunch of lemons that might be really sour, but if you know how to change emotional water into emotional wine you will be the magician of your life.

Yes, this whole parenting thing can be challenging, taxing and exhausting at times. Your beliefs and patterns are what get in the way and make things really hard. Your beliefs and patterns may cause impatience, intolerance and just general grouchiness. Don't let that deter you. This is all pretty common. Whether you see life as a discovery and adventure or you see it is hard, challenging and painful will determine your perceived outcome and that of your child's.

Remember you are the model from which they create their identity. This is not to make you feel guilty or overwhelmed. This is simply to point out the facts. If you don't like the way your life has been or the way you were parented then be different! But don't just modify your parenting; create a whole new paradigm of parenting for your family. In this book we have tried to lay out a foundation and a model for you to make your own. The most important things are:

1. Become aware of your patterned behaviors and beliefs

2. Be aware of how you feel internally and to your child
3. Love your child for who they are not who or how you believe they should be
4. Don't be a wimpy parent
5. Don't be a controlling or aggressive parent
6. Be honest and integrit
7. Be clear in your communication
8. Don't be afraid to be disliked by your child
9. Don't let your fears interfere with your parenting
10. Be a heartfelt/centered parent
11. Be kind and patient with yourself and your partner (if you have one)
12. Love yourself first and foremost

FINAL NOTE

Being a parent is often something no one is prepared for. It is however something anyone can learn if their heart is in it. At times you will find it is difficult or challenging to maintain a relationship, a career and be a parent. Remind yourself that this is all part of the journey.

When you find yourself frustrated and at your wits end remind yourself this: "It is my patterns and belief systems that are causing my difficulty. If I change these I will view this experience in a different way. All human beings do something similar. I have done nothing wrong and yet I have not been taught how this works. I am in discovery of both myself and how to parent."

- Never judge yourself or your child.
- It is the love of yourself that will allow you to deeply love your child.
- It is the love for your child that will allow you to learn from them.
- It is your love of life that will teach your child to love life.
- It is your love, clarity, consistency, unconditional acceptance and integrity that will teach your child to love themselves.

Love your child with all of your heart, be aware of and change your dysfunctional beliefs systems and behavior patterns but most of all;

Love and accept yourself unconditionally

Acknowledgements

A special thanks to Teamwork Wins Ltd (www.teamworkwins.org) for permission to use excerpts from their "Kid's Manual" and to work with the children and parents they serve while using the information in this book.

Teamwork Wins Ltd is a nonprofit organization assisting children with Invisible Challenges™ to become self-directed, self-maintaining, self-sustaining, free-thinking, creative individuals. An organization that helps children "who don't fit in", in a world that teaches people to be like others and not to stand out. They teach children to be who they are, not who they are told they should be, and to share their unique beauty and gifts with the world.

Thanks also to the parents who have worked with and sent their children to TWW for opening their hearts and sharing their lives, insights, learnings experiences and wisdom.

Most of all, many thanks to Nancy Baker and Annmarie Serratore for their love and assistance in compiling and putting this book together as well as a thanks to all the transcribers for their time and love.

MICHAEL CAVALLARO

Michael Cavallaro' s life work has been finding ways for people to integrate their spiritual nature with their everyday lives. For almost 40 years, through classes, workshops, lectures, books, audios, articles and private consultations he has helped thousands of people lead healthier, happier lives by finding practical solutions to various challenges.

His training as a family intervention counselor and clinical hypnotherapist has given him insight into established approaches to problems. The exploration of a variety of spiritual practices, traditional and non-traditional methods, combined with his own experience and insights inspired him to integrate and apply ancient wisdom with modern life.

Michael's background is as varied as his interests. He has worked in the fields of construction, management, finance, insurance and more; taught in schools and prisons and currently teaches classes in artistic expression. He serves as an Educational Consultant for Teamwork Wins, Ltd, a non-profit organization that guides individuals with **Invisible Challenges™** in becoming self-directed, free-thinking, creative individuals. Artistically, Michael has recorded several music CD's and creates unique, energy filled artwork. All these interests are brought together with the intent of bringing light to the world and assisting others in finding joy in their existence and the connection to their own true selves.

Though he is an international speaker, his true gifts stand out most powerfully in intimate workshops and individual sessions. Here Michael's ability to see clearly past the facades and into the ways humans block and defend themselves with their fears, shames and beliefs truly comes out. His way of expressing what each person knows within their own heart but never fully admits allows participants the opportunity to shed what's not working in their life and let their own light shine.

He lives in Pennsylvania with his wife Adele and is the founder of Living Concepts, LLC.

Michael is available for book signings, workshops and public appearances as well as private consulting. For more information or to design a program for you or your organization, contact admin@adeleandmichael. com or call 215.680.2351.

RESOURCES

"The 55 Concepts, A Guide to Conscious Living" by Michael Cavallaro is packed with concepts that can assist in changing the way in which you parent and the way in which your life works. If both you and your child use and apply the concepts, you will notice a difference in your relationship.

Teamwork Wins, Ltd is a 501(c)3 non-profit organization guiding individuals with Invisible Challenges™ in becoming self-directed, self-sustaining, free-thinking and creative. The organization teaches functional skills through group activities.

Living Concepts is a multi-faceted organization devoted to assisting those who desire to become more conscious and chose to clear what's not working in their life in order to become self-directed creators of their human experience. The assistance provided is an integration of your human experience with the inner divine wisdom that is innate to everyone. Through individual or group work one can go beyond changing behaviors or thoughts to changing beliefs, patterns and the way they perceive the world to a place of creating and living the life they want. Classes, workshops, courses, individual and group sessions, books, audios and free resources are available at the website. (www. adeleandmichael.com)

If you have questions about what you have learned in this book email us at admin@adeleandmichael.com. We offer private consultations and for a minimum fee, we also provide a monthly service to answer questions or reword statements so that you can try these techniques and practice them at home. For a minimal fee, we also provide a monthly service — we will answer questions or reword statements so that you can communicate to your child more clearly and kindly and know that you are being reasonable.

It may be very helpful to seek third party assistance with some of life's complications in these matters. When doing so interview those you are seeking assistance from and use your intuition as to whether they are a match for you or not.

Adele and Michael LLC

PO Box 374

Red Hill, PA 18076

215.680.2351

www.adeleandmichael.com

admin@adeleandmichael.com

Made in the USA
Middletown, DE
09 March 2019